A Family Guide to the Bible

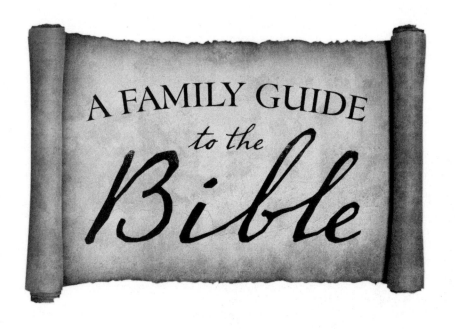

CHRISTIN DITCHFIELD

CROSSWAY BOOKS

WHEATON, ILLINOIS

To parents everywhere who have the confidence that a love for the Word of God is the most important thing they can teach their children—and who have the courage to ask for help when they need it.

May God open your heart and mind to all the wonders of His Word, and give you all the wisdom and inspiration and creativity you need to share them with your children in a way that will impact their lives for all eternity.

CONTENTS

INTRODUCTION

When you first flip open the pages of the Bible, it can be a thrilling experience. Inside you find incredible stories that capture your imagination, amazing characters that touch your heart, powerful truths that challenge and inspire you, words that seem to come alive and leap right off the page!

But getting into the Bible can also be confusing, overwhelming, and even intimidating. After all, it was written in a very different time (thousands of years ago), in a very different place (thousands of miles away), in a culture completely foreign to our own. If you didn't grow up in a home where you were taught all the finer points of biblical theology—and even if you did—you may find there are huge gaps in your knowledge base, gaps that make it difficult for you to truly grasp what you're reading yourself, let alone explain it to your children or grandchildren, your Sunday school class, or a children's church group.

Yet it's crucial that we try . . . and try . . . and try again. Because for one thing, the Bible is the most influential and widely-read book in the history of the world. Being familiar with its contents is part of being a well-educated, well-rounded, well-read individual. More importantly, the Bible's truths are timeless—and still tremendously relevant to us today. Reading the Bible is how we come to know the God of the universe, our Creator. The Bible tells us who He is and what He's like, why He created us and what He expects of us. It reveals to us the sinfulness

of our own hearts—the pride, the selfishness, the rebellion—and introduces us to the Savior who can deliver us and help us be all that we were
meant to be.

There are literally hundreds of fabulous Bible commentaries, handbooks, and encyclopedias written by Bible scholars available to us today.
And if you've got the time and inclination, you can spend hours getting
lost in their pages, learning all kinds of fascinating facts and information. But unfortunately, for most of us, time is the one thing we don't
have much of. And frankly the thought of wading through some of those
eight hundred-page epics can be just as daunting as the original task. Talk
about information overload!

A Family Guide to the Bible was written to help busy parents, grandparents, and teachers with the basics: what's in the Bible, where to find
it, and how it all fits together. It's intended to be simple, family friendly,
and easy to understand and follow. Hopefully one day you'll have the
time to dig into some of those more detailed resources and reference
books. But this is a place to start, a first step in a lifelong journey—a
great adventure of faith!

The first three chapters of *A Family Guide to the Bible* give you a little
background information. "The History of the Bible" explains how we
got the book we hold in our hands today. "The Authority of the Bible"
discusses how we know we can trust it. And "The Message of the Bible"
provides an overview of the greatest story ever told, from Genesis to
Revelation—start to finish.

Next, we'll take a brief look at what's in each of the sixty-six books
that make up *the* book we call the Bible. Who wrote this particular book?
When and where? What are the highlights? Things to know? You'll find
it all right here.

The last section offers lots of practical tips and suggestions on things
like choosing a translation, using a Bible concordance or encyclopedia,
and organizing your own personal Bible study and/or family devotions.
There are Bible reading plans, maps and charts, and lists of Scriptures
that tell you where to find familiar Bible stories or verses that address
specific topics such as "What the Bible Says about Heaven."

It is my heartfelt hope and prayer that *A Family Guide to the Bible* will truly be a blessing, a help to you and your family, as each of you comes to know Jesus Christ more deeply, personally, and powerfully through the pages of His Word.

Christin Ditchfield

1

THE HISTORY OF THE BIBLE

Where Did It Come From?

"And we have the word of the prophets . . . men spoke from God as they were carried along by the Holy Spirit."

2 Peter 1:19, 21

*T*he word "Bible" comes from the Greek word *biblios*, meaning "book." Christians often refer to this book as "the Word of God," because we believe that it is literally God's Word, His message, or as some have said, His love letter to mankind. Every chapter, every verse, every word of Scripture was inspired by God himself.

But how did it come to us? How did we get the book that we hold in our hands today? Did it simply drop down from heaven one day? Was it delivered on somebody's doorstep by an angelic messenger?

The Bible was actually written over a period of more than 1,500 years by as many as forty different authors. God spoke to these men, and they wrote down what He said. He directed them, motivated them, moved them to write—and they responded by picking up their pens. Inspired by the Spirit of God, these men recorded the history of God's people, His commandments and decrees, prayers and poetry and songs of praise, letters of encouragement and instruction, and prophecies of things to come. At first these words were written on tablets of stone and clay, later on scrolls made of papyrus (plant fiber) and vellum (animal skins).

Over time, as new words—new scrolls—were added, they were gathered together and kept in places of honor in temples and synagogues and churches, to be brought out and read during worship services and special ceremonies. Local congregations of believers treasured them. The scrolls were also carefully copied by hand by scribes and scholars, then passed on to other communities, countries, and cultures down through the ages. Eventually scholars came up with systems to organize the scrolls, either into categories or chronological order. They divided the Scriptures into sections—chapters and verses and books—that not only made it simpler to find specific passages and study them, but also made it easier to check and cross-check to avoid errors in copying.

By AD 400, many different documents were circulating among the churches, each purporting to be Scripture. The greatest church leaders, religious historians, and Bible scholars of the day came together for a series of church councils. Their goal was to determine which of these writings were truly worthy of being considered sacred Scripture—which were the most respected, the most widely-regarded, the ones that could be verified as authentic, the ones that were consistent with established biblical teaching. They considered the external testimony (what others throughout history had thought of these books) and the internal testimony (what the books said about themselves and each other). And these church leaders prayed. They fervently prayed that God himself would guide them and give them wisdom and discernment.

When all was said and done, the church council had established what is known as the biblical "canon"—a collection of books, each of which had been recognized as meeting a certain standard or specific criterion. These same books make up the Bible we read today.

There are sixty-six individual books in the Bible, divided into two sections called "testaments." The word "testament" means "covenant" or "agreement"—as in a legally binding contract. The Old Testament is

God's covenant or commitment to mankind from the time of creation to the fall of Israel (when it ceased to be an independent nation and its people were sent into exile), approximately 1500 BC to 400 BC. There are thirty-nine books in the Old Testament, written mostly in Hebrew and organized into five different categories: the books of the Law (also known as the Law of Moses or "the Torah"), the Histories, Poetry and Wisdom, Major (longer length) Prophets, and Minor (shorter length) Prophets.

Fig. 1.1 The Old Testament

The Books of the Law	2 Chronicles	Ezekiel
	Ezra	Daniel
Genesis	Nehemiah	
Exodus	Esther	**Minor Prophets**
Leviticus	**Poetry and**	Hosea
Numbers	**Wisdom**	Joel
Deuteronomy	Job	Amos
History	Psalms	Obadiah
Joshua	Proverbs	Jonah
Judges	Ecclesiastes	Micah
Ruth	Song of Solomon	Nahum
1 Samuel		Habakkuk
2 Samuel	**Major Prophets**	Zephaniah
1 Kings	Isaiah	Haggai
2 Kings	Jeremiah	Zechariah
1 Chronicles	Lamentations	Malachi

The books of the Old Testament are sometimes referred to as "the Jewish Scriptures" because—along with "rabbinic tradition" (commentary and teachings on the Scriptures by religious leaders)—they are the foundation of the Jewish faith. Devout Jews still study and revere these books and observe these laws today.

Four hundred years after the last book of the Old Testament was written, the New Testament picks up the story with the birth of Jesus, the long-awaited Messiah or "deliverer," whose coming was foretold by the prophets of old. The New Testament is God's new covenant or commitment to His people—a fulfillment of promises made in the old covenant. "In the past God spoke to our forefathers through the prophets at many times and in various ways, but in these last days he has spoken to us by his Son . . ." (Hebrews 1:1–2).

The twenty-seven books of the New Testament were originally written in Greek sometime between AD 48 and AD 95. They are arranged into five categories: the Gospels, History, Paul's Letters (letters written by the apostle Paul), General Letters (letters written by other apostles or disciples of Jesus), and Prophecy.

Fig. 1.2 The New Testament

The Gospels	Galatians	James
Matthew	Ephesians	1 Peter
Mark	Philippians	2 Peter
Luke	Colossians	1 John
John	1 Thessalonians	2 John
History	2 Thessalonians	3 John
Acts	1 Timothy	Jude
	2 Timothy	**Prophecy**
Paul's Letters	Titus	Revelation
Romans	Philemon	
1 Corinthians	**General Letters**	
2 Corinthians	Hebrews	

Over the years, some Christians have mistakenly come to the conclusion that there is no need to study the Old Testament because it *is* "old," and therefore (supposedly) no longer valid. We don't live under the law of Moses or abide by all the rules and regulations established in Leviticus. We're not under the terms of the old covenant, but the new. However, Jesus Himself corrected this misunderstanding or misapplication of truth when He said: "Do not think that I have come to abolish the Law or the Prophets; I have not come to abolish them but to fulfill them. I tell you the truth, until heaven and earth disappear, not the smallest letter, not the least stroke of a pen, will by any means disappear from the Law until everything is accomplished" (Matthew 5:17–18).

As someone once observed:

The New is in the Old concealed; the Old is in the New revealed.

The authors of the New Testament quote the Old Testament literally hundreds and hundreds of times—some scholars have identified as many as two thousand comparable passages! In His preaching and teaching, Jesus quoted from at least twenty-two different books of the Old Testament.

Everything that the Old Testament teaches us about who God is and what He requires of us is absolutely still valid. His ultimate plan and purpose for mankind is still the same. Furthermore, Christianity was born out of Judaism. Knowing our history is key to understanding our present and our future. So both the Old and the New Testament have tremendous value to followers of Jesus today.

When the church councils first met to establish the biblical canon, there were some writings from both the Old Testament and the New Testament era that they chose not to include—books whose authorship couldn't be verified and whose content couldn't be authenticated, and books that were not historically regarded as Scripture by either Jewish or Christian religious leaders. Centuries later, the Roman Catholic Church decided to include some of these books in the Catholic Bible. They are referred to by Protestant Christians as the Apocrypha ("Apocrypha"

Fig. 1.3 The Apocryphal or Deuterocanonical Books

Tobit	Baruch
Judith	Additions to Daniel
Additions to Esther	1 Maccabees
Wisdom of Solomon	2 Maccabees
Ecclesiasticus	

originally meant "secret" or "hidden" writings, and many of these books have a mystical tone.) Roman Catholics call them the "deuterocanonical" or "second canon" books.

During the Middle Ages, the Greek and Hebrew Bible was translated into Latin. Monks living in monasteries devoted their lives to making copies of the Bible the only way they could—by hand! It was painstaking work. It took years to create a single copy of the sacred Scriptures from start to finish. Consequently, copies of the Bible were costly and precious and rare. Only the wealthiest individuals—bishops and kings and queens—could own Bibles of their own. A local church would be glad to have even one copy for the congregation to share. It would be kept on display, and only the priest would know enough Latin to be able to read it.

From the 1300s to the 1500s, a handful of courageous and dedicated Bible scholars began the work of translating the Scriptures into "the language of the common man"—English or German or French, depending on their nationality. These scholars believed that everyone, not just a privileged few, should have access to the powerful, life-changing truths of the Bible for themselves. The translators' efforts were greatly assisted by Johann Gutenberg's invention of the printing press, which revolutionized the process of book publishing—no more copying page after page by hand! (The Gutenberg Bible was printed in 1455.) However, these Bible scholars often found themselves caught up in a political power struggle as corrupt church leaders opposed and outlawed their work. If ordinary people could read the Bible for themselves, they might challenge the authority of the church and question some of its more questionable (and unbiblical) teachings! Many Bible translators were falsely accused of heresy, tortured, and killed for their commitment to the Scriptures, including William Tyndale, "the Father of the English Bible."

In the 1600s, King James commissioned a committee of fifty-four Bible scholars to create an accurate, authoritative, modern English translation of the Bible. It was first published in 1611, and became known as the King James or "Authorized" Version. For over three hundred years, it was considered *the* English language Bible.

The twentieth century brought advances in technology, new archaeological discoveries and information, and a renewed interest in Bible translation. Today we have dozens of contemporary English language translations and paraphrases. (For more on this, see "Choosing a Translation," on page 259.) The Bible has been translated into two thousand other languages, as well.

Sadly, there are still as many as four thousand people groups that don't have access to the Bible in their own language, and there are still countries and cultures hostile to the Christian faith, in which mere possession of a Bible is a capital offense.

The Reverend Billy Graham once said that perhaps an even greater tragedy is the fact that the Bible remains a "closed book" to millions of people "either because they leave it unread or because they read it without applying its teachings to themselves. . . . The Bible needs to be opened, read and believed."[1]

We need to remember what an incredible privilege it is to hold in our hands the Word of God Himself, His message, His love letter to us—to be able to read it for ourselves, learn to understand it, and apply it to our own lives today.

1. Quoted in Henrietta C. Mears, *What the Bible Is All About* (Ventura, CA: Regal/Gospel Light, 1998), 10.

2

THE AUTHORITY OF THE BIBLE

Can We Trust It?

*T*he Bible claims to be the Word of God—His message to mankind. Many books of the Bible begin with the phrase, "And the Word of the Lord came to. . . ." Others state that God said to the author, "Write in a book all the words I have spoken to you" (Jeremiah 30:2). King David claimed, "The Spirit of the LORD spoke through me; his word was on my tongue" (2 Samuel 23:2). Peter, one of Jesus' disciples explained, "You must understand that no prophecy of Scripture came about by the prophet's own interpretation. For prophecy never had its origin in the will of man, but men spoke from God as they were carried along by the Holy Spirit" (2 Peter 1:20–21).

The Bible also says about itself:

All Scripture is God-breathed and is useful for teaching, rebuking, correcting and training in righteousness. (2 Timothy 3:16)

For the word of God is living and active. Sharper than any double-edged sword, it penetrates even to dividing soul and spirit, joints and marrow; it judges the thoughts and attitudes of the heart. (Hebrews 4:12)

But if the Bible we hold in our hands today is literally thousands of years old, if it's been copied and copied and recopied—translated from old languages we don't read or speak—can we really trust it? Can we rely on it as our authority on life and faith? Maybe the original was inspired, but how do we know the copy we have today hasn't lost something in the translation? That it isn't full of errors and mistakes?

Scholars and skeptics through the ages have asked these same questions. Entire books have been written on the subject. Many of today's most brilliant, educated theologians and apologists ("defenders of the faith") started out to prove that we couldn't trust the Bible, that it wasn't accurate or authoritative or true. Somewhere along the way they became convinced of the exact opposite; they were overwhelmed by the evidence to the contrary. Here are just a few of their "arguments"—their insights and observations on why we can trust in the accuracy and authority of the Scriptures we have today.

Unity. Apart from divine intervention, it's impossible to believe there's any way that forty different authors over 1,500 years could write with the unity of thought and purpose that we find in the Scriptures. The worldview, the doctrines, and the teachings are all completely consistent with each other. There's no true conflict or contradiction, no real disagreement. Wherever it appears at first glance that there might be some sort of conflict or minor discrepancy, it turns out there's usually a fairly simple explanation for it. For instance, each of the four Gospels (Matthew, Mark, Luke, and John) tells the story of Jesus' earthly ministry. Many times, the Gospel writers provide word-for-word accounts of specific events and incidents. But then there are instances in which they seem to differ in what was said or who was present at the time. That doesn't mean one is right and another is wrong. Guided by the Holy Spirit, each writer chose to include the details that seemed most appropriate and relevant to him—and what he was trying to communicate to his readers. Just like the old story about the seven blind mice describing an elephant, each one's perspective might be different—but still correct! All together, they give us the full picture.

Accuracy. The scribes who first copied the Scriptures and the scholars who translated them did so with great reverence and respect for the original documents. They were meticulous in their attention to detail; they went to elaborate lengths, taking extraordinary care to ensure the accuracy of their work. Today we still have thousands of copies of Scripture made by hand before AD 1500, and they are all the same. In 1947, a shepherd discovered the Dead Sea Scrolls in a desert cave. These were copies of Scripture dating back sometime between 100 BC–AD 100, older than any other copies previously known to exist. And they are virtually identical to copies made thousands of years later. There is no variation in the doctrine or teachings.

History. For years, secular historians dismissed certain books of the Bible or certain passages of Scripture on the basis that there was no historical evidence to confirm the existence of such-and-such a city or such-and-such a king. They said there was no proof that these people mentioned in the Bible ever existed. But in the last two hundred years, archaeologists have made some amazing discoveries. They have uncovered records of long-lost cities, previously unknown kings, and entire races of people that history forgot, but the Bible didn't. Time after time, archaeological discoveries have supported and confirmed the biblical account.

Prophecy. There is also the fact that the Bible contains hundreds of prophecies—many of which have already clearly been fulfilled, with events taking place just as the prophets said they would. Long before the events happened, these prophets predicted the rise and fall of nations, empires, rulers, and kings—and their words came true. How else could they possibly know all that they knew, unless God really did speak to them, revealing the future often in specific and minute detail.

Of course it's true that not every contemporary translation of Scripture is as accurate as it could be or should be. There are individuals and organizations that have approached the translation of the Bible with an agenda. By changing certain words and phrases—adding some and omitting others—they have imposed their own views onto the Scripture and inserted their own teachings into the text. So it *is* important to choose an accurate, reliable translation for Bible reading. Some of the most widely read, reputable English translations are the King James Version, the New International Version, the English Standard Version, and the New American Standard Bible. (For more on choosing a translation, see pages 259–261 of this book.) When exploring a particularly difficult or complex passage of Scripture, it's a good idea to compare multiple translations to get a better feel for the original meaning of the text. (For more on studying the Bible, see chapter 6.)

Ultimately, as Christians we believe that the same God who inspired His servants to pick up their pens and record His words in the first place is still alive and well and at work in the world today. He is fully capable of guarding the transmission of His Word from generation to generation, preserving it and protecting it, so that His children can walk in His truth today just as they have for centuries.

3

THE MESSAGE OF THE BIBLE

What Is It All About?

*W*ritten over 1,500 years, by as many as forty different authors, all of the sixty-six individual books of the Bible combine to tell a single story, the story of God's love for humankind. It's the story of God's desire to enter into a "love relationship" with us—one in which He loves us and we love Him—with a passion to outrival the greatest human love stories of all time.

The first words of the Bible are, "In the beginning, God. . . ."

God is eternal and everlasting. He has always been. He will always be. At some point in time, many thousands and thousands of years ago, He decided to create the heavens and the earth—the universe as we know it, with all the galaxies and all the stars and planets hurtling through time and space. He created supernatural beings called "angels" to fill the heavens. God wanted to show His glory and majesty and wisdom and power. He wanted to share His boundless love. So He made Adam and Eve—the first man and first woman—and gave them a beautiful home in the garden of Eden, a lush paradise of perfection. God gave Adam and Eve authority over all the "beasts of the field and the birds of the air"—the animals with whom they shared the earth. He gave them the responsibility to care for their garden. He also gave them free will—the ability to think and choose for themselves what they would do, the ability to give and receive love freely. There was only one rule—one fruit of one tree that they weren't supposed to touch. But even one rule was too much for Adam and Eve to follow. They were easily tempted and led astray. For they were not alone in the garden.

Earlier there had been a rebellion in heaven. One of the archangels, Lucifer, had sought God's power and glory for himself. When God cast him out of heaven, Lucifer took a third of the angels with him. From then on, they were known as demons. And God made it clear that their ultimate judgment, their final punishment, was still to come. But until such time as He saw fit to end it, they would be engaged in a mighty battle of epic proportions.

For though he was powerless to take on God himself in all his glory, Lucifer saw an opportunity to hurt God—to wound His heart—by destroying the beauty of His creation and turning His precious children against Him. Lucifer found that he could fill them with greed and pride and rebellion and spur them on to defiance and disobedience. He appeared as a serpent in the garden of Eden and tempted Eve to eat the forbidden fruit. Eve gave it to Adam, and their innocence was lost. So was the sweet fellowship—the precious relationship—they had enjoyed with God. They were cast out of Eden. Adam and Eve and all of their descendants were sentenced to struggle and labor and pain—and eventually to face old age and death, instead of eternal life.

God was not caught off guard by this turn of events. He knew all along that given a choice, this is what the human heart would choose. But so great was His mercy and love that from the beginning He made a way to set things right. He put a plan in motion to rescue the human race—to save people from their sins and from themselves. As He sent them out of Eden, God told Adam and Eve that He would undo the damage they had done. One of their "seed"—their descendants—would do what they had not been able to do: obey. Through His obedience, He would save humankind. And He would crush the serpent forever.

Lucifer—also known as Satan or "the devil"—was free for the time being. Through the ages, he would continue to wreak havoc on creation, filling men's hearts and minds with evil, luring them away from the God who loved them and longed to hold them close to His heart. And God would allow it to happen, because it ultimately served His purposes—to test human beings and reveal what was in their hearts, to give them a legitimate choice as to who or what they would serve, and to help His children learn and grow in their relationship with Him. (An example of this is found in the story of Job.)

Adam and Eve felt the consequences of their sin right away. They had been created to populate the earth, and they had many, many children of their own. But sadly, few of their children learned from their parents' mistakes. Few of their children and their children's children chose to walk with God. Too many of them fell for the devil's lies, over and over again. Only a few generations later, the earth was full of wickedness—so much so that for a moment, God regretted ever having created human beings in the first place. He decided to wipe them all from the face of the earth—all except one righteous family. With Noah, God would start all over again. By faith, Noah built the ark just as God directed him to, and Noah and his whole family were saved. God was moved by Noah's courage and obedience. He hung a rainbow in the sky as a symbol of His promise never to destroy the earth with a flood again.

Hundreds of years later, the evil in the world had again become overwhelming. But this time God did something different. Instead of wiping all the wicked people from the face of the earth, He chose a righteous man to start a family—a family that would become a tribe, a people, and eventually a nation—that would be set apart for God himself. Out of all the people in the world, they would be *God's* people. He would teach them to know Him and to walk in His ways. He would nurture them and protect them and provide for them. He would bless those who blessed them and curse those who cursed them. God would hold them up as a shining example of what He wanted all humankind to be—an example of the kind of relationship He longed to have with all the peoples of the earth.

God chose Abraham, a man of exceptional faith and courage and conviction. He asked Abraham to leave his home and his country and everything he knew to go to a new land that God would show him, a land Abraham had never seen or heard of before. In this land, God would bless him and make him a great nation. His descendants would be as numerous as the stars in the sky and the sand on the seashore. All that Abraham had to do was trust God—receive all the blessings God wanted to give him—and walk in His ways. To seal the deal, God made a "covenant" with Abraham, a legally binding contract. And then when Abraham was 100 years old and his wife, Sarah, was 90, God gave them the first of their descendants. He gave them a child in their old age—a miracle baby, Isaac. When Isaac was a teenager, God tested Abraham's faith in and obedience to Him. God asked him to sacrifice Isaac, to give up his only son—the child through whom God's promises were supposed to be kept. Though he was heartbroken at the request, Abraham determined to do as God asked—only to find at the last minute that God had provided a substitute sacrifice to take Isaac's place. This was only a hint of things to come.

God gave Isaac twin sons, Jacob and Esau. The brothers fought each other for their father's blessing—the spiritual "birthright" belonged to Esau, but Jacob wanted it more. So the promise God made to Abraham would be fulfilled through the younger brother, not the older. God changed Jacob's name to Israel and gave him twelve sons: Reuben, Simeon, Levi, Judah, Zebulun, Issachar, Dan, Gad, Asher, Naphtali, Joseph, and Benjamin. Their descendants were so numerous, they became "tribes"—the twelve tribes—all of them the "children (and grandchildren and great-grandchildren) of Israel."

Jacob (Israel) made it all too obvious that Joseph was his favorite son—and Joseph's brothers hated him for it. They sold Joseph into slavery in Egypt and told his father he was dead. But God was with Joseph. In a series of miraculous events, Joseph went from prison inmate to prime minister, second only to the king of Egypt in wealth and power and authority. In time, Joseph forgave his brothers for what they had done to him. He brought the whole family to Egypt, where he could provide for them during a great famine. (These are the stories of the book of Genesis.)

Four hundred years later, there were over a million descendants of Abraham, Isaac, and Jacob living in Egypt. The Egyptians were afraid that these "Hebrew" people would take over their country, so they forced them into slavery. But God had not forgotten His promise to Abraham. God sent Moses to deliver the people and bring them out of slavery in Egypt, back to the land He had promised their ancestors. It took ten miraculous and horrific plagues to humble Pharaoh's heart and convince him to let the people go. The last of these plagues was particularly poignant. God struck down the firstborn son of every living creature in the land of Egypt, saving only those of the Hebrews who marked their doorposts with the blood of a sacrificial lamb. When God saw the blood, He "passed over" their houses. To this day, the Jewish people commemorate this miracle with the feast of "the Passover." And when all was said and done, another miracle took place: the Red Sea parted, and Moses led the people across on dry land.

The children of Israel had all but forgotten their culture, their heritage, and their faith. The former slaves were not yet strong enough to stand on their own as a nation. So God led them into the desert, to test them and teach them and train them. There, He renewed with them the covenant or contract He had made with Abraham. He gave them the Ten Commandments and the "Law of Moses"—a system of justice and rituals for work, worship, and family life. These things would set them apart from the other nations of the earth and help them to set an example of the kind of purity and holiness that pleases God. God reminded the children of Israel that if they would faithfully obey His commandments, they would be His very own—His chosen people. He would bless them and protect them and provide for them.

But the people didn't trust God; they constantly questioned Him and doubted Him. Their rebellion and disobedience turned what should have been a twelve-day trip to the Promised Land into forty years of wandering in circles under the hot desert sun. Even so, God did not abandon them. Like a loving Father, He disciplined them—and then comforted

them—time and time again. God told them that although their generation would not live to see it, their children and grandchildren would
inherit the Promised Land. (All of these stories are found in Exodus,
Leviticus, Numbers, and Deuteronomy.)

After the death of Moses, Joshua led the people out of the desert and
into Abraham's country, Canaan, the Promised Land. As God directed
them, the children of Israel drove out the heathen people living there
and took possession of the land. They divided it into regions for each
of the twelve tribes. God had set apart the tribe of Levi to serve Him in
the tabernacle (or Tent of Meeting). So the Levites had no land of their
own; instead, their families were given certain cities in the lands held by
each of the other tribes. And the tribe of Joseph had come to be known
by the names of his two sons. They were the half-tribes of Ephraim and
Manasseh. (This story is found in the book of Joshua.)

As time went on, the children of Israel continued to waver in their
faith and their commitment to God. When they wandered away from
Him and disobeyed Him, He allowed their enemies to triumph over
them in battle, to capture them and enslave them—just as He had said
He would. But when they repented of their sins, when they returned
to God and cried out to Him for deliverance, He rescued them—just
as He had said He would. From time to time, God sent His people
"judges"—mighty warriors like Samson, Gideon, and Deborah to deliver
them from the hands of their enemies, to administer justice, and then
to preside over the people in times of peace. (These are the stories of the
book of Judges.)

It was in the days of the judges that a young Moabite widow came to
know the God of Israel through the faith of her mother-in-law. She also
became a living example of God's power to rescue, redeem, and restore.
(This is the story of the book of Ruth.)

Another woman brought her miracle baby—a long-awaited answer to
prayer—to the tabernacle (the Tent of Meeting) to dedicate him to the
service of God. As a child, Samuel first heard the voice of God calling
to him in the middle of the night. He would grow up to become a great
prophet and judge over all Israel. But as Samuel's days were drawing to
an end, the people of Israel decided they no longer wanted to be led by

a judge who was a servant of an invisible King (God). They wanted an earthly king, a human king, like those of the nations around them.

God told Samuel to give the people what they asked for—exactly what they wanted. On the outside, Saul appeared to be everything a king should be. He was tall, dark, and handsome. He had a commanding presence and an air of authority. But on the inside, he was weak, jealous, greedy, and proud. His heart was not committed to God. Eventually, King Saul descended into madness, and a shepherd boy took his throne.

David was "the least of his brothers" in age, in appearance, and in strength. But he was a king on the inside, where it counts—a man of courage and character and integrity, a man "after God's own heart." Though he was far from perfect, David never lost his passion for God, his commitment or desire to please Him. As a teenager, with nothing more than a slingshot, David defeated the giant Goliath. He went on to become a mighty warrior and Israel's greatest king. (These stories are told in 1 and 2 Samuel and 1 Chronicles.) David also wrote beautiful songs of praise and worship—heartfelt prayers—that have touched the lives of millions of people from that day to this. (These are found in the book of Psalms.)

David's son, King Solomon, was the wisest man and the wealthiest king the world has ever seen. He compiled all the wisdom God had given him and others to share with the generations to come. (These are the books of Proverbs, Ecclesiastes, and Song of Songs.) And Solomon fulfilled his father's greatest dream by building a magnificent temple— no longer a tent—in which the children of Israel could meet to worship God.

Sadly, Solomon's son lacked his father's wisdom. Rehoboam's foolishness—his arrogance and pride—literally tore the country apart. Only the two tribes of Judah and Benjamin remained loyal to Rehoboam and agreed to serve him as king. Their region became known as Judah, the southern kingdom. The other ten tribes chose to follow one of Solomon's advisors, Jeroboam, as the new king of Israel, the northern kingdom. One people, divided into two countries, with two separate kings.

At times Judah and Israel were at war with each other; at times they were at peace. At times they obeyed God and kept His commandments—

particularly when their kings were righteous men who faithfully served God. But when their kings were wicked men, men who flouted God's commandments and worshiped idols instead, the people did the same. God sent the prophets Elijah and Elisha to demonstrate His mighty power—His infinite superiority to their worthless idols—and to urge them to return to Him once more. (These stories can be found in 1 and 2 Kings and 2 Chronicles.)

Even when His people turned their backs on Him, God didn't turn His back on them. He remembered the promise He had made to Adam and Eve, to Abraham and Isaac and Jacob. He remembered the covenant He had made with the children of Israel, even if they didn't. So in spite of their rejection of Him, their rebellion against Him, He never abandoned them. He sent many prophets—messengers—to remind the people of how much He loved them, of all the things He had done for them, and of all that they had promised to do for Him. God's prophets made it very clear just where the people had gone wrong, what it was that displeased God, and how they could make things right. They reminded the people that their Messiah was coming, their Deliverer was on the way. In the meantime, the prophets warned the people that if they didn't turn from their sin, God would allow them to suffer the consequences. He would discipline them. In fact, He would even remove His blessing, His protection from them, and let them face their enemies on their own. (These are the messages of Isaiah, Ezekiel, Hosea, Joel, Amos, Obadiah, Jonah, Micah, Nahum, Habakkuk, and Zephaniah.)

Sometimes the people took the words of the prophets to heart. They repented—temporarily. But ultimately, the people would not listen. They would not turn away from their sin. And so God allowed their enemies to triumph over them. The kingdom of Israel fell to the Assyrians in 722 BC and ceased to exist. Judah was conquered by the Babylonian Empire in 586 BC. The beautiful temple Solomon had built was desecrated and destroyed, the towns and villages burned to the ground, and most of the people killed or carried off in chains.

Jeremiah, the "weeping prophet," cried out to God in agony, expressing his people's heartache and despair. At the same time, he remembered that God had predicted that all of this would take place. And God had promised that after a time—seventy years, to be precise—His people would be set free. They would see their homeland again. (This is the message of Jeremiah and Lamentations.) Furthermore, God had not forgotten His promise to send a Messiah, a Deliverer, who would set His people free once and for all.

God's people were humbled by what had happened to them. Living in exile, a remnant struggled to remain true to Him, to keep His commandments, and to be a light in the dark world that surrounded them. These people discovered that God was still with them, even in their captivity. Shadrach, Meshach, and Abednego refused the king's command to bow before a massive idol. As punishment, they were thrown into a fiery furnace—and lived to tell about it! Daniel continued his ministry of intercession and prayer, even when it was outlawed. He survived a night in the lion's den. (These stories are found in the book of Daniel.) And an orphaned Jewish girl named Esther won the world's most famous beauty pageant. She became the Queen of Persia. Her position gave her the power and influence to foil a secret plot to annihilate the entire Jewish race. (This is the story of the book of Esther.)

Exactly seventy years after they were exiled, a Persian king named Cyrus gave permission for any of God's people who so desired to return to their homeland. They were allowed to resettle and rebuild the city of Jerusalem and the temple of their God. Among the settlers was Ezra, a scribe and priest who carefully instructed the people in God's law. A few years later, Ezra was joined by Nehemiah, a man who had been the king's cupbearer in Babylon. Newly appointed as the governor of Jerusalem, Nehemiah supervised the rebuilding of the city walls. (These are the stories found in Ezra and Nehemiah.)

Throughout this time, God continued to speak words of instruction, correction, and encouragement through His prophets. (These are the messages of Haggai, Zechariah, and Malachi.)

Then came the "silent years"—over four hundred of them—when God said nothing. Empires rose and fell. God's people continued to live in the land He had given them. But they never regained the prosperity—or independence—of their past. Their country was occupied; they were ruled by "puppet kings," clearly under the authority and control of the

Roman Empire. Now more than ever, they longed for their Messiah, the Deliverer God had promised who would set them free. Decades passed. Centuries passed. And nothing happened. There were no visions, no prophets or prophecies, no miracles, nothing.

Some grew tired of waiting. They gave up, bitterly concluding that God had forsaken them. Some tried to bring about their own deliverance through religious or political reform. Others simply got caught up in the dailiness of living. They had jobs to do, bills to pay, kids to raise. They were too busy for what must have seemed like fairy tales or wishful thinking. Nothing even remotely miraculous had ever happened in their lifetime—or their parents' or grandparents' or great-grandparents'. It was as hard for them to believe the supernatural stories of the Old Testament as it can be for some today. Somehow it just didn't seem real. A remnant remained faithful. A few watched and waited. And waited. And waited.

"But when the fullness of time had come, God sent forth his Son . . ." (Gal. 4:4, ESV).

The angel Gabriel appeared to a young woman named Mary and told her that she had been chosen to be the mother of God's Son. God sent Jesus to do what Adam had failed to do—to live a life of perfect obedience to God. Jesus set the example for all humankind. And He did so much more. He explained where God's people had gotten off track, how they had become consumed with the outward appearance of holiness—following all the rules and regulations to a T—when God wanted purity in their hearts. He told them that God wanted to establish a new covenant—a new contract—with His people, this one based not on following God's law but living in His love. They would be God's people, not because they followed His commandments perfectly (something they could never do anyway) but because they trusted in His Son—whose obedience to God would count for everyone.

In the thirty-three years of His earthly ministry, Jesus healed the sick, raised the dead, cast out demons, and calmed the storms. He called a group of disciples to follow Him, twelve especially: Simon Peter, Andrew, James, John, Philip, Thomas, Bartholomew (Nathanael), Matthew (Levi), James the younger, Simon, Thaddeus, and Judas. They would be His witnesses, testifying to all that they had seen and heard when they were with Him and carrying on His ministry after He had gone.

And then Jesus willingly laid down His life. He took the punishment for the sins of the world. Just as He had with Abraham and Isaac, God had provided a substitute. To save His people, He sacrificed His One and Only Son. Everyone who believed in Him and trusted in Him would be "covered" by the blood of Jesus. That is, God would see the blood of the sacrificial Lamb—the Lamb of God—and would "pass over" the people's sins and forgive them.

Jesus was brutally crucified—He suffered and died. But then on the third day, He rose from the dead in power and glory. He appeared to His disciples for forty days afterward, preparing them to carry on the work of the kingdom of God. Then He ascended into heaven, leaving them with the task of spreading the good news—proclaiming His salvation. He also gave them some very precious promises of His own. Jesus promised He would send God's Holy Spirit to give them the power to build His kingdom here on earth. He said that He himself would be with them in Spirit—He would never leave them or forsake them. And one day, He promised, He would come again. This time He would be coming for His own, gathering everyone who has believed in Him to live with Him in heaven forever. (The stories of Jesus are found in Matthew, Mark, Luke, and John.)

Just as Jesus promised, the Holy Spirit moved powerfully through the early church, the first Christians, as they carried out the Great Commission: preaching the good news of the gospel of Jesus Christ to everyone who would listen. People of many different cultures and countries answered God's call, finding their way to Him through His Son. Thousands and thousands became true believers.

The enemies of God were horrified and tried to put a stop to it. But their attempts backfired. The more suffering and persecution the church faced, the faster and stronger it grew. People were drawn to a truth so powerful, a faith so real, a relationship so precious, that it was worth dying for. Saul was a Jewish leader who arrested and even executed many of the first Christians. But on the road to Damascus, he had a miraculous encounter with Jesus himself—and his life was turned upside down.

Saul became Paul, the most famous apostle and Christian missionary. He traveled thousands of miles to preach the gospel in Europe and Asia and the Middle East. He endured every kind of persecution and suffering himself, for the privilege of sharing with others the life-changing power of knowing Jesus and trusting in Him. (These stories are told in the book of Acts.)

As he traveled from place to place, Paul kept in contact with the churches he had founded. As God gave him wisdom, Paul wrote them letters of encouragement and instruction. Sometimes he explained difficult doctrinal or theological issues; other times he offered very practical advice on family and church life. (These letters include Romans, 1 and 2 Corinthians, Galatians, Ephesians, Philippians, Colossians, and 1 and 2 Thessalonians.) The churches that received these letters often shared them with others, passing them on from one town or village, from one congregation to another.

Paul also wrote letters to individuals, to young pastors Timothy and Titus and to Philemon, the owner of a runaway slave. (These letters are 1 and 2 Timothy, Titus, and Philemon.) And he may have written a powerful sermon on the role of Jesus as our "high priest"—how He is the fulfillment of all the Old Testament prophecies and the mediator of our new covenant with God. (This is the book of Hebrews.)

Paul wasn't the only one writing down all the wisdom God had given him to share with the church. James, one of Jesus' younger brothers and the leader of the church in Jerusalem, wrote that "faith without works is dead" and that our actions speak louder than our words. (This is the book of James.) Peter, one of the original twelve disciples, wrote several letters encouraging the church to stand strong in times of suffering. (These are 1 and 2 Peter.) Jude, another of Jesus' brothers, warned believers to watch out for false teachers. And likewise, John the Beloved, who also wrote the gospel that bears his name, urged believers to resist worldliness and false teachings and to walk in the light of God's love. (These letters are 1, 2, and 3 John.)

John was the only one of the twelve disciples to live to be an old, old man—nearly all of the others died a martyr's death. Almost at the end of his life, living in exile on the isle of Patmos, John suddenly had a magnificent vision—a revelation—of how the world would end, how Jesus would come again, and how God would create a glorious new heaven and a new earth, a paradise for His people that would never end. (This is the message of the book of Revelation.)

John's prophecy is yet to be fulfilled. God's people waited thousands of years for Jesus to come to earth the first time. And it has been more than two thousand years since He left, promising that He would come again.

> But do not forget this one thing, dear friends: With the Lord a day is like a thousand years, and a thousand years are like a day. The Lord is not slow in keeping his promise, as some understand slowness. He is patient with you, not wanting anyone to perish, but everyone to come to repentance. (2 Peter 3:8–9)

After all these years, God's heart toward humankind is the same. It's a heart of love. To this day, He longs for each and every one of us to come to know Him—to receive the love that He has for us and to give Him our love in return.

Down through the ages and to this very day, those who are His keep their eyes on the skies . . . for, "Behold, I am coming soon!" (Revelation 22:12).

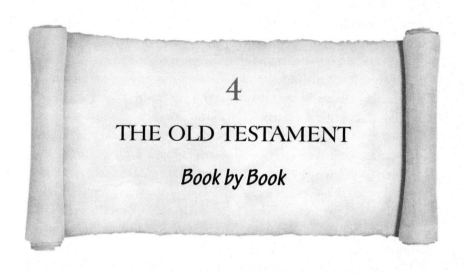

4

THE OLD TESTAMENT

Book by Book

GENESIS

■ **The Book:** Genesis

■ **The Author:** Moses

■ **The Audience:** The people of God

■ **The Setting:** The lands of the Middle East, 1450 BC–1400 BC

■ **The Story:** Genesis means "beginnings." This is the story of how it all began—how God created the world and all who live in it, and how He chose from them a people for His very own. There were problems right from the start, but God had a plan. It would take centuries, but over time His plan would unfold, His purposes would be revealed, and His promises would be fulfilled—every last one.

■ **The Message:** "In the beginning God created the heavens and the earth" (1:1). In the first five days, He puts the sun, moon, and stars in the sky. He separates the seas from dry land and covers the land with living, growing things—plants and animals. Then on the sixth day, "God created man in His own image, in the image of God he created him; male and female he created them" (1:27). On the seventh day, He rests. "God saw all that He had made, and it was very good" (1:31). God gives Adam and Eve—the first man and first woman—a beautiful home in the garden of Eden, a paradise of perfection. He also gives them authority over all the "beasts of the field and all the birds of the air." He gives them the responsibility to care for the garden and the gift of His presence, His friendship. There is only one rule, one fruit of one tree that they aren't supposed to touch. But even one rule is too much for Adam and Eve to follow. Satan—the devil—appears as a serpent and tempts Eve to eat the forbidden fruit. Eve gives it to Adam, and their innocence is lost. So is the sweet fellowship—the precious friendship—they have enjoyed with God. Adam and Eve are cast out of Eden. As a result of their sin, they and all of their descendants are sentenced to struggle and labor and pain—eventually to face old age and death, instead of eternal life (3:1–24). But God is merciful. He promises to punish the serpent for his part in the fall of man and to make a way to reconcile humankind to Himself. God tells the snake, "I will put enmity between you and the woman, and between your offspring and hers; he will crush your head, and you will strike his heel" (3:15). Adam and Eve feel the consequences of their sin right away. Life is much harder than they ever imagined it could be. Created to populate the earth, they have many, many children. But few of their children learn from their parents' mistakes. In a fit of jealousy and rage, their first son Cain murders his brother Abel (4:1–16). Few of Adam and Eve's other children and grandchildren and great-grandchildren chose to walk with God.

Only a few generations later, the earth is full of wickedness—so much so that for a moment, God regrets ever having created human beings in the first place. He decides to wipe them all from the face of the earth—all except one righteous man and his family. With Noah, God will start all over again. God directs Noah to build an ark—a huge ship—and gather into it animals of every shape and kind. Rain falls for forty days and forty nights, until the whole earth is flooded. Only those on the ark—Noah and his family—survive. God is pleased with Noah's obedience. He hangs a rainbow in the sky as a symbol of His promise never to destroy the earth with a flood again (6:1–9:17). "Then God blessed Noah and his sons, saying to them, 'Be fruitful and increase in number and fill the earth'" (9:1). Unfortunately, Noah's descendants do not disperse and fill the earth as God commanded them. Instead, they gather on one plain, in one city, building a great tower to reach into heaven. When God sees this, He confuses their language—He gives them many different languages—so that they will have to separate themselves (according to language groups) and spread out over the earth (11:1–9).

When the wickedness of humankind again becomes overwhelming, God calls another righteous man to start a family—a family that will become a tribe, a people, and eventually a nation set apart for God. He will teach them to know Him and walk in His ways, and they will be a shining example of the kind of relationship God longs to have with all the people of the earth. God chooses Abram, a man of exceptional faith and courage and conviction. He asks Abram to leave his home and his country and everything he knows to go to a new land that God will show him, a land Abram has never seen or heard of before. In this land, God will richly bless him. His descendants will be as numerous as the stars in the sky, the sand on the seashore. All that Abram has to do is trust God—receive all the blessings God wants to give him—and walk in His ways. God changes Abram's name to Abraham—"father of many nations"—and makes a "covenant" with him, a legally binding contract (12:1–15:21). Circumcision will be the outward, physical sign that Abraham and his descendants agree to the contract (17:1–27). As time passes, Abraham and his wife Sarah remain childless. The couple decides to try to make God's promise come true on their own by having Abraham start a family with Sarah's servant, Hagar. But Ishmael is not the son God promised (16:1–16). Nearly fourteen years later, when Abraham is 100 years old and his wife, Sarah, 90, God gives them what He considers to be the first of their descendants—a child in their old age, a miracle baby they name Isaac (18:1–15; 21:1–21). When Isaac is a young man, God tests Abraham's faith in and obedience to Him. He asks him to literally sacrifice Isaac, to give up his precious son, the "child of the promise." Though he is heartbroken at the request, Abraham determines to do as

God asks. On the way to the altar, Isaac notices they have no animal to offer as a sacrifice. Abraham tells him: "God himself will provide the lamb for the burnt offering, my son" (22:8). His words are prophetic. At the last moment, God does indeed provide a substitute sacrifice to take Isaac's place (22:1–19).

Later, God gives Isaac and his wife, Rebekah, twin sons, Jacob and Esau. The brothers fight each other for their father's blessing. The spiritual "birthright" belongs to Esau, the oldest, but Jacob wants it more. He tricks his brother into selling it to him and then tricks his father into giving it to him. So the promise God made to Abraham will be fulfilled through the younger brother, not the older (24:1–28:22). Jacob marries two sisters, Leah and Rachel. The first one he is tricked into marrying; the second he loves and labors for (29:1–30). In spite of Jacob's flaws, God is with him and blesses him for the sake of his father and grandfather. God gives Jacob visions of angels coming to and going from earth on a ladder that stretches to heaven (28:10–22). Later, Jacob wrestles with an angel in a contest not only of strength, but of persistence and determination— and Jacob wins (32:22–31)! God changes Jacob's name to Israel and gives him twelve sons: Reuben, Simeon, Levi, Judah, Zebulun, Issachar, Dan, Gad, Asher, Naphtali, Joseph, and Benjamin (29:31–36:43).

As a young man, Joseph begins to have visions and dreams of his own that seem to say God has destined him for greatness. Jacob (Israel) makes it all too obvious that Joseph is his favorite son—lavishing him with gifts such as a richly ornamented robe, a "coat of many colors," and Joseph's brothers hate him for it (37:1–11). They sell Joseph into slavery in Egypt and tell their father he is dead. But God is with Joseph. In a series of miraculous events, Joseph goes from slave and prison inmate to prime minister, second only to the king of Egypt in wealth and power and authority. Joseph interprets Pharaoh's dreams, warning him of a great famine soon to come—and under Joseph's guidance, the Egyptians begin storing up food in preparation (37:12–36; 39:1–41:57). When the famine hits and Joseph's brothers come to Egypt to buy food, they do not recognize the new ruler of Egypt as their own flesh and blood. Joseph tests his brothers to see if their hearts have changed, and finding that they have, he reveals himself to them and forgives them for what they had done to him (42:1–45:28). "'You intended to harm me, but God intended it for good to accomplish what is now being done, the saving of many lives. So then, don't be afraid. I will provide for you and your children.' And he reassured them and spoke kindly to them" (50:20–21). Joseph brings the whole family to Egypt, his father and his brothers' households (46:1–50:26). Their descendants will become so numerous that they will identify themselves as "tribes"—the twelve tribes—all of them the "children (and grandchildren and great-grandchildren) of Israel." Though they will live in Egypt for generations, Joseph reminds his family that their relocation is only temporary. One day God Himself will lead them out of Egypt and back to the land He promised to Abraham, Isaac, and Jacob (50:24).

Key Verse or Passage

"I will establish my covenant as an everlasting covenant between me and you and your descendants after you for the generations to come, to be your God and the God of your descendants after you." (Genesis 17:7)

More on This Story in the Bible: The story of God's people—"the children of Israel"—continues in Exodus, Leviticus, Numbers, and Deuteronomy. There are references to the events described in Genesis throughout the Bible, sometimes with more detail or further explanation of their significance. A concordance or a study Bible can help you find specific references and learn more.

Words to Know:

covenant: A promise, an agreement, a legally-binding contract.

blessing: All the good things God gives to His people—His protection and provision; the act of pronouncing or bestowing God's favor on others. In the Bible, words of blessing (and cursing) have a kind of power that can make them come true.

birthright: The special rights, privileges, and possessions inherited by the first-born son in Bible times; the birthright included a special blessing from the father and the authority to take over leadership of the family.

▥ **Did You Know?** Bible scholars call Genesis 3:15 the "protoevangelium"—the first good news, the first promise of a Savior. At the very same time that Adam and Eve learned of the curse their sin had brought on the world—almost in the same breath—God promised that one day the curse would be broken. One of their descendants would do what they had failed to do: live a life of perfect obedience to God. By doing so, He would crush the serpent and destroy the power of sin and death forever (see Romans 5:12–21)!

▥ **Making the Connection:** The never-ending conflict in the Middle East—the hostility between Jews and Arabs today—goes all the way back to Genesis. The Jewish people are the descendants of Abraham's son, Isaac, "the child of the promise" born through Abraham's wife, Sarah. The Arab nations are descendants of Abraham's son, Ishmael, born of a human attempt to bring about the fulfillment of the promise through the Egyptian slave girl, Hagar. In the New Testament, the apostle Paul explains that Sarah and Hagar were meant to be a living object lesson, an illustration of God's plan of redemption for all humankind (Galatians 4:21–31). Hagar represents the first covenant, the old covenant, which was based on obedience to the Law. God gave us the old covenant to show us how, in our human nature, we were all slaves to sin, unable to keep God's commandments. No matter how hard we tried, we could never be good enough on our own to earn God's favor. Sarah represents the new covenant, based on God's grace—His mercy extended to us through our faith in Jesus, His Son. Jesus was good enough for all of us. And then He took the penalty for our sin in our place. Now everyone who believes in Him and trusts in Him becomes a child of the promise, a descendant of "the free woman," an heir to the new covenant—regardless of the nationality of their birth.

EXODUS

▥ **The Book:** Exodus

▥ **The Author:** Moses

The Audience: The people of God

The Setting: The land of Egypt, 1446 BC–1440 BC

The Story: The book of Exodus tells how the children of Israel (the descendants of Jacob) became slaves in the land of Egypt and how God raised up Moses to deliver them from Pharaoh's oppression. The members of this family were numerous enough now to be called a nation, and Moses would lead them to a country of their own. But first he would have to convince Pharaoh to let his people go. And he would have to teach the people to know and love and serve the Lord their God.

The Message: Jacob (Israel) and his sons (the children of Israel) first arrived in Egypt as honored guests, but their descendants have become so numerous that the Egyptians now feel threatened by them. A new Pharaoh takes control by forcing the Israelites into slavery and later attempting to kill all of their baby boys at birth (1:1–22). When Moses is born, his mother hides him in a basket floating on the river, under the watchful eye of his sister, Miriam. Pharaoh's daughter finds the baby, adopts him, and raises him in the palace as her son (2:1–10). When Moses is grown, he tries to come to the aid of his people, murdering an Egyptian he sees mercilessly beating a Hebrew. But the Hebrews don't appreciate Moses' interference, and Pharaoh is furious—so Moses flees to the desert, where he finds shelter among the Midianites and starts a new life and a family of his own (2:11–25).

When Moses is 80 years old, God speaks to him from a burning bush: "I have indeed seen the misery of my people in Egypt. I have heard them crying out because of their slave drivers, and I am concerned about their suffering. So I have come down to rescue them from the hand of the Egyptians and to bring them up out of that land into a good and spacious land, a land flowing with milk and honey. . . . So now, go. I am sending you to Pharaoh to bring my people the Israelites out of Egypt" (3:7–8, 10). Moses is to tell the people that their God—whose name is "I AM"— has sent him to them. No longer young and brash and arrogant, Moses protests that he is not the man for the job. God promises to empower him and enable him to accomplish this seemingly impossible task— showing him all kinds of signs and wonders, including turning his staff into a snake. But Moses still resists, and God finally agrees to send Moses' brother Aaron to assist him and serve as his spokesman (4:1–17). When Moses returns to Egypt, he meets with the leaders of the twelve tribes of Israel and tells them all that God has said and done. Then he and Aaron approach Pharaoh with a request to let the people leave Egypt to offer sacrifices to God in the desert. Pharaoh flatly refuses—he "hardens his heart"—just as God told Moses he would (4:18–7:13).

God strikes the Egyptians with ten plagues to reveal His awesome power to them and to His own people. Plagues of blood, frogs, gnats, flies, livestock, boils, hail, locusts, darkness—and the one that makes Pharaoh finally relent, the death of every firstborn son in all of Egypt (7:14–12:39). After 430 years in Egypt, the children of Israel, who now number in the millions, begin their journey back to the land of their ancestors. Pharaoh quickly regrets letting them go and chases them to the edge of the Red Sea. God supernaturally parts the waters so that His people can cross on dry land, but when the Egyptians try to follow, they are drowned (12:40–14:31). "Then Moses and the Israelites sang this song to the LORD: 'I will sing to the LORD, for he is highly exalted. The horse and its rider he has hurled into the sea. The LORD is my strength and my song; he has become my salvation. He is my God, and I will praise him, my father's God, and I will exalt him'" (15:1–2).

In the wilderness God continues to miraculously provide for and intervene on behalf of His people, though their true nature is revealed as they become increasingly ungrateful and unappreciative. He sends them "manna"—bread from heaven—every day. When they complain that they want meat, He sends them quail (16:1–36). When they stop in a place where there is no water, the people accuse Moses (and God) of bringing them out in the desert to die. God makes a spring of water come gushing out of a rock (17:1–7). When a nearby people, the Amalekites, attack the Israelite camp, Moses lifts up his staff, and God empowers His people to triumph in battle (17:8–16). Moses finds himself serving not only as the people's spiritual and political and military leader, but as judge and justice of the peace. A visit from his father-in-law, Jethro, convinces Moses to delegate some of his authority and establish a hierarchy of leadership among the twelve tribes (18:1–27).

In three months time, the people reach Mount Sinai, where God displays His mighty power in thunder and lightning, smoke and fire and earthquakes (19:1–25). Through Moses, He gives the people instructions for holy living—rules and regulations for worship, community life, and family life—including the Ten Commandments. This system of laws will set them apart from other nations and make them a shining example of the kind of purity and holiness that pleases God (Exodus 20:1–23:33). All the people confirm their covenant—their commitment—to love and serve God. "Everything the LORD has said we will do" (24:3).

"The LORD said to Moses, 'Come up to me on the mountain and stay here, and I will give you the tablets of stone, with the law and commands I have written . . ." (24:12). God gives Moses very specific and detailed instructions for the creation of the tabernacle or "Tent of Meeting," where the people are to bring their offerings and sacrifices in worship (25:1–38:31). The ark of the covenant will hold the Ten Commandments and other sacred objects. Curtains will separate the courtyard and common areas from the Holy Place and the Most Holy Place, where the Spirit of God will dwell. Moses is up on the mountain a long time— forty days and forty nights—receiving all of these instructions. Back at the camp, the people grow impatient waiting for him—they want to get moving. "They gathered around Aaron and said, 'Come, make us gods who will go before us. As for this fellow Moses who brought us up out of Egypt, we don't know what has happened to him'" (32:1). Aaron makes a golden calf for them, and the people offer sacrifices and bow down and worship it. As Moses is coming down the mountain with his assistant, Joshua, he hears the drunken revelry that the people's "worship" has degenerated into. When he sees what has happened, he explodes with righteous anger, smashing the stone tablets God gave him and then destroying the golden calf. He severely reprimands Aaron and sends the Levites who are still faithful to God to rid the camp of those who have led the people astray (32:1–35). Moses goes back up on the mountain to meet with God again, and God writes His commandments on two new tablets to replace the ones Moses broke. After spending so much time in the presence of God, Moses begins to glow with His radiance (33:7–34:5).

When Moses returns to the camp, he calls all the people together and shares with them the instructions God has given for the construction of the tabernacle. When the work is complete, Moses holds a dedication ceremony and ordains Aaron and his sons as priests (35:1–40:33). A cloud appears over the Tent of Meeting; God's glory fills the tabernacle in such a powerful way that even Moses cannot enter. "In all the travels of the Israelites, whenever the cloud lifted from above the tabernacle, they would set out; but if the cloud did not lift, they did not set out—until the day it lifted. So the cloud of the LORD was over the tabernacle by day, and fire was in the cloud by night, in the sight of all the house of Israel during all their travels" (40:36–38).

Key Verse or Passage

"I am the LORD your God, who brought you out of Egypt, out of the land of slavery. You shall have no other gods before me. You shall not make for yourself an idol in the form of anything in heaven above or on the earth beneath or in the waters below. . . . You shall not misuse the name of the LORD your God. . . . Remember the Sabbath day by keeping it holy. . . . Honor your father and your mother. . . . You shall not murder. You shall not commit adultery. You shall not steal. You shall not give false testimony. . . . You shall not covet. . . ." (The Ten Commandments, Exodus 20:2–17)

More on This Story in the Bible: To learn how the children of Israel came to live in Egypt, read Genesis 37–50. Leviticus, Numbers, and Deuteronomy continue their story. References to these books—"the Law of Moses"—can be found throughout the Bible. Moses also wrote Psalm 90. The Gospels tell us that almost 1,500 years after he died, Moses appeared walking and talking with Jesus on the Mount of Transfiguration (Matthew 17:1–13; Mark 9:2–13; Luke 9:28–36). Other New Testament Scriptures shed further light on Moses' experience with the children of Israel (see Stephen's speech to the Sanhedrin in Acts 7:17–53 and the book of Hebrews, particularly Hebrews 11:24–26). Hebrews also explains how all of the instructions for the creation of the tabernacle and institution of the sacrifices and the ordination of the high priest were meant to foreshadow the coming of Jesus—the ultimate sacrifice, the true

High Priest, the presence of God dwelling not just *among*, but *within* the hearts of His people.

▓ Words to Know:

plague: a sudden widespread disaster; a highly infectious disease.

exodus: the departure or exit of a large group of people all at once.

covenant: a promise, an agreement, a legally-binding contract.

the tabernacle or Tent of Meeting: the tent that served as the place of worship for the children of Israel during their wilderness wanderings and early days as a nation. (Later it was replaced by a more permanent structure—the temple.)

▓ Did You Know?

Did You Know? As the children of Israel began their wilderness wanderings, they grumbled and complained that God had brought them out of slavery in Egypt only to let them starve in the desert. God, in His mercy, provided for them by sending bread from heaven. This miraculous food was like nothing they had ever seen, which it is why they called it "manna"—meaning "what is it?" Every day it appeared on the ground like the dew. "Each morning everyone gathered as much as he needed," and they were fed (Exodus 16:21). But there was one thing about the manna—it didn't keep. They couldn't store it up and save it for a rainy day. The Israelites had to gather a fresh supply every morning. They had to look to God and trust Him to provide for each new day. In that tradition, Jesus taught His disciples to pray: "Give us today our daily bread . . ." (the Lord's Prayer, Matthew 6:9–13). He also taught them that there was more to the story of God providing for the *physical* hunger of their ancestors in the desert. The Israelites' experience was symbolic—it pointed to the day when God would fulfill His people's *spiritual* hunger. "I tell you the truth, it is not Moses who has given you the bread from heaven, but it is my Father who gives you the true bread from heaven. For the bread of God is he who comes down from heaven and gives life to the world.' . . . Jesus declared. 'I am the bread of life. He who comes to me will never go hungry, and he who believes in me will never be thirsty'" (John 6:32–33, 35; see also John 6:48–51). Only He can know and understand and fulfill the deepest longings of the human heart.

■ **Making the Connection:** Today, Jewish people all over the world still celebrate the feast or festival of the Passover, commemorating the day when the angel of death "passed over" the Israelites' houses—which were marked with the blood of a sacrificial lamb—and struck down all the firstborn sons of the Egyptians (Exodus 12:1–42). It's what led to their deliverance from slavery in Egypt. But Passover has special meaning for Christians, as well. The New Testament explains that Jesus is the pure and spotless "Lamb of God" who was sacrificed to deliver us from our slavery to sin (see John 1:29; 1 Corinthians 5:7; Hebrews 9:11–10:18; and 1 Peter 1:18–21). Jesus' blood "covers" us; it marks us and sets us apart as His. So when God looks at us, He sees the blood of Jesus and "passes over" or forgives and forgets our sin, as something that has already been paid for. Jesus took the punishment in our place when He died on the cross and then was raised from the dead. So in a very real sense, the Christian celebration of Passover is Easter.

LEVITICUS

■ **The Book:** Leviticus

■ **The Author:** Moses

■ **The Audience:** The people of God

■ **The Setting:** The Sinai Peninsula, 1445 BC–1400 BC

■ **The Story:** On Mount Sinai God not only gave Moses the Ten Commandments, He gave him a whole system of laws—rules and regulations—that would keep His people pure and holy, set apart for Him. These laws would keep the children of Israel from adopting the evil practices of the nations around them, including idol worship, orgies, and child sacrifice. The laws would also prepare them to understand and recognize their need for a Savior (Hebrews 10:1–23).

■ **The Message:** "The Lord called to Moses and spoke to him from the Tent of Meeting . . ." (1:1). Moses gives the people God's instructions for bringing Him burnt offerings, grain offerings, fellowship offerings, sin offerings, and guilt offerings (1:2–7:38). Then the children of Israel gather together for a dedication service at the tabernacle (or Tent of Meeting), in which Aaron and his sons are formally ordained as priests (8:1–9:21). "When they came out, they blessed the people; and the glory of the LORD appeared to all the people" (9:23). However, it doesn't take long for two of Aaron's sons to disobey God's thorough and detailed instructions. Nadab and Abihu show their disrespect for God by burning incense without permission—and it costs them their lives. They are literally consumed by God's holy fire (10:1–2). "Among those who approach me I will show myself holy; in the sight of all the people I will be honored . . ." (10:3).

God gives His people further instructions on "clean" (healthy or permissible) foods and "unclean" foods. He describes procedures for purification after childbirth and cleansing from skin diseases, mildew, and bodily discharges (11:1–15:33). God also directs the people to observe an annual nationwide day of fasting and repentance for their sins—the Day of Atonement (16:1–34). Then there are more instructions for holy living. God is very specific about what He expects from His people in their behavior and their relationships. He establishes clear guidelines on everything from health and hygiene to sexuality to lawsuits and debt relief. He explains the appropriate punishments for particular sins. Through Moses, God gives the people instructions for the observance of a number of feasts and holiday celebrations (17:1–25:55). God promises that He has many blessings and rewards in store for those who walk in obedience to His commandments—not the least of which is the reassurance of His constant presence: "I will walk among you and be your God, and you will be my people" (26:12). The consequences for disobedience are just as clearly spelled out (26:14–45). "These are the commands the LORD gave Moses on Mount Sinai for the Israelites" (27:34).

Key Verse or Passage

"Consecrate yourselves and be holy, because I am the LORD your God. Keep my decrees and follow them. I am the LORD, who makes you holy." (Leviticus 20:7–8)

▦ **More on This Story in the Bible:** The story of the children of Israel that began in Genesis, Exodus, and Leviticus continues in Numbers and Deuteronomy. In the New Testament, the book of Hebrews explains how many of the rules and rituals established in Leviticus were meant to prepare God's people for the coming of the Messiah—Jesus—and help them understand what He accomplished for them through His suffering and sacrificial death.

▦ **Words to Know:**

"**clean**": pure and uncontaminated; a person who was "clean" could participate in ceremonial worship and other aspects of community life, while a person who was "unclean" could not (at least, not until they'd been *made* clean by following the instructions God had given in the Law).

holy/holiness: perfect and pure, set apart for (and by) God.

consecrate: to set apart or dedicate to the service of God.

atonement: the act of paying for one's mistakes and making things right; reconciling or restoring relationships that have been damaged by wrongdoing.

▦ **Did You Know?** Leviticus means "of the Levites." The tribe of Levi was set apart by God to serve Him as priests. The Levites led the community in worship, offered their sacrifices, and cared for the tabernacle (and later the temple) itself.

▦ **Think about It:** These instructions that God gave the children of Israel were for a specific people living in a specific time—and for a very specific purpose. It's a mistake to take a verse here or there out of context— particularly verses that clearly address cultural and not moral or spiritual issues—and insist that they are still binding to believers today. We are no longer "under the Law" and obligated to the terms of the old covenant or contract (Galatians 3:24–26; Hebrews 9:15). It's also a mistake to completely ignore or disregard these instructions, as they reveal a great deal about the character and nature of God and His purpose for mankind. The moral principles at the heart of the Law are timeless and eternal.

▨ **Making the Connection:** Today it's a holiday we know as Yom Kippur. In the Old Testament, it was referred to as the Day of Atonement. This was a solemn day of fasting, prayer, and repentance. The nation of Israel gathered together to confess its sins—both corporate and individual—to seek atonement and reconciliation with God. This was the only day of the year that the priest could step beyond the veil in the temple and enter into the Holy of Holies—the place where the presence of God rested. The priest represented the people and served as a mediator on their behalf. He sacrificed a goat as a sin offering and sprinkled its blood on the mercy seat. Outside, he laid his hands on another goat and confessed Israel's sin once again. This "scapegoat" was taken outside of town and allowed to wander away in the wilderness, symbolically carrying their sins away with him.

The Bible tells us that when Jesus died on the cross, He became a sacrifice for us. He paid the penalty for our sin completely, once and for all. He removed the barrier that separated us from God (see Hebrews 9–10). In fact, Matthew 27:51 tells us that at the moment He died, "the curtain of the temple was torn in two from top to bottom." Because of the blood of Jesus, we have all been given access to the Holy of Holies. We can enter the presence of God without fear or shame. Our sins have been forgiven, blotted out, washed away in the blood of the Lamb. A day of sorrow has become a day of celebration.

NUMBERS

▨ **The Book:** Numbers

▨ **The Author:** Moses

▨ **The Audience:** The people of God

▨ **The Setting:** From Mount Sinai to the Plains of Moab, 1445 BC–1400 BC

▨ **The Story:** Numbers gets its name from the "numbers" of people counted in the first census of the children of Israel after they left Egypt. God had miraculously delivered them from four hundred years of slavery, and now He was about to lead them into the land He had promised to give the descendants of Abraham, Isaac, and Jacob. Unfortunately, the people's rebellion and disobedience would keep them wandering in the wilderness instead.

The Message: As the children of Israel prepare to leave Mount Sinai and set out for the Promised Land, God tells Moses to take a census to count the number of men eligible to serve in the army (1:1–54). He gives instructions on the position—in relation to the tabernacle—that each of the tribes should take as they travel and where they should pitch their tents (2:1–34). There are more detailed instructions for the priests— the Levites—and rules and regulations for the community as a whole (3:1–6:27; 15:1–41; 18:1–19:22). All the people gather for a special ceremony dedicating the tabernacle (7:1–9:23). And now their journey begins in earnest.

Sadly, there is trouble right from the start. The people constantly grumble and complain. Some say they are sick of manna, the miraculous bread of heaven that God sends them each day. They want meat! So God sends them a storm of quail; the birds pile up on the ground three feet deep. Now the people have so much meat, they literally choke on it (11:4–35). Next, Aaron and Miriam chafe under their younger brother's leadership; they're resentful of Moses' position and influence. After all, God has spoken through them, too. They start a rebellion disguised as concern over Moses' marriage to a Cushite (or Midianite) woman—an outsider. But God silences them and makes it very clear that He is the one who has chosen Moses to lead the people. He makes a distinction between Moses and the others who serve him. "When a prophet of the LORD is among you, I reveal myself to him in visions, I speak to him in dreams. But this is not true of my servant Moses; he is faithful in all my house. With him I speak face to face . . ." (12:6–8).

When the children of Israel arrive at the borders of Canaan, the Promised Land, Moses sends twelve men (representing each of the twelve tribes) to go ahead of them and scout out the lay of the land (13:1–33). Ten of the spies return discouraged by the size and strength of the people they will have to drive out in order to take possession of the land. Two of the spies, Joshua and Caleb, see things differently: "The land we passed through and explored is exceedingly good. If the LORD is pleased with us, he will lead us into that land, a land flowing with milk and honey, and will give it to us. . . . Do not be afraid of the people of the land, because we will swallow them up. Their protection is gone, but the LORD is with us . . ." (14:7, 9). But the children of Israel *are* afraid, so afraid that they flat-out refuse to enter the Promised Land. After all the miraculous things God has done for them, they still don't trust Him. So God says they will have to wander in the desert until every member of their generation—except for Joshua and Caleb—has died. "For forty years—one year for each of the forty days you explored the land—you will suffer for your sins and know what it is like to have me against you" (14:34). Their children will be the ones to inherit the Promised Land. When the people realize the cost of their disobedience, they do an abrupt about-face. They decide they will obey God, after all. Moses warns them that it's too late and that God is not with them, but the people try to enter the Promised Land anyway—only to be driven out by its fierce inhabitants. There is nothing for them to do now but return to the desert (14:1–45).

Once again, the people grumble and complain—this time crying out for water. *Why did you bring us out into this desert to die? We would have been better off in Egypt!* God tells Moses to speak to a rock and command water to spring forth from it. But in his anger and frustration with the people, Moses strikes the rock instead. The people get the water they've been clamoring for, but Moses loses his own privilege of entering the Promised Land (20:1–13).

The kings of nearby nations grow nervous, watching this vast people moving up and down along their borders—and sometimes across or through their lands. They have heard what happened to the Egyptians. Those who try to attack the Israelites are utterly destroyed (21:1–3, 21–35). The king of Moab calls for Balaam, a "prophet-for-hire" to come and curse the people of God. But along the way, Balaam's donkey rises up to rebuke him! And when Balaam finally arrives where the Israelites are camped, he speaks only the words God has put in his mouth—words of blessing instead of cursing (22:1–24:25).

As the forty years of wilderness wandering draw to a close, God tells Moses to take another census and count the people who will enter the

Promised Land. He gives instructions for dividing the land among the twelve tribes and appoints Joshua to be Moses' successor (26:1–27:23; 32:1–42). God reminds the people how to present their offerings and sacrifices and how to celebrate their national holy days (holidays)—the Passover, the Feast of Weeks, the Feast of Trumpets, the Feast of Tabernacles, and the Day of Atonement (28:1–29:40). Moses recounts all the steps and stages of the Israelites' journey from Egypt to the Promised Land— every stop along the way (33:1–56). And he describes the geographical boundaries that God has established—north, south, east, and west—for the land God is giving His people as their inheritance (34:1–29).

Key Verse or Passage

"The LORD bless you and keep you; the LORD make his face shine upon you and be gracious to you; the LORD turn his face toward you and give you peace." *(Numbers 6:24–26)*

More on This Story in the Bible: The book of Numbers continues the story of Moses and the children of Israel that begins in Exodus and Leviticus and is remembered in Deuteronomy. Some of the most significant events in Israel's history inspired the Psalms; others are explained in the New Testament book of Hebrews.

Words to Know:

The tabernacle or Tent of Meeting: the tent that served as the place of worship for the children of Israel during their wilderness wanderings and early days as a nation. (Later it was replaced by a more permanent structure—the temple.)

Levites: the descendants of Jacob (Israel) who were set apart by God to serve Him as priests. The Levites aren't counted among the twelve tribes to receive their own territory in the Promised Land; instead they get cities in each of the other tribes' territories.

sanctuary: a holy place set apart for worship; the tabernacle.

oracle: a prophecy, a parable, or a proverb.

blessing: all the good things God gives to His people, including His protection and provision; the act of pronouncing or bestowing God's favor on others. In the Bible, words of blessing (and cursing) have a kind of power that can make them come true.

Think about It: Balaam—the "prophet-for-hire"—was prevented from cursing God's people outright. No matter how much he tried, he could only speak the words God allowed him to, words of blessing instead of cursing (22:1–24:25). So Balaam came up with another plan to please his employers, a much more subtle strategy to destroy God's chosen people (31:16). Balaam suggested that the Moabites use "wine, women, and song" to seduce the children of Israel. Israelite men who got involved with Moabite women would find themselves worshiping Moabite gods in order to please their paramours. Then there would be no need for Balaam to curse them—they would bring a curse upon themselves. God would punish them severely for their sin. Sadly, Balaam's strategy was all too effective then—and it still is today (25:1–18).

Making the Connection: At one point, when the children of Israel rebelled against God, He allowed a plague of venomous snakes to attack them, and many people died. When those who were still living repented and asked God to forgive them, He stopped the plague. God told Moses to craft a bronze snake and hang it up high on a pole. Anyone who had been bitten could look up and be healed and live (21:4–9). Thousands of years later, Jesus would point to this event in Israel's history as one that was meant to be symbolic of His mission and ministry: "Just as Moses lifted up the snake in the desert, so the Son of Man must be lifted up, that everyone who believes in him may have eternal life" (John 3:14–15).

DEUTERONOMY

The Book: Deuteronomy

The Author: Moses

The Audience: The people of God

The Setting: The Plains of Moab, between 1401 BC and 1400 BC

■ **The Story:** Deuteronomy means "second law" or "repetition of the law." In this series of sermons, Moses reviews everything that has happened to the children of Israel—all the lessons they have learned—from the time they left Egypt until they arrived at the Promised Land. In what is, in essence, his farewell address, Moses reminds the people to keep all of God's commandments and honor their covenant with Him.

■ **The Message:** Moses begins with a history lesson—a review of how far the children of Israel have come since their days as slaves in Egypt and the battles they have fought and won. Their parents and grandparents lost their chance to enter the Promised Land; now it is their turn (1:1–4:14). An incredible adventure lies ahead of them: "The LORD your God, who is going before you, will fight for you, as he did for you in Egypt, before your very eyes, and in the desert. There you saw how the LORD your God carried you, as a father carries his son, all the way you went until you reached this place" (1:30–32). Moses reminds the people what an incredible privilege it is to know God the way they know God, to experience His presence and His power the way that they have (4:32–40). He repeats the Ten Commandments that God gave him on Mount Sinai and reminds the people of the commitment they made to love and serve God always (5:1–33; 6:1–25).

God says it is vitally important that the children of Israel drive out all of the heathen nations living in the Promised Land, and that they do not make treaties with them or intermarry with them. Otherwise, they will become just like them—when they are *supposed* to be different. "For you are a people holy to the LORD your God. The LORD your God has chosen you out of all the peoples on the face of the earth to be his people, his treasured possession" (7:6). God didn't choose them because they were the most numerous people, the most powerful people, or even the most spiritual people. On the contrary: "It is not because of your righteousness or your integrity that you are going in to take possession of their land; but on account of the wickedness of these nations, the LORD your God will drive them out before you . . ." (9:5). "It was because the LORD loved you and kept the oath he swore to your forefathers that he brought you out with a mighty hand and redeemed you from the land of slavery . . ." (7:8).

Moses says, "Remember how the LORD your God led you all the way in the desert these forty years, to humble you and to test you in order to know what was in your heart, whether or not you would keep his commands. He humbled you, causing you to hunger and then feeding you with manna, which neither you nor your fathers had known, to teach you that man does not live on bread alone but on every word that comes from the mouth of the LORD. Your clothes did not wear out and your feet did not swell during these forty years. Know then in your heart that as a man disciplines his son, so the LORD your God disciplines you" (8:2–5). The children of Israel must remember their past as they move into their future. "When you have eaten and are satisfied, praise the LORD your God for the good land he has given you. Be careful that you do not forget the LORD your God, failing to observe his commands, his laws and his decrees that I am giving you this day" (8:10–11).

Moses reminds the people of how—when he was up on Mount Sinai receiving the Ten Commandments—they provoked God to anger by worshiping a golden calf (9:7–29). In his own frustration with the people, Moses smashed the original stone tablets and God had to give him new ones (10:1–11). "And now, O Israel, what does the LORD your God ask of you but to fear the LORD your God, to walk in all his ways, to love him, to serve the LORD your God with all your heart and with all your soul, and to observe the LORD's commands and decrees that I am giving you today for your own good?" (10:12–13).

Moses tells the people, "When you enter the land the LORD your God is giving you, do not learn to imitate the detestable ways of the nations there. Let no one be found among you who sacrifices his son or daughter in the fire, who practices divination or sorcery, interprets omens, engages in witchcraft, or casts spells, or who is a medium or spiritist or who consults the dead. Anyone who does these things is detestable to the LORD, and because of these detestable practices the LORD your God will drive out those nations before you. You must be blameless before the LORD your God" (18:9–13). God strictly—and repeatedly—forbids

His people to engage in idolatry, the worship of other gods (4:15–31; 13:1–18; 16:21–17:7).

Moses repeats God's instructions on everything from marriage and divorce to crime and punishment to the proper procedures for offering sacrifices and celebrating holy days (12:1–32; 14:1–26:19). God makes it very clear that there are blessings (rewards) for obedience and curses (punishments) for disobedience (28:1–19). God is giving them a choice; it is up to them to make a decision: "Now what I am commanding you today is not too difficult for you or beyond your reach. It is not up in heaven, so that you have to ask, 'Who will ascend into heaven to get it and proclaim it to us so we may obey it?' Nor is it beyond the sea, so that you have to ask, 'Who will cross the sea to get it and proclaim it to us so we may obey it?' No, the word is very near you; it is in your mouth and in your heart so you may obey it. See, I set before you today life and prosperity, death and destruction. . . . Now choose life, so that you and your children may live" (30:11–15, 19).

Moses records all of these things for future generations in the Book of the Law (31:9–12). Then he blesses each of the twelve tribes and the nation of Israel as a whole: "Who is like you, a people saved by the LORD? He is your shield and helper and your glorious sword . . ." (33:29). Moses commissions his successor, Joshua: "The LORD himself goes before you and will be with you; he will never leave you nor forsake you. Do not be afraid; do not be discouraged" (31:8). Moments before Moses' death, the Lord leads him to the top of Mount Nebo where he can look out over the Promised Land and see it with his own eyes—even though he will not be allowed to enter it (1:37; 34:1–4). "Since then, no prophet has risen in Israel like Moses, whom the LORD knew face to face, who did all those miraculous signs and wonders the LORD sent him to do in Egypt—to Pharaoh and to all his officials and to his whole land. For no one has ever shown the mighty power or performed the awesome deeds that Moses did in the sight of all Israel" (34:10–12).

Key Verse or Passage

"Hear, O Israel: The LORD our God, the LORD is one. Love the LORD your God with all your heart and with all your soul and with all your strength. These

commandments that I give you today are to be upon your hearts. Impress them on your children. Talk about them when you sit at home and when you walk along the road, when you lie down and when you get up. Tie them as symbols on your hands and bind them on your foreheads. Write them on the doorframes of your houses and on your gates." (Deuteronomy 6:4–9)

More on This Story in the Bible: The stories that Moses retells in Deuteronomy are first found in Exodus, Leviticus, and Numbers. They continue in the book of Joshua. Some of the most significant events in Israel's history inspired the Psalms; others are explained in the New Testament book of Hebrews.

Words to Know:

holy/holiness: perfect and pure, set apart for (and by) God.

blessings: all the good things God gives to His people, including His protection and provision; the act of pronouncing or bestowing God's favor on others. In the Bible, words of blessing (and cursing) have a kind of power that can make them come true.

Did You Know? Deuteronomy 34:7 tells us, "Moses was a hundred and twenty years old when he died, yet his eyes were not weak nor his strength gone." When the time came, God Himself buried Moses. "To this day no one knows where his grave is" (34:6). Perhaps the reason Moses' burial place is a secret is that God did not want it to become a shrine—a setting for idolatry and misplaced worship—or a target for desecration by Israel's enemies. Interestingly, in the New Testament, Jude refers to an argument that took place over the body of Moses between Michael the archangel and the devil. Jude mentions the story to remind his readers that human beings should have a proper respect for the power of supernatural beings—both good and evil—and remember that the authority to rebuke evil beings comes only from God (see Jude 9).

Making the Connection: The words of Deuteronomy 6:4–9, along with Deuteronomy 11:13–21 and Numbers 15:37–41, make up "the shema"—the Jewish confession of faith. These sacred verses are the centerpiece of all morning and evening prayers recited by devout Jews today. In Matthew 22:36–38, Jesus said that all of the Law could be summed up in Deuteronomy 6:5, "Love the Lord your God with all your heart and with all your soul and with all your strength" and in Leviticus 19:18, "Love your neighbor as yourself."

Think about It: Many people are familiar with the instructions God gave Moses regarding the appropriate punishment for criminal behavior in Deuteronomy 19:21: "life for life, eye for eye, tooth for tooth. . . ." The law made provision for those who caused harm to others accidentally or unintentionally. But those who willfully, recklessly, or deliberately violated God's commandments and committed crimes against the people of the community had to be punished—in such a dramatic way that it would deter others from following in their footsteps (Deuteronomy 19–25).

But in the New Testament, Jesus made it clear that this law established to punish criminals was not license to hate or harbor bitterness and unforgiveness in our hearts. It doesn't give individuals the right to pursue vengeance or retribution: "You have heard that it was said, 'Eye for eye, and tooth for tooth.' But I tell you, Do not resist an evil person. If someone strikes you on the right cheek, turn to him the other also. And if someone wants to sue you and take your tunic, let him have your cloak as well. If someone forces you to go one mile, go with him two miles. Give to the one who asks you, and do not turn away from the one who wants to borrow from you. . . . I tell you: Love your enemies and pray for those who persecute you . . ." (Matthew 5:38–42; 44). Ultimately, it is God's responsibility to settle the score (Romans 12:19).

JOSHUA

The Book: Joshua

The Author: Unknown—possibly Joshua

The Audience: The people of God

The Setting: The land of Canaan, between 1405 BC and 1383 BC

The Story: After the death of Moses, Joshua led the children of Israel into the Promised Land. But before they could settle into their new country and establish themselves as a nation, they had to drive out the heathen peoples living there. It was a daunting task, but God said He would be with them every step of the way.

The Message: As Joshua takes over the leadership of the children of Israel, God appears to him and says: "I will give you every place where you set your foot. . . . No one will be able to stand up against you all the days of your life. As I was with Moses, so I will be with you; I will never leave you nor forsake you" (1:3, 5). God urges Joshua: "Be strong and courageous. . . . Do not let this Book of the Law depart from your mouth; meditate on it day and night, so that you may be careful to do everything written in it. Then you will be prosperous and successful" (1:7–8).

The people prepare to cross the Jordan River and enter the Promised Land; Joshua sends spies out ahead to determine what opposition they may face—specifically from the heavily fortified city of Jericho. When the spies reach the city, they find shelter in the home of Rahab, a prostitute, who hides them from the king's soldiers. Rahab tells the spies, "I know that the LORD has given this land to you and that a great fear of you has fallen on us, so that all who live in this country are melting in fear because of you" (2:9). She asks the spies to spare her and her family, just as she has spared them (2:12–21).

Forty years after the children of Israel left Egypt, a new generation is ready to take possession of the Promised Land. As they step into the Jordan River, God parts the waters just as He did at the Red Sea (3:1–17). On the other side, the people build a memorial with stones from the dry riverbed to help them remember this historic day and God's miraculous intervention on their behalf (4:1–24). The children of Israel realize that during their wilderness wanderings, they have neglected to circumcise their sons in keeping with the covenant God made with Abraham. Before they go any further, the whole nation must be circumcised at once (5:1–12).

Joshua has an encounter with a supernatural being—"the Commander of the Lord's Army"—who gives him a unique strategy for conquering the city of Jericho: "March around the city once with all the armed men. Do this for six days. . . . On the seventh day, march around the city seven times, with the priests blowing the trumpets. When you hear them sound a long blast on the trumpets, have all the people give a loud shout; then the wall of the city will collapse . . ." (6:3–5). Joshua and the people follow God's instructions to the letter, and the city wall crumbles, just as God said it would. The armies of Israel rush in to attack the stunned inhabitants of the now defenseless city (6:20–21). "But Joshua spared Rahab the prostitute, with her family and all who belonged to her . . . and she lives among the Israelites to this day" (6:25).

After the battle of Jericho, the children of Israel move on to attack Ai—a much smaller, weaker city. But to their shock and dismay, they are soundly defeated (7:1–5). Joshua cries out to God for an explanation, and God reveals to him that there is sin in the camp. Some of His people have disobeyed his commands and kept for themselves plunder from the city of Jericho—things that were supposed to be "devoted" to destruction. God wants His people to understand that even one person's sin can negatively impact the entire community. Therefore, the guilty party— Achan and his family—must pay with their lives for their disobedience (7:6–26). Once Achan's sin has been dealt with, Joshua and the armies of Israel set up an ambush for the people of Ai. This time they destroy the city utterly and completely (8:1–29). Afterward, the people sacrifice offerings to show their gratitude to God and renew their covenant with Him (8:30–35).

Now God had told His people not to make any peace treaties with the heathen people living in or around Canaan because He wanted all of them driven out. But the men of Gibeon deceive Israel's leaders into believing that they are from a far off country, and an unfortunate alliance is made (9:1–27). In battle against the five kings of the Amorites God again displays His awesome power, throwing Israel's enemies into confusion, raining hail down on them from the sky, and—in answer to Joshua's prayer—making the sun stand still for a full day, so that Israel has the time and the daylight to fight to victory (10:1–15).

Under Joshua's leadership and with God's mighty power, the children of Israel have defeated thirty-one kings and captured their cities

(12:1–24). But there are still some battles to be fought, some kings and kingdoms to defeat. Through Joshua, God gives the people specific instructions to go on and finish what they started and then divide the land into territories for each of the tribes (13:1–22:34).

Joshua calls together the elders and leaders of the tribes to give them what will turn out to be his "farewell address"—his last opportunity to counsel and advise the people he has cared for and faithfully led all these years (23:1–24:27). He recounts their history and reminds the people of God's goodness to them in the past, all the miracles He has done on their behalf, the mercy and grace He has shown them. Joshua speaks of the great opportunities ahead for them and their children in the Promised Land. And he challenges them to decide once and for all whether or not they will worship the One true God. Joshua says they can serve other gods if they want to. "But as for me and my household, we will serve the Lord" (24:14–15). The people reply, "We too will serve the Lord, because he is our God" (24:18). Joshua cautions the people against making promises they can't keep—but they insist: "We will serve the Lord our God and obey Him" (24:24). So Joshua leads the people in a ceremony renewing their covenant with God. And then at the age of 110, Joshua breathes his last. "Israel served the Lord throughout the lifetime of Joshua and of the elders who outlived him and who had experienced everything the Lord had done for Israel" (24:31).

Key Verse or Passage

"Be strong and courageous. Do not be terrified; do not be discouraged, for the Lord your God will be with you wherever you go." (Joshua 1:9)

More on This Story in the Bible: The book of Joshua continues the story of the children of Israel that begins in Exodus, Leviticus, Numbers, and Deuteronomy. Some of the most significant events in Israel's history inspired the Psalms; others are explained in the New Testament book of Hebrews.

Words to Know:

consecrated: set apart or dedicated to the service of God.

circumcision: a visible, physical sign of the covenant or contract between God and His people. Circumcision represented the people's willingness to walk in obedience to God's commandments. To be uncircumcised was to be disobedient and rebellious—it was a rejection of God and His commandments. Sometimes the Bible uses the word symbolically—for instance, when it describes people as having "circumcised" or "uncircumcised" hearts.

inheritance: the land that God gave the children of Israel to fulfill His promise to their ancestors, Abraham, Isaac, and Jacob.

Think about It: Sometimes it's hard for us to understand the very matter-of-fact way in which the books of the Old Testament (including Joshua) describe the horrific slaughter of thousands and thousands of people in acts of war. It helps to remember that "the earth is the Lord's, and everything in it, the world, and all who live in it" (Psalm 24:1). God has the right to judge the nations and to use one nation to punish or even destroy another in order to accomplish His ultimate purpose for mankind—His plan of salvation and redemption. It's important to note that God did not call His people to engage in a never-ending "holy war" to achieve world domination. He commanded them to drive out the pagan people living at a specific time in a specific place, for a specific purpose. The people that He set apart for destruction were people who engaged in unspeakable wickedness, every kind of evil and immorality—including child sacrifice. God took their land away from them and gave it to His chosen people, so that the nation of Israel could be a shining example of the kind of purity and holiness that pleases God—the kind of purity and holiness He longs to see in every nation, in all of humankind. When God's people rebelled against Him and engaged in the same wickedness as their predecessors, they met the same fate—they were driven out of their homeland by the other nations that came after them. From beginning to end, the Scriptures make it clear that while God is just, He is also merciful. Those who obey Him experience His blessing. Those who disobey—and then repent—experience His forgiveness. God calls men and women from every tribe and nation to come to know Him and love Him and worship Him "in spirit and in truth" (John 4:23; Revelation 5:9).

■ **Making the Connection:** Joshua told God's people: "If serving the Lord seems undesirable to you, then choose for yourselves this day whom you will serve, whether the gods your forefathers served beyond the River, or the gods of the Amorites, in whose land you are living. But as for me and my household, we will serve the Lord" (24:15). The children of Israel needed to understand that they couldn't live on the faith of a previous generation. And neither can we. As someone once put it, God has no grandchildren. You can be His child—you can choose to have a personal relationship with Him. But you can't be His grandchild. You can't inherit a relationship with God. You have to choose for yourself whom you will serve!

JUDGES

■ **The Book:** Judges

■ **The Author:** Unknown—possibly Samuel

■ **The Audience:** The people of God

■ **The Setting:** The land of Canaan, between 1086 BC and 1004 BC

■ **The Story:** After the death of Joshua, God's people went back and forth between obedience and disobedience, faithfulness to Him and unfaithfulness. From time to time, God raised up "judges"—mighty warriors who led the people to victory in battle, presided over them in peace, and taught them to obey God's commandments.

■ **The Message:** The children of Israel did not obey God's instructions to drive out all of the heathen people living in the Promised Land (1:1–2:5). During Joshua's lifetime, the people had served the Lord. But "after that whole generation had been gathered to their fathers, another generation grew up, who knew neither the LORD nor what he had done for Israel" (2:10). The people sinned against God, and He allowed their enemies to triumph over them—until they repented and cried out to Him for deliverance (2:11–3:5). "Whenever the LORD raised up a judge for them, he was with the judge and saved them out of the hands of their enemies as long as the judge lived; for the LORD had compassion on them as they groaned under those who oppressed and afflicted them. But when the judge died, the people returned to ways even more corrupt than those of their fathers, following other gods and serving and worshiping them. They refused to give up their evil practices and stubborn ways" (2:18–19).

Othniel defeats the king of Aram, and Ehud defeats the king of Moab (3:7–30). Shamgar saves the Israelites from the Philistines (3:31). Then for twenty years, the children of Israel are oppressed by Jabin, the king of Hazor. When the men of Israel are too fearful to obey God's command to attack Jabin's army at Mount Tabor, God gives the victory to a woman instead. "Deborah, a prophetess, the wife of Lappidoth, was leading Israel at that time. She held court under the Palm of Deborah . . . and the Israelites came to her to have their disputes decided" (4:4–5). Barak, the commander of Israel's army, won't go without her—so Deborah rides out into battle with him. "On that day God subdued Jabin, the Canaanite king, before the Israelites" (4:23).

To defeat the Midianites, God chooses an unlikely hero; Gideon is fearful and fainthearted. But God assures him over and over again, "I will be with you" (6:16). Gideon gathers an army of thirty-two thousand men. God whittles it down to three hundred—"in order that Israel may not boast against me that her own strength has saved her" (7:2). God sends the superstitious Midianites terrifying nightmares that convince them they are sure to fall to the Israelites in battle. On the day of the attack, He throws the Midianites into such confusion that they turn on each other, and Gideon's men hardly have to lift their swords (7:7–25).

Gideon's son, Abimilech, murders seventy of his own brothers and tries to set himself up as Israel's first king—but his surviving brother rallies the people to rebel against his leadership, and God Himself orchestrates his downfall (9:1–56). Next, Tola and then Jair become Israel's judges (10:1–5). Jephthah is a mighty warrior whose military exploits are overshadowed by the foolish vow he makes to sacrifice whatever comes out of the door to greet him when he returns home victorious. "Whatever" turns out to be his beloved daughter (10:6–12:7). Judges Ibzan, Elon, and Abdon are men of means, influential in their communities, and capable leaders each in his own time (12:8–15).

Samson is a man set apart by God from birth; his long hair is a symbol of the obedience to God that gives him the supernatural strength to defeat Israel's enemies time and time again (13:1–15:20). Samson rules Israel for twenty years before lust leads him astray. In an attempt to please a deceitful woman named Delilah, he shares with her the secret of his strength. She promptly has his hair cut and turns him over to the Philistines, who blind the weakened warrior and throw him in chains. Samson cries out to God for the chance to make things right. His hair grows back, and his strength returns in time for him to pull down on his head an entire temple full of three thousand Philistines. "Thus he killed many more when he died than while he lived" (16:30).

After Samson's death, the children of Israel descend further and further into wickedness and sin. Just as the heathen nations had once tortured them, they now commit unspeakable acts of violence and terror on each other. Left to themselves, without strong leadership, they abandon their faith—their commitment to God—utterly and completely (17:1–21:25).

Key Verse or Passage

"In those days Israel had no king; everyone did as he saw fit." (Judges 21:25)

More on This Story in the Bible: The events described in the book of Ruth take place during the time of the Judges. Several of the Judges are mentioned among the great men and women of God in the "hall of faith" in Hebrews 11. Israel's last and greatest Judge was Samuel; his story can be found in 1 Samuel 1:1–25:1.

Words to Know:

subdue: to conquer someone or something and bring them under control.

oppression: the cruel and unjust exercise of power or authority to weigh someone or something down.

▦ **Did You Know?** In the days of the Old Testament, the Spirit of the Lord "came upon" specific men and women at specific times to empower them to accomplish specific things. But today, thanks to Jesus, the Bible tells us God's Holy Spirit lives in and through all believers—all the time! (For more on the Holy Spirit in the New Testament era, see John 14–16, 1 Corinthians 12–14, and the book of Acts—"the acts of the Holy Spirit.")

▦ **Think about It:** Sometimes Christians talk about "putting out a fleece" as Gideon did in Judges 6:36–40—asking God for a miraculous sign before making an important decision or choosing a certain course of action. There's no doubt that God does still speak through signs and wonders today. He also speaks to us through His Holy Spirit, through other believers, and through the pages of His Word. The Bible teaches that it is always appropriate to ask God for guidance and direction (James 1:5). It is not always appropriate to ask for a miraculous sign (Mark 8:11–12). We may or may not get one. Sometimes we may receive "false signs" that do not come from God (Mark 13:22). That's why it's important to really get to know God and learn to recognize His voice. Spend time in His Word so that you'll know what kinds of things He does and does not say!

RUTH

▦ **The Book:** Ruth

▦ **The Author:** Unknown

▦ **The Audience:** The people of God

▦ **The Setting:** The land of Canaan, between 1046 BC and 1035 BC

▦ **The Story:** In the days of the Judges, a young Moabite widow named Ruth left her own country and family and faith to follow in the footsteps of her Hebrew mother-in-law, Naomi. Ruth's story is one of love, loyalty, and faithfulness in friendship. As she made sacrifices for Naomi's sake, it was Ruth who ended up blessed—with a wonderful new husband and the privilege of becoming a part of Jesus' family tree!

■ **The Message:** A severe famine had driven an Israelite named Elimelech to take his wife, Naomi, and sons, Mahlon and Kilion, to live in the neighboring country of Moab. Within ten years, Elimelech and his sons had died—leaving Naomi and her daughters-in-law, Ruth and Orpah, as widows (1:1–5). Hearing that the famine is over at last, Naomi decides she will return to her homeland. Her daughters-in-law plan to accompany her, but Naomi insists it would be better for them to return to their own families and remarry among their own people (1:6–13). Orpah offers her mother-in-law a tearful farewell, but Ruth refuses to go: "Don't urge me to leave you or to turn back from you. Where you go I will go, and where you stay I will stay. Your people will be my people and your God my God . . ." (1:16–17).

The two women journey to Bethlehem, where the townspeople rush to greet them. Naomi's friends grieve with her in the loss of her husband and sons (1:19–22). Ruth goes to work in the fields picking up the grain the harvesters have left behind (2:2). When the owner of the fields arrives, he notices the Moabite woman right away (2:5–6). Boaz greets Ruth warmly and extends his personal invitation to her to continue gleaning in his fields. He suggests she stay close to his servant girls (where she'll be safe) and urges her to help herself to the food and water he has provided for his workers (2:8–9). Ruth is amazed by his kindness: "Why have I found such favor in your eyes that you notice me—a foreigner?" (2:10). Boaz replies, "I've been told all about what you have done for your mother-in-law since the death of your husband—how you left your father and mother and your homeland and came to live with a people you did not know before. . . . May you be richly rewarded by the LORD, the God of Israel, under whose wings you have come to take refuge" (2:11–12). Throughout the day, Boaz continues to watch over Ruth. He quietly instructs his servants to drop extra stalks of grain where Ruth will find them (2:14–16).

When Naomi hears of the kindness of Boaz, she reflects on the fact that he is a relative—a member of the family—and therefore eligible to marry Ruth in place of Mahlon. In fact, he is culturally and morally obligated to do so. At Naomi's suggestion, in the middle of the night, Ruth slips onto the threshing floor where Boaz has fallen asleep. When he awakens to find her lying at his feet, Ruth asserts her claim on his affection and protection (3:1–10). Boaz is honored by her request. He tells her that if it were up to him, he would marry her in a heartbeat—only he isn't quite the next of kin. There is another man who is technically first in line. This man must be given a chance to accept or reject Ruth's hand (3:11–13). Promising to speak to him at once, Boaz helps Ruth slip away before the dawn—before anyone else sees her and misunderstands the purpose of her visit (3:14–18).

As it turns out, the man who is the closest relative chooses not to exercise his right, so Boaz becomes the "kinsman-redeemer." He assumes the responsibility of buying back Mahlon's property and taking Mahlon's widow—Ruth—as his wife (4:1–12). Soon after Boaz and Ruth are married, God blesses them with a son—Obed. All the women of the town gather to congratulate Naomi and rejoice with her in the birth of her grandson. "May he become famous throughout Israel! He will renew your life and sustain you in your old age. For your daughter-in-law, who loves you and who is better to you than seven sons, has given him birth" (4:14–15). One day Obed will become the father of Jesse, and Jesse will become the father of David—Israel's greatest king (4:21–22).

Key Verse or Passage

"Don't urge me to leave you or to turn back from you. Where you go I will go, and where you stay I will stay. Your people will be my people and your God my God." (Ruth 1:16)

More on This Story in the Bible: Learn more about the time in which Ruth lived—"the days of the Judges"—by reading the book of Judges. For more on God's heart to bring everyone—even Gentiles (non-Jewish people)—to Himself, see Isaiah 49:6, Romans 3:29, and Revelation 5:9.

Words to Know:

> **glean:** to gather grain that has been left behind by reapers; the Law required that the "gleanings" be left for the poor and for foreigners

(immigrants) who might not have any other means to provide food for themselves and their families.

redeem: to free or deliver another person from difficulty, danger, or bondage, usually by paying a ransom (in essence, "buying" the person and/or their property back at a price).

kinsman-redeemer: the nearest blood relative who by Law had the right to buy back a piece of property or an individual who had been sold into slavery to pay a debt, in order to keep the property (and the person) in the family.

Did You Know? From the beginning, Boaz was especially kind and gracious to Ruth—even though she was a foreigner, an "outsider." Perhaps it was because he understood a little of what she was going through. After all, his mother had been a foreigner—an outsider—when she came to live with the Israelites after the fall of Jericho. Rahab was the woman who hid the spies that Joshua sent to scout out the city in advance of one of the most amazing battles in history (read Rahab's story in Joshua 2:1–21 and 6:1–25.)

Making the Connection: Just as Boaz became Ruth's "kinsman-redeemer," Jesus became ours! The Bible tells us that Jesus is our "older brother" (Romans 8:29; Hebrews 2:11). As our nearest blood relative, He took it upon Himself to redeem us and restore us to our rightful place in the family of God. We had sold ourselves into slavery to sin (Romans 6:16). But with His death on the cross, Jesus made the ultimate sacrifice; He paid the ultimate price to ransom us—to buy us back—and set us free from the power of sin once and for all (Romans 6:17–18; Mark 10:45; Revelation 5:9). Truly He is our Kinsman-Redeemer.

1 SAMUEL

The Book: 1 Samuel

The Author: Unknown

The Audience: The people of God

▨ **The Setting:** Written from Israel, approximately 1050 BC–750 BC

▨ **The Story:** God raised up the prophet Samuel to lead the children of Israel as the last of the judges and to anoint and establish Israel's first kings—Saul and David. When Saul failed to walk in obedience to God's commandments, God (through Samuel) withdrew His favor from him and appointed David to take Saul's place. But Saul wouldn't give up his throne without a fight. For the better part of fifteen years, he and David played an epic game of cat and mouse. Saul hunted David all over and around the country, seeking to destroy him. But David's sense of honor wouldn't allow him to engage or attack King Saul—committing an act of treason—so David lived on the run and in hiding, waiting for the day God Himself would deal with Saul once and for all.

▨ **The Message:** Samuel is born in answer to prayer, and from his childhood is dedicated to the service of God (1:1–2:11). As a boy, Samuel hears the voice of God calling to him in the night, and he answers: "Speak, for your servant is listening!" (3:10). God calls young Samuel to rebuke the high priest, Eli, for failing to restrain his sons (who are also priests) from committing all kinds of atrocities in the tabernacle, or Tent of Meeting (2:12–3:21). Eli's sons are the ones responsible for carrying the ark of the covenant into battle like a lucky charm—and losing it to the Philistines! "The Israelites were defeated and every man fled to his tent. . . . The ark of God was captured and Eli's two sons, Hophni and Phinehas, died" (4:10–11). Quite literally "plagued" by the presence of the ark, the Philistines send it back over the border, where it is stored in the house of a man named Abinidab (5:1–7:1). Still a young man, Samuel becomes prophet, priest, and ruler over all Israel. During his ministry, he calls God's people to repent of the idolatry and sin that they have once again fallen into, and return to the Lord (7:2–17).

As Samuel's days come to an end, the people ask him to appoint a king—"such as other nations have"—to take his place (8:1–22). At God's direction, Samuel anoints Saul, "an impressive young man without equal among the Israelites" to be their first king (9:1–11:15). Though Saul's appearance and presence—and military victories—quickly win the confidence of his people, it soon becomes clear that his heart is not fully committed to God. On several significant occasions, he directly disobeys God and then tries to appease Him with "gifts" (11:1–15:35). Samuel confronts the king: "To obey is better than sacrifice. . . . For rebellion is like the sin of divination, and arrogance like the evil of idolatry. Because you have rejected the word of the LORD, he has rejected you as king" (15:22–23). God tells Samuel to anoint a young shepherd boy named David and declare him Israel's future king (16:1–13).

Strangely enough, David finds himself called into Saul's service; he is asked to play some of the beautiful psalms he has written in order to soothe the troubled king, who is now tormented by an evil spirit (16:14–23). Next David finds himself taking supplies to the battlefield, where he turns out to be the only one brave enough to stand up to a giant named Goliath. "David said to the Philistine, 'You come against me with sword and spear and javelin, but I come against you in the name of the LORD Almighty, the God of the armies of Israel . . .'" (17:45). David goes on to become a mighty warrior, leading Saul's armies to victory over all their enemies. Saul grows jealous and tries to kill David, but David escapes with the help of Jonathan—Saul's son and heir and David's dearest friend (18:1–20:42). "Don't be afraid," Jonathan says to David. "My father Saul will not lay a hand on you. You will be king over Israel, and I will be second to you. Even my father Saul knows this" (23:17). Many of the soldiers who have served under David's command share Jonathan's conviction. They rally around David and become his most loyal supporters—his servants and soldiers and bodyguards.

Over the next few years, David and his men and their families live in hiding, moving from place to place, taking refuge wherever they can find it—even at times, among the Philistines. Many of the Israelites are sympathetic to and supportive of David; others are less so (21:1–23:29; 25:1–44; 27:1–12; 29:1–30:31). At various times and in various places, David and his men engage in battle against the Philistines and the Amalekites, watching over and protecting and providing for the people of Israel, as well as themselves and their families. On several occasions, David actually has the opportunity to kill King Saul—but he considers it a sin to do so (24:1–22; 26:1–25). "Who can lay a hand on the LORD's anointed and be guiltless? As surely as the Lord lives . . . the LORD himself will strike him; either his time will come and he will die, or he will go into battle and perish. But the LORD forbid that I should lay a hand on the LORD's anointed" (26:9–11). Saul does, in fact, die on the battlefield shortly afterward. After consulting a medium for guidance, he commits suicide rather than be taken captive by the Philistines (28:1–25; 31:1–13). And David—the shepherd boy—becomes king.

Key Verse or Passage

"But when they said, 'Give us a king to lead us,' this displeased Samuel; so he prayed to the LORD. And the LORD told him: 'Listen to all that the people are saying to you; it is not you they have rejected, but they have rejected me as their king. . . . Listen to them and give them a king.'" (1 Samuel 8:6–7, 22)

■ **More on This Story in the Bible:** The story continues in 2 Samuel (1 and 2 Samuel were originally one volume). For more on the life of David, see 1 Chronicles and the book of Psalms.

■ **Words to Know:**

anoint: to mark as being chosen by or set apart for God.

prophesy: to speak under the influence or by the divine inspiration of God.

uncircumcised: circumcision was a visible, physical sign of the covenant or contract between God and His people, representing the people's willingness to walk in obedience to God's commandments. To be uncircumcised was to be disobedient and rebellious—or in the case of Goliath and the Philistines, "heathen."

■ **Making the Connection:** The people of Israel were tired of being led by God and His prophets. They wanted a king like those of all the other nations. And God gave them what they asked for. On the outside, Saul appeared to be everything they wanted—everything a king should be. He was tall, dark, and handsome. He had a commanding presence and an air of authority. But on the inside, he was weak, jealous, greedy, and proud.

Next God gave Israel the king of His choosing—a man after His own heart—David. When Samuel was sent to anoint him, he thought there must be some mistake. This teenage shepherd boy didn't look anything like a king. God told Samuel, "Man looks at the outward appearance, but the Lord looks at the heart" (1 Samuel 16:7).

Hundreds of years later God sent His people the King of kings, the Messiah, their long-awaited Deliverer. But they didn't recognize Him. He didn't look like a king. Isaiah 53:2–3 tells us, "He had no beauty or majesty to attract us to him, nothing in his appearance that we should desire him. He was despised and rejected by men, a man of sorrows, and familiar with suffering. Like one from whom men hide their faces, he was despised, and we esteemed him not."

It's one of the greatest tragedies in human history. The Son of God Himself came unto His own, and they would not receive Him (John 1:1–11). God's people rejected Him because He didn't "look right." Of course, we can't point the finger because the truth is, we still make that same mistake today. We often miss God's leading and direction in our lives because it doesn't look the way we thought it would. We still judge other people and other circumstances by appearances, without giving any thought to what's beneath the surface. Maybe it's time we stop and take another look!

2 SAMUEL

■ **The Book:** 2 Samuel

■ **The Author:** Unknown

■ **The Audience:** The people of God

■ **The Setting:** Written from Israel, approximately 1050 BC–750 BC

■ **The Story:** After the death of King Saul, David was finally able to take the throne God had promised to give him years earlier. This is the story of the reign of Israel's greatest king—his miraculous victories, his humbling failures and defeats—and his passionate, unwavering commitment to serve God through it all.

▨ **The Message:** In spite of everything that has happened between them, David is truly grieved to learn of Saul's death—and of the death of Jonathan, Saul's son and David's dearest friend (1:1–27). David rules from Hebron in Judah until he and his men are able to thoroughly defeat Saul's surviving sons and supporters (2:1–4:12). "All the tribes of Israel came to David at Hebron and said, 'We are your own flesh and blood. In the past, while Saul was king over us, you were the one who led Israel on their military campaigns. And the LORD said to you, 'You will shepherd my people Israel, and you will become their ruler' . . . and they anointed David king over Israel" (5:1–3). David recovers the city of Jerusalem from the Jebusites and designates it the new capital of Israel, the royal city— "the City of David" (5:6–9). "And he became more and more powerful, because the LORD God Almighty was with him" (5:10).

David continues his military conquests over the Philistines, the Moabites, the Ammonites, the Arameans, the Amalekites, and the Edomites, enlarging and establishing his kingdom (5:17–25; 8:1–18; 10:1–19). He brings the ark of the covenant to Jerusalem and restores it to a place of honor in Israel's ceremonial worship (6:1–23). King David hates the thought of living in a palace, while God—the King over all kings—is worshiped in a tent. He wants to build a magnificent temple worthy of such a great and mighty God. God tells David that He has never asked His people to build Him a house—and that David is not the one to do it. But He is honored by David's devotion to Him, and He will build *David* a "house": "I took you from the pasture and from following the flock to be ruler over my people Israel. I have been with you wherever you have gone, and I have cut off all your enemies from before you. Now I will make your name great, like the names of the greatest men of the earth. . . . When your days are over and you rest with your fathers, I will raise up your offspring to succeed you. . . . I will establish his kingdom. He is the one who will build a house for my Name, and I will establish the throne of his kingdom forever" (7:8–9, 12–13).

Not long afterward, David makes one of his most famous and tragic mistakes: he commits adultery with Bathsheba and has her husband killed on the battlefield before the sin can be discovered (11:1–27). The prophet Nathan rebukes David with a parable that reveals to the king just how cruel and heartless and wicked his actions have been. Devastated, David throws himself on the mercy of God—asking for and receiving forgiveness, but at the same time understanding that there will be bitterly painful consequences for his actions (12:1–31).

In his later years, David's children bring him great heartbreak, hurt, and disappointment. His over-indulgence of them, his failure to discipline them and hold them accountable for their actions, seems to give them license to brutalize, attack, and destroy each other. David's beloved son Absalom even goes so far as to organize a vast conspiracy—a revolt—against his father that has the king and those loyal to him fleeing for their lives (13:1–17:29). Eventually, David's forces overcome Absalom, but to the king it is a hollow victory that costs his son's life (18:1–19). Again David goes to war against the enemies of Israel and attempts to rebuild and restore his kingdom, righting wrongs done by his predecessor Saul (19:9–21:22). Once again, he errs in conducting a census to determine his military strength—rather than recognizing God as the source of His might. God sends a plague that threatens to wipe out the kingdom, but David immediately repents—and God relents (24:1–25).

David praises God for His faithfulness to him over his lifetime (22:1–51). "The LORD is my rock, my fortress and my deliverer; my God is my rock, in whom I take refuge, my shield and the horn of my salvation. He is my stronghold, my refuge and my savior . . ." (22:2–3). As his days draw to a close, David utters his last words—words of praise and tribute to "God, the Rock, my Savior" (22:47–23:7).

Key Verse or Passage

"Now then, tell my servant David, 'This is what the LORD Almighty says: I took you from the pasture and from following the flock to be ruler over my people Israel. I have been with you wherever you have gone, and I have cut off all your enemies from before you. Now I will make your name great, like the names of the greatest men of the earth.'" (2 Samuel 7:8–9)

More on This Story in the Bible: The story begins in 1 Samuel (1 and 2 Samuel were originally one volume). For more on the life of David, see

1 Chronicles and the book of Psalms. His son Solomon's story continues in 2 Chronicles and 1 Kings.

▨ Words to Know:

lament: a dirge; a poem or song of sadness and mourning often sung at a funeral.

sovereign: the ultimate authority, the supreme power.

oracle: a prophecy, a parable, or a proverb.

▨ Did You Know?

After David was confronted about his sin with Bathsheba, he poured out his heart to God in true humility and repentance. "Have mercy on me, O God, according to your unfailing love; according to your great compassion blot out my transgressions. Wash away all my iniquity and cleanse me from my sin. . . . Create in me a pure heart, O God, and renew a steadfast spirit within me." For generations, David's heartfelt prayer—Psalm 51—continues to resonate with those who have stumbled in their walk with God and has helped many to find their footing again—and the strength to carry on.

▨ Making the Connection:

Israel's first king, Saul, was a terrible disappointment to his people. Though he began under the anointing of God, with great promise and potential, he did not finish well. As the years passed, he grew bitter and angry; he was consumed by jealousy, fear, and suspicion. His days were cut short. In summing up Saul's life, the Scripture makes this observation: "Saul died because he was unfaithful to the LORD; he did not keep the word of the LORD and even consulted a medium for guidance, and did not inquire of the LORD. So the LORD put him to death and turned the kingdom over to David son of Jesse" (1 Chronicles 10:13–14).

Twice this passage refers to the fact that Saul did not seek God's guidance—he did not inquire of the Lord. He went his own way and did what seemed best to him. Faced with a crisis, he sought answers from a medium—a witch—who conducted a séance for him. This was detestable to the Lord. It was an insult to Him. He had chosen Saul to be king. He had placed him in his position of authority. And yet Saul failed to look to the Lord for direction. He would not acknowledge the truth of the Scripture that says, "The LORD gives wisdom, and from his mouth came knowledge and understanding" (Proverbs 2:6). Saul's kingdom was taken from him and given to David, a man after God's own heart (1 Samuel 13:14). In contrast to his predecessor, David routinely inquired of the Lord (see, for example, 2 Samuel 2:1; 5:19–23). In Psalm 25:4–5, he prayed, "Show me your ways, O LORD, teach me your paths; guide me in your truth and teach me, for you are God my Savior, and my hope is in you all day long." May that be our prayer, as well.

1 KINGS

The Book: 1 Kings

The Author: Unknown

The Audience: The people of God

The Setting: Written from exile, approximately 590 BC–570 BC

The Story: King Solomon took the throne of his father David and ruled wisely, but Solomon's son didn't follow in his footsteps. Rehoboam's foolishness split the kingdom in two. Ten tribes rebelled and made Jeroboam the king of Israel, the northern kingdom. Only two tribes stay with Rehoboam, becoming Judah, the southern kingdom. In both Israel and Judah, one king followed another. Some remained faithful to God; others led the people into idol worship and sin. The prophet Elijah spoke on God's behalf, performing miracles to demonstrate God's power, calling the kings and their people to return to Him.

The Message: On his deathbed, King David appoints his son Solomon to take his place as ruler over all Israel: "'I am about to go the way of all the earth,' he said. 'So be strong, show yourself a man, and observe what the LORD your God requires: Walk in his ways, and keep his decrees and commands, his laws and requirements, as written in the Law of Moses, so that you may prosper in all you do and wherever you go'" (2:2–3).

Not long afterward, God appears to the new king in a dream and says, "Ask for whatever you want Me to give you." Instead of asking for fame and fortune, Solomon humbly confesses that he feels unequal to the task of ruling this great nation. He wants to do what is right in the eyes of the Lord and take good care of His people. Solomon says, "Give your servant a discerning heart to govern your people and to distinguish between right and wrong . . ." (3:9). God is pleased with this request: "I will do what you have asked. I will give you a wise and discerning heart, so that there will never have been anyone like you, nor will there ever be. Moreover, I will give you what you have not asked for—both riches and honor—so that in your lifetime, you will have no equal among kings" (3:12–13). Solomon's splendor does indeed become legendary (3:1–4:34; 7:1–12; 9:10–11:43).

King Solomon fulfills his father's dream by building a glorious and magnificent temple to replace the tabernacle as the center of worship and prayer in Israel (5:1–6:38; 7:13–9:9). At the dedication ceremony, Solomon prays,

> O LORD, God of Israel, there is no God like you in heaven above or on earth below—you who keep your covenant of love with your servants who continue wholeheartedly in your way. You have kept your promise to your servant David my father; with your mouth you have promised and with your hand you have fulfilled it—as it is today. . . .
> But will God really dwell on earth? The heavens, even the highest heaven, cannot contain you. How much less this temple I have built! Yet give attention to your servant's prayer and his plea for mercy, O LORD. . . . May your eyes be open toward this temple night and day. . . . Hear the supplication of your servant and of your people Israel when they pray toward this place. Hear from heaven, your dwelling place, and when you hear, forgive." (8:23–24, 27–30)

Unfortunately Solomon's devotion to God wavers in his later years; to appease his many foreign wives, he engages in the idol worship that is at the heart of their cultures and customs (11:1–13).

Solomon's son, Rehoboam, cruelly oppresses his people, and ten of the tribes rebel against him—establishing their own kingdom, "Israel," and appointing Jeroboam to rule over them. Only two tribes remain loyal to Solomon's son, who is now king of "Judah" (12:1–33). The subsequent kings of Judah and Israel wander far away from the path God set before them, ignoring or disobeying His commandments and breaking their covenant promises to Him (13:1–16:28). Then Ahab becomes king of Israel, and he does "more evil in the eyes of the LORD than any of those before him. He not only considered it trivial to commit the sins of [his ancestors], but he also married Jezebel daughter of Ethbaal king of the Sidonians, and began to serve Baal and worship him" (16:30–33). The people of Israel follow suit.

God calls a prophet named Elijah to rise up and demonstrate God's mighty power among His people, confronting Queen Jezebel's prophets— prophets of Baal—and calling down fire from heaven to consume a soaking wet sacrifice on the heights of Mount Carmel (18:16–46). Vengeful Jezebel threatens to kill Elijah, but God hides His prophet and protects him, revealing Himself to Elijah in a powerful new way: "The LORD said, 'Go out and stand on the mountain in the presence of the LORD, for the LORD is about to pass by.' Then a great and powerful wind tore the mountains apart and shattered the rocks before the LORD, but the LORD was not in the wind. After the wind there was an earthquake, but the LORD was not in the earthquake. After the earthquake came a fire, but the LORD was not in the fire. And after the fire came a gentle whisper. When Elijah heard it, he pulled his cloak over his face . . ." (19:11–13). After his encounter with God on the mountain, Elijah is joined by a young man named Elisha, who will serve as his assistant and apprentice (19:19–21).

In spite of Ahab's wickedness, God delivers the king's enemies into his hands and enables him to triumph in battle. Yet Ahab refuses to acknowledge God in his victory and ignores specific directions God has given him (20:1–43). Jezebel helps Ahab acquire a choice piece of property by falsely accusing, arresting, and executing the innocent landowner. Elijah confronts Ahab with this sin and pronounces God's judgment on the king and queen, describing the disgraceful death decreed for the two of them and every last one of their descendants (21:1–28).

Shortly afterward, despite dire warnings from the prophet Micaiah, Jehoshaphat, king of Judah, and Ahab, king of Israel, join forces to attack the king of Aram at Ramoth Gilead. Ahab is mortally wounded by an arrow shot at random, and his son Ahaziah takes his throne (22:1–22:53).

Key Verse or Passage

"Now, O LORD my God, you have made your servant king in place of my father David. But I am only a little child and do not know how to carry out my duties. Your servant is here among the people you have chosen, a great people, too numerous to count or number. So give your servant a discerning heart to govern your people and to distinguish between right and wrong. For who is able to govern this great people of yours?" (1 Kings 3:7–9)

More on This Story in the Bible: The book of 1 Kings picks up the story of the nation of Israel from 1 and 2 Samuel, and continues on in 2 Kings. (The two books, 1 and 2 Kings, were originally a single volume.) For nearly 350 years, God called on the people and their kings to walk in obedience to His commandments, warning them through the words of the prophets what would happen if they did not (see Isaiah, Jeremiah, Ezekiel, Hosea, Amos, Obadiah, Micah, Nahum, Habakkuk, Zephaniah, and Zechariah). More on the kings of Judah mentioned in 1 and 2 Kings can also be found in 2 Chronicles.

Words to Know:

> **wisdom:** knowledge of what is right or true; sound judgment, insight, and discernment.

> **annals:** historical records.

> **prophet:** a person who speaks for God or a god.

Making the Connection: Queen Jezebel is one of the most reviled women in all of Scripture, not only because of her own wickedness, but because of the way she used her influence to lead others into sin—and ultimately, to slaughter (1 Kings 16:31; 18:16–19:9; 21:1–29). But the Bible tells us we reap what we sow, and Jezebel did not escape God's justice or judgment in the end (see 1 Kings 21:23 and 2 Kings 9:14–37). Look up her name in any dictionary today, and you'll learn that a "jezebel" is an impudent, cruel, vicious, scheming, and shamelessly evil woman. Thousands of years later, she is still remembered as a shame and a disgrace!

Think about It: The Bible tells us that the prophet Elijah once complained that he was the only servant of God still living in the land. It seemed like everyone else had turned back from God and abandoned faith. Elijah was the only one left—or so he thought. But then God told him there were seven thousand others that the prophet knew nothing about—courageous men and women who were living out their faith day by day, even in the face of overwhelming opposition (1 Kings 18:4; 19:14–18).

Elijah wasn't the only one. And neither are we. There are people all over the world who share our faith, our values, our hopes and dreams—people of God who are committed to what they believe in, willing to take a stand for what is good and right and true (1 Peter 5:8–10). For all the headline-grabbing evil and immorality that goes on in our world today, there are still those who daily practice acts of kindness and generosity, heroism and self-sacrifice. We can be proud to be counted among them.

2 KINGS

The Book: 2 Kings

The Author: Unknown

The Audience: The people of God

The Setting: Written from exile, between 590 BC and 550 BC

The Story: Elisha carried on the ministry of Elijah, demonstrating the mighty power of God and calling Israel to return to Him. The line of kings continued in both Israel and Judah, until their wickedness grew so great that God allowed Israel to be destroyed by the Assyrians in 722 BC and Judah to be conquered by the Babylonians in 586 BC. God's people were sent into exile, living as servants, slaves, or second-class citizens in other kingdoms. For many years, both nations simply ceased to exist.

The Message: As the days of Elijah's ministry draw to a close, he begins to prepare his assistant, Elisha, to carry on in his place. "As they were walking along and talking together, suddenly a chariot of fire and horses of fire appeared and separated the two of them, and Elijah went up to heaven in a whirlwind" (2:11). God immediately confirms the transfer of Elijah's spiritual leadership and authority to Elisha, by empowering Elisha to perform awe-inspiring miracles, both great and small. He heals the sick, raises the dead, provides food for the hungry, and leads the people to victory in battle (2:13–8:15).

Elisha sends another prophet to declare Jehu king of Israel and commission him to carry out God's judgment on the house of King Ahab and Queen Jezebel—including their son-in-law, Ahaziah, king of Judah. "When Athaliah the mother of Ahaziah saw that her son was dead, she proceeded to destroy the whole royal family" (11:1). A priest and his wife rescue one of the infant princes and raise him secretly in the temple, until his grandmother can be overthrown (11:1–20). "Joash was seven years old when he began to reign. . . . Joash did what was right in the eyes of the LORD all the years Jehoiada the priest instructed him" (11:21; 12:2). Meanwhile, the kings of Israel do what is "evil in the eyes of the Lord," leading the people further and further into sin—until God allows the northern kingdom to be conquered and destroyed by the Assyrians (13:1–25; 14:23–29; 15:8–31; 17:1–40). "All this took place because the Israelites had sinned against the LORD their God, who had brought them up out of Egypt. . . . They worshiped other gods and followed the practices of the nations the LORD had driven out before them. . . . They did wicked things that provoked the LORD to anger" (17:7–8, 11).

The southern kingdom lasts a few hundred years longer, in part because of a few kings who earnestly try to walk in God's ways and set a good example for their people (14:1–22; 15:1–7, 32–38). "Hezekiah trusted in the LORD, the God of Israel. There was no one like him among all the kings of Judah, either before him or after him. He held fast to the LORD and did not cease to follow him; he kept the commands the LORD had given Moses. And the LORD was with him; he was successful in whatever he undertook . . ." (18:5–7). God gives Hezekiah a miraculous and mighty victory over Sennacherib, king of Assyria, and later extends Hezekiah's life by healing him of a deadly disease (18:1–20:21). Unfortunately, his son, Manasseh, becomes one of Judah's most infamous kings. "He bowed down to all the starry hosts and worshiped them. He built altars [to sacrifice to other gods] in the temple of the LORD. . . . He sacrificed his own son in the fire, practiced sorcery and divination, and consulted mediums and spiritists. He did much evil in the eyes of the LORD, provoking him to anger" (21:3–4, 6). Manasseh's son, Amon, walks in wickedness as well, until he is assassinated by his own officials (21:17–26).

By contrast, Amon's son, Josiah, "was eight years old when he became king. . . . He did what was right in the eyes of the LORD and walked in all the ways of his father David, not turning aside to the right or to the left" (22:1–2). In restoring the desecrated temple, the young king rediscovers the Book of the Law and calls the entire nation to repent and renew their covenant with God (22:1–23:30). "Neither before nor after Josiah was there a king like him who turned to the LORD as he did—with all his heart and with all his soul and with all his strength, in accordance with all the Law of Moses" (23:25). Sadly, the kings who succeed him do not share his devotion to God; they turn to idol worship instead.

In time, the kings of Judah become subject to the Babylonians. A series of failed rebellions lead to a series of sieges, until the city of Jerusalem and the temple of King Solomon are completely and utterly destroyed. The few people of Judah who are not killed or taken prisoner escape to Egypt (23:36–25:30). Just like her sister-nation, Israel, centuries earlier, "so Judah went into captivity, away from her land" (25:21).

Key Verse or Passage

"O LORD, God of Israel, enthroned between the cherubim, you alone are God over all the kingdoms of the earth. You have made heaven and earth."
(2 Kings 19:15)

More on This Story in the Bible: The book of 2 Kings picks up the story of God's people in both the northern and southern kingdoms from the account that begins in 1 Kings. (The two books were originally a single volume.) For nearly 350 years, God called on the people and their kings to walk in obedience to His commandments, warning them through the words of the prophets what would happen if they did not (see Isaiah, Jeremiah, Ezekiel, Hosea, Amos, Obadiah, Micah, Nahum, Habakkuk, Zephaniah, and Zechariah). More on the kings of Judah mentioned in 2 Kings can also be found in 2 Chronicles.

Words to Know:

annals: historical records.

prophet: a person who speaks for God or a god.

siege: a devastating attack; the surrounding of a city or fortress, cutting off its communications and supplies and compelling it to surrender.

Did You Know? Have you heard the expression "to carry on the mantle" or "the mantle has been passed to . . ."? It comes from 2 Kings 2:1–13. When Elijah was taken up to heaven in a chariot of fire, his cloak (or "mantle") fell to the ground, where Elisha picked it up—physically and symbolically carrying on the ministry and the legacy of the man of God who had gone before him.

Think about It: The king of Aram grew furious when he discovered that all of his secret battle plans and strategies were being revealed by God to the prophet Elisha—who in turn revealed them to the king of Israel, enabling the people of God to outsmart and outmaneuver their enemies. So in the middle of the night, the king of Aram sent a mighty army to surround the city where Elisha was staying, intending to capture and kill him.

> When the servant of the man of God got up and went out early the next morning, an army with horses and chariots had surrounded the city. "Oh, my lord, what shall we do?" the servant asked.
>
> "Don't be afraid," the prophet answered. "Those who are with us are more than those who are with them." And Elisha prayed, "O LORD, open his eyes so he may see." Then the LORD opened the servant's eyes, and he looked and saw the hills full of horses and chariots of fire all around Elisha. (2 Kings 6:15–17)

God had sent His own supernatural heavenly army to protect them. The Bible tells us that there is a spiritual battle going on all around us—a battle between the forces of good and evil—even if we aren't always aware of it. The good news is that "the one who is in you is greater than the one who is in the world" (1 John 4:4). When we find ourselves "under attack"—frightened, overwhelmed, or discouraged by the challenges we face, we need to ask God to open our eyes and give us faith to see what He is already doing on our behalf. We can trust Him to give us the victory (Psalm 44:6–8).

1 CHRONICLES

■ **The Book:** 1 Chronicles

■ **The Author:** Ezra

■ **The Audience:** The people of God returning from captivity and exile

■ **The Setting:** Written from the land of Judah, 450–425 BC

■ **The Story:** God's people had been living in exile for seventy years. When they finally returned to their devastated homeland, they were nothing like the glorious nation they had once been. They wondered if God was still with them—if His plans and purposes were still in place, if His covenant with them was still in force. To affirm them, Ezra the priest retold the story of King David and his son Solomon, drawing parallels between the two of them and Moses and Joshua, who had served God centuries before. Ezra encouraged the people to see God's hand at work down through the ages and to trust Him to accomplish His purposes for them in the years to come.

■ **The Message:** Ezra begins with the genealogy—the historical records—of God's people, from Adam to Abraham to the twelve sons (twelve tribes) of Israel to the ancestors of Saul, Israel's first king (1:1–9:44). He tells how Saul died and how David became king in his place (10:1–11:9). A great hero in his own right, David leads a group of "mighty men"—legendary warriors—who serve under him and support his claim to the throne (11:10–12:40). God gives them victory after victory as they battle

Israel's enemies (14:8–17; 18:1–20:8). And "David reigned over all Israel, doing what was just and right for all his people" (18:14).

David wants to restore Israel's worship of the One True God. Many years before, the ark of the covenant—the symbol of God's presence among His people—had been lost in battle to the Philistines and then recovered and stored in the home of a God-fearing man in Kiriath Jearim. David decides to have the ark brought back to the city of Jerusalem, but he fails to inquire as to the proper way to transport the sacred object, and the oversight costs a man his life (13:1–14). Sometime later, David tries again to recover the ark. This time, he does it the right way (15:1–29). All the people of Israel rejoice, and in the celebration David offers up a beautiful psalm of praise: "Sing to the LORD, all the earth; proclaim his salvation day after day. Declare his glory among the nations, his marvelous deeds among all peoples. For great is the LORD and most worthy of praise. . . . Splendor and majesty are before him; strength and joy in his dwelling place. . . . Give thanks to the LORD, for he is good; his love endures forever" (16:23–25, 27, 34).

The desire of David's heart is to build a magnificent temple worthy of so great a Savior. God tells David that He has never asked His people to build Him a house—and that David is not the one to do it. But He is honored by David's devotion to Him, and He will build *David* a "house": "I took you from the pasture and from following the flock, to be ruler over my people Israel. I have been with you wherever you have gone, and I have cut off all your enemies from before you. Now I will make your name like the names of the greatest men of the earth. . . . When your days are over and you go to be with your fathers, I will raise up your offspring to succeed you, one of your own sons, and I will establish his kingdom. He is the one who will build a house for me, and I will establish his throne forever" (17:7–8, 11–12).

Not long afterward, David makes a serious mistake. He sins by taking a census of the people in order to determine his strength—rather than recognizing God as the source of His might. God sends a plague that threatens to wipe out the kingdom, but David immediately repents and takes responsibility for his actions. He comes face-to-face with the angel of the Lord on a piece of property belonging to a man named Araunah.

David wants to build an altar on the spot, and Araunah offers to give his land to the king. But David insists on paying full price for it. "I will not take for the LORD what is yours, or sacrifice a burnt offering that costs me nothing" (21:24). God hears David's prayer and forgives him and ends the plague.

As time goes on, David determines: "My son Solomon is young and inexperienced, and the house to be built for the Lord should be of great magnificence and fame and splendor in the sight of all the nations. Therefore I will make preparations for it." He gives Solomon thorough and detailed instructions for carrying on the work after he is gone (22:1–19; 28:1–21). David organizes the Levites into divisions responsible for supervising the construction of the temple, serving in it as priests, officials and judges, treasurers, gatekeepers, and musicians (23:1–26:32). The king donates a great deal of his own wealth—his material resources—toward the project, and he invites his people to do the same. He is thrilled to see them rise to the challenge, giving freely and wholeheartedly, with much rejoicing. At a special ceremony, David thanks them and blesses them. "Then David said to the whole assembly, 'Praise the LORD your God.' So they all praised the LORD, the God of their fathers; they bowed low and fell prostrate before the LORD and the king" (29:20).

"David son of Jesse was king over all Israel. He ruled over Israel forty years—seven in Hebron and thirty-three in Jerusalem. He died at a good old age, having enjoyed long life, wealth and honor. His son Solomon succeeded him as king" (29:26–28).

Key Verse or Passage

"Praise be to you, O LORD, God of our father Israel, from everlasting to everlasting. Yours, O LORD, is the greatness and the power and the glory and the majesty and the splendor, for everything in heaven and earth is yours. Yours, O LORD, is the kingdom; you are exalted as head over all. Wealth and honor come from you; you are the ruler of all things. In your hands are strength and power to exalt and give strength to all. Now, our God, we give you thanks, and praise your glorious name." (1 Chronicles 29:10–13)

■ **More on This Story in the Bible:** For more on the life of King David, see 1 and 2 Samuel and the book of Psalms. The story of the kings of Israel and Judah continues in 2 Chronicles (which was originally a part of 1 Chronicles), and is also told in 1 and 2 Kings. Ezra, "the chronicler," also wrote the book of the Bible that bears his name. For nearly 350 years, God called on the people and their kings to walk in obedience to His commandments, warning them through the words of the prophets what would happen if they did not (see Isaiah, Jeremiah, Ezekiel, Hosea, Amos, Obadiah, Micah, Nahum, Habakkuk, Zephaniah, and Zechariah). After their captivity, He spoke to them through Haggai, Zechariah, and Malachi.

■ **Words to Know:**

chronicle: a detailed history or record of events.

genealogy: a record of a person's family history.

anointed: marked as being chosen by or set apart for God.

■ **Did You Know?** Originally, the ark of the covenant contained the Ten Commandments and the Book of the Law, the flowering staff of Aaron, and some of the manna with which God had fed the children of Israel in the wilderness. The ark was kept in the Holy of Holies—the Most Holy Place—inside the tabernacle or "Tent of Meeting" (Exodus 25:10–22). Carried by the Levites, the ark went before the children of Israel into the Promised Land (Joshua 3:1–4:24). It was marched around the walls of Jericho, before they came tumbling down (Joshua 6:13–20). Centuries later, without God's instruction or permission, the Israelites carried the ark into battle as a talisman against the Philistines and lost it in the battle (1 Samuel 4:1–22). Literally plagued by its presence in their country, the Philistines sent it back over the border into Kiriath Jearim. Then David brought the ark to Jerusalem and Solomon built a temple for it. By this time, the only thing still in it was the Ten Commandments (2 Chronicles 5:10).

Later, when the city of Jerusalem was conquered by the Babylonians and the temple of Solomon reduced to rubble, the ark of the covenant disappeared. Was it destroyed? Carried off to Babylon? Secreted away by survivors of the siege? Today the final resting place of the ark is still a mystery that inspires treasure hunters and conspiracy theorists—and movie makers—around the globe!

Jeremiah once prophesied that the day would come when the ark would not be missed—or even remembered—because there would be no need for it. In that day, God would dwell freely in and among all of His people, rather than in one particular place (Jeremiah 3:14–18).

2 CHRONICLES

■ **The Book**: 2 Chronicles

■ **The Author**: Ezra

■ **The Audience**: The people of God returning from captivity and exile

■ **The Setting**: Written from the land of Judah, 450–425 BC

■ **The Story**: God's people had been living in exile for seventy years. Returning to their devastated homeland, they were nothing like the glorious nation they had once been. They needed the encouragement that God was still with them, that His plans and purposes were still in place, and that His covenant with them was still in force. So Ezra the priest retold the story of King David and his son Solomon and all the kings of Judah who followed after them. Ezra drew parallels between the construction of the tabernacle and the construction of the temple to show the continuity of God's plan through the ages and to encourage the people to continue to walk in obedience to His commands. Every time even the most wicked of the kings repented and returned to God, He forgave him and restored His people to a right relationship with Him. Ezra promised God could and would do the same again.

■ **The Message**: "Solomon son of David established himself firmly over his kingdom, for the LORD his God was with him and made him exceedingly great" (1:1). Soon afterward God appears to the new king in a dream and says, "Ask for whatever you want me to give you." Solomon replies, "LORD God . . . you have made me king over a people who are as numerous as the dust of the earth. Give me wisdom and knowledge, that I may lead this people, for who is able to govern this great people of yours?" (1:9–10). God is pleased with Solomon's request: "Since this is your heart's desire and you have not asked for wealth, riches or honor, nor for the death of your enemies, and since you have not asked for a long life but for wisdom and knowledge to govern my people over whom I have made you king, therefore wisdom and knowledge will be given you. And I will also give you wealth, riches and honor, such as no king who was before you ever had and none after you will have" (1:11–12). King Solomon's splendor does indeed become legendary (1:13–17; 8:1–9:31).

King Solomon fulfills his father's dream by building a glorious and magnificent temple to replace the temporary structure of the tabernacle (or Tent of Meeting) as the center of worship and prayer in Israel (2:1–7:22). At the dedication ceremony, God tells Solomon, "I have chosen and consecrated this house that my name may be there forever. My eyes and my heart will be there for all time. And as for you, if you will walk before me as David your father walked, doing according to all that I have commanded you and keeping my statutes and my rules, then I will establish your royal throne, as I covenanted with David your father, saying, 'You shall not lack a man to rule Israel'" (7:16–18, ESV).

Solomon's son Rehoboam cruelly oppresses his people, and ten of the tribes rebel against him—establishing their own kingdom, "Israel," and appointing Jeroboam to rule over them. Only two tribes remain loyal to Solomon's son, who is now king of "Judah" (10:1–12:16). Rehoboam's son Abijah turns to God during his three-year reign and finds the help he needs to overcome his enemies (13:1–22). The Spirit of God comes upon King Asa, and he urges his nation to turn away from idolatry and return to worship of the One true God. But faced with a personal crisis, he fails to seek God for himself (15:1–16:13). In spite of a brief, ill-fated alliance with Ahab king of Israel, King Jehoshaphat serves God faithfully and experiences His deliverance on the battlefield, as God utterly destroys those who have dared attack His people (17:1–21:1). "The fear of God came upon all the kingdoms of the countries when they heard how the Lord had fought against the enemies of Israel. And the kingdom of Jehoshaphat was at peace, for his God had given him rest on every side" (20:29–30). Kings Jeroboam and Ahaziah adopt the idolatry practiced by their sister nation, Israel, and bring God's judgment upon themselves and the kingdom of Judah. Young King Joash serves God faithfully, as long as he is under the guidance and direction of the priest who helped raise him—but afterward, he falls into idolatry and sin (22:1–24:27). King Amaziah follows the Lord, "but not wholeheartedly" (25:2). For a time Uzziah does what is right, "but after Uzziah became powerful, his pride led to his downfall . . ." (26:16). King Jotham serves the Lord, but King Ahaz leads the people back into idol worship (27:1–28:27).

King Hezekiah trusts in the Lord; he becomes one of Judah's most devout and faithful kings (29:1–32:33). His son Manasseh, however, becomes one of Judah's most infamous kings. "He bowed down to all the starry hosts and worshiped them. He built altars [to sacrifice to other gods] in the temple of the LORD. . . . He sacrificed his sons in the fire, . . . practiced sorcery, divination and witchcraft, and consulted mediums and spiritists. He did much evil in the eyes of the LORD, provoking him to anger" (33:3–6). Yet taken captive and subjected to torture at the hands of his enemies, Manasseh repents. He humbles himself before God and cries out for mercy—and God hears his prayer. Afterward, Manasseh tries to undo the evil he had done, restoring the temple he had desecrated and urging the people of Judah to return to God with him (33:10–20).

Sadly, Manasseh's change of heart has little impact on his son, Amon (33:21–25). But his grandson, Josiah, accomplishes what Manasseh could not. "While he was still young, he began to seek the God of his father David . . ." (34:3). Josiah destroys the people's idols and smashes their altars, purifying the land and beginning a full-scale renovation of the temple. The young king rediscovers the Book of the Law and calls the entire nation to repent and renew its covenant with God (34:1–35:27).

Unfortunately, Josiah's descendants do not share his devotion. The kings of Judah and their people become more and more unfaithful to God. "The LORD, the God of their fathers, sent word to them through his messengers again and again, because he had pity on his people and on his dwelling place. But they mocked God's messengers, despised his words and scoffed at his prophets until the wrath of the LORD was aroused against his people and there was no remedy. He brought up against them the king of the Babylonians. . . . God handed all of them over to

Nebuchadnezzar. . . . He carried into exile to Babylon the remnant, who escaped from the sword, and they became servants to him and his sons until the kingdom of Persia came to power. The land enjoyed its sabbath rests; all the time of its desolation it rested, until the seventy years were completed in fulfillment of the word of the LORD. . ." (36:15–17, 20–21).

Key Verse or Passage

"If my people, who are called by my name, will humble themselves and pray and seek my face and turn from their wicked ways, then will I hear from heaven and will forgive their sin and will heal their land." (2 Chronicles 7:14)

More on This Story in the Bible: The book of 2 Chronicles picks up the story from 1 Chronicles (the two books were originally one volume). Ezra, "the chronicler," also wrote the book of the Bible that bears his name. For more on King Solomon and the kings of Judah, see 1 and 2 Kings. For nearly 350 years, God called on the people and their kings to walk in obedience to His commandments, warning them through the words of the prophets what would happen if they did not (see Isaiah, Jeremiah, Ezekiel, Hosea, Amos, Obadiah, Micah, Nahum, Habakkuk, Zephaniah, and Zechariah). After their captivity, He spoke to them through Haggai, Zechariah, and Malachi.

Words to Know:

chronicle: a detailed history or record of events.

wrath: anger or fury.

entreaty: an earnest or urgent request, a petition or appeal.

Making the Connection: King Jehoshaphat and his tiny nation found themselves in dire circumstances: their enemies had gathered a vast army against them and were soon approaching. The king called the people of Judah to fast and pray. Young and old, men, women, and children—they all gathered at the temple to stand before the Lord.

King Jehoshaphat cried out to God, reminding Him of His promise to care for them. He declared the nation's commitment to wait on the Lord for His deliverance, even as they faced imminent attack. Then the king concluded his prayer with these simple words: "We are powerless against this great horde that is coming against us. We do not know what to do, but our eyes are on you" (2 Chronicles 20:12, ESV).

So many times, we find ourselves completely overwhelmed by the circumstances of life—distressed, discouraged, even devastated by what has taken place right before our very eyes. In our prayers for ourselves or our loved ones or our nation, let's remember the words of King Jehoshaphat: "We do not know what to do, but our eyes are on you." The Scripture says that those who look to the Lord are radiant; their faces are never covered with shame (Psalm 34:5). They will not be abandoned or forsaken (2 Corinthians 4:8–10, 16–18). As King Jehoshaphat and his people waited on God, they received this precious promise from Him: "Do not be afraid or discouraged because of this vast army. For the battle is not yours, but God's. . . . Stand firm and see the deliverance the LORD will give you . . ." (20:15, 17). May we have the courage and faith to do the same!

EZRA

The Book: Ezra

The Author: Ezra

The Audience: The people of God returning from exile

The Setting: The land of Judah in 440 BC

The Story: For years God's people lived in captivity and exile, but at last they were released and allowed to return to their homeland. Nearly sixty years after the first group of exiles returned to Judah, a priest named Ezra arrived with a second group to help lead the new community of faith and supervise the reconstruction of the temple.

The Message: Ezra begins by explaining how the exiles first returned to Judah, including a copy of the decree issued by Cyrus, king of Persia, instructing them to rebuild the temple. Then "everyone whose heart God had moved—prepared to go up and build the house of the LORD in Jerusalem" (1:5). As soon as they got their families settled, the people began working on the reconstruction of the temple. It was a time of both joy and sadness: joy over the restoration God had begun in them and through them, sadness over all that their disobedience had cost them. "And all the people gave a great shout of praise to the LORD, because the foundation of the house of the LORD was laid. But many of the older priests and Levites and family heads, who had seen the former temple, wept aloud. . . . No one could distinguish the sound of the shouts of joy from the sound of weeping, because the people made so much noise. And the sound was heard far away" (3:11–13).

The leaders of neighboring countries grew alarmed. They feared that God's people might once again become a powerful nation, a force to be reckoned with. "Then the peoples around them set out to discourage the people of Judah and make them afraid to go on building. They hired counselors to work against them and frustrate their plans . . . " (4:4–5). They also sent letters back and forth to successive kings of Persia, falsely accusing the Jewish people of illegally rebuilding their homeland and plotting a rebellion. For a time, the work in Jerusalem came to a stand-still (4:24). Then, during the reign of King Darius, a search of the royal archives revealed that God's people had indeed been given permission to rebuild the temple—in fact they had been commanded to do so. Darius sent a wealth of resources to help with the rebuilding and decreed that the work should be completed immediately! "Then the people of Israel—the priests, the Levites and the rest of the exiles—celebrated the dedication of the house of God with joy" (6:16).

Now, many years later, Ezra has been appointed by King Artaxerxes to take gifts and offerings from the treasury in Persia to the temple in Judah and help establish the growing community. "And you, Ezra, in accordance with the wisdom of your God, which you possess, appoint magistrates and judges to administer justice to all the people of Trans-Euphrates—all who know the laws of your God. And you are to teach any who do not know them" (7:25–27).

To his horror, Ezra discovers that many members of the first group of exiles have blatantly disobeyed the Law and intermarried with neighboring people of other faiths—the very sin that had (ultimately) led to their downfall and exile in the first place. So Ezra rebukes the people, fasting and praying and crying out to God for mercy on their behalf (Ezra 9). Chastened, the people respond by divorcing their unbelieving spouses and committing themselves to renewed obedience to God's Law.

Key Verse or Passage

"With praise and thanksgiving they sang to the LORD: 'He is good; his love to Israel endures forever.' And all the people gave a great shout of praise to the LORD, because the foundation of the house of the LORD was laid." (Ezra 3:11)

More on This Story in the Bible: For more on the return of the exiles and their efforts to rebuild their homeland, read the book of Nehemiah (Ezra, the priest, and Nehemiah, the governor, worked together side by side.) And Haggai, Zechariah, and Malachi prophesied to God's people during this time. Most Bible scholars believe Ezra was also "the chronicler" who recorded the history of Israel and Judah in 1 and 2 Chronicles.

Words to Know:

scribe: a writer; a person carefully trained to make copies of important manuscripts and documents by hand (before the invention of the printing press).

offerings: gifts given to God and His work.

diligence: steady, earnest, careful work; a consistent effort to accomplish something.

consecrated: set apart or dedicated to the service of God.

Did You Know? More than a hundred years before it happened, God spoke through His prophets and warned His people that one day they would be conquered by the Babylonians. As Ezra points out, Jeremiah had specified the length of their captivity to the day—seventy years (Ezra 1:1; Jeremiah 25:11–14). And before Cyrus was even born, Isaiah named him as the Persian emperor who would one day defeat the Babylonians, release God's people, and give them permission to rebuild their homeland (Isaiah 44:28–45:3).

■ **Think about It:** Some people have misunderstood or misinterpreted events like those described in Ezra 9–10, concluding that the Bible frowns on or even forbids interracial marriage. But actually, according to the Bible, there really is only one race: the human race. We're all physically and spiritually descended from the same two people, Adam and Eve. Different people groups have distinguishing characteristics and cultures, but deep down we're the same. What the Bible forbids is interfaith marriage—being "unequally yoked" or "partnered" with unbelievers (2 Corinthians 6:14). Throughout history, whenever God's people married outside their faith, they found themselves wandering away from Him—giving in to pressure from their unbelieving spouses to compromise their principles and disobey God's laws. This was particularly devastating in the Old Testament era, when God was trying to establish a people who would serve as a shining example of His holiness to the surrounding nations. In Ezra's time, the people came up with a radical, extreme "solution": to separate themselves from their unbelieving families. It seemed necessary at the time, to get the nation back on track. But in the New Testament era, it's a different story. Christians are told not to automatically separate from or divorce their unbelieving spouses; instead, we're urged to set a good example and try to "win" our whole families to faith in Christ (1 Corinthians 7:12–16; 1 Peter 3:1–2).

NEHEMIAH

■ **The Book:** Nehemiah

■ **The Author:** Nehemiah

■ **The Audience:** The people of God returning from exile

■ **The Setting:** The land of Judah in 430 BC

■ **The Story:** Nehemiah was living in Babylon, serving as cupbearer to the king. He heard that the exiles who had returned to Judah had given up rebuilding the temple and that the walls of Jerusalem still lay in ruins. Nehemiah was given permission to leave the king's court to supervise the rebuilding of the city walls. As the new governor, he worked closely with Ezra to get the people of God back on track.

The Message: Nehemiah tells the story of how he first learned of the trouble in Jerusalem and how God gave him favor with the king, who granted Nehemiah's request to go and help his people (1:1–2:10). The surrounding communities had been engaging in psychological warfare— using threats and ridicule and intimidation—to keep God's people from rebuilding their homeland. So Nehemiah keeps his purpose in coming a secret and conducts his first inspection of the city walls in the dead of night (2:11–16). Afterward he gathers all of the people together to urge them to pick up their tools and finish what they started so long ago. "Come, let us rebuild the wall of Jerusalem, and we will no longer be in disgrace" (2:17). The people respond enthusiastically and begin organizing work crews at once (3:1–32).

"But when Sanballat, Tobiah, the Arabs, the Ammonites . . . heard that the repairs to Jerusalem's walls had gone ahead and that the gaps were being closed, they were very angry. They all plotted together to come and fight against Jerusalem and stir up trouble against it. But we prayed to our God and posted a guard day and night to meet this threat" (4:7–9). Nehemiah makes a stirring speech to the community: "Remember the Lord, who is great and awesome, and fight for your brothers, your sons and your daughters, your wives and your homes" (4:14). Encouraged, the people of God determine to stand firm, despite the opposition they may encounter. "From that day on, half of my men did the work, while the other half were equipped with spears, shields, bows and armor. . . . Those who carried materials did their work with one hand and held a weapon in the other, and each of the builders wore his sword at his side as he worked . . ." (4:16–18).

With the rebuilding underway, Nehemiah finds that there are other things in the community that need his attention. He ends the unlawful oppression of the poor and exposes government corruption (5:1–19). Sanballat and Tobiah continue to make trouble, engaging in all kinds of political intrigue—including an attempt on Nehemiah's life. But in spite of everything, the work on the wall is finally completed (6:1–15). "When all our enemies heard about this, all the surrounding nations were afraid and lost their self-confidence, because they realized that this work had been done with the help of our God" (6:16). All of the people gather for a huge celebration—a dedication ceremony and worship service. Ezra the priest reads aloud from the Law of Moses and the people renew their covenant relationship with God, their commitment to walk in obedience to Him (8:1–10:39).

Before he returns to Babylon, Nehemiah carries out some final reforms in the community (11:1–13:31). It has been an enormously difficult task to get the people back on track. Nehemiah asks God not to let his efforts go unnoticed or unrewarded: "Remember me for this also, O my God, and show mercy to me according to your great love" (13:22).

Key Verse or Passage

"This day is sacred to our Lord. Do not grieve, for the joy of the LORD is your strength." (Nehemiah 8:10)

More on This Story in the Bible: For more on the return of the exiles and their efforts to rebuild their homeland, read the book of Ezra (Ezra, the priest, and Nehemiah, the governor, worked together side by side.) Haggai, Zechariah, and Malachi prophesied to God's people during this same time.

Words to Know:

usury: lending money and charging the borrower an excessive or even illegal amount of interest.

intimidate: to frighten or fill with fear; using the threat of violence to keep someone from doing something.

sacred: dedicated to or set apart for the worship of God; holy.

Making the Connection: God's people were vulnerable because their defenses were down—the city walls lay in ruins. Their enemies used fear and intimidation to discourage the people and keep them from regrouping and rebuilding. The weight of their despair prevented them from rising up to be the people God meant for them to be. Nehemiah taught God's people to keep their eyes on Him and refuse to listen to all the threats and accusations made by their enemies. Nehemiah reminded the people of the value and significance of what they were fighting for. And he had them take turns literally "standing in the gap"—with weapons drawn—so that others could concentrate on rebuilding the protective barriers.

The Bible tells us we all have an enemy—Satan—who tries to use fear, hopelessness, discouragement, and despair to subdue vulnerable believers today. But we can fend him off using the same strategy that worked for Nehemiah. Somehow we've got to keep our focus firmly on the God who loves us and strengthens us and protects us and defends us. We've got to tune out the lies and tune in to the truth. We need to take turns "standing in the gap" on behalf of our friends and family, our brothers and sisters in Christ. Pray for them, encourage them, support them, shield them. In a spiritual sense, stand between them and the enemy of their souls. "The weapons we fight with are not the weapons of the world. On the contrary, they have divine power to demolish strongholds" (2 Corinthians 10:4; see also Ephesians 6:10–18). Will you stand in the gap for someone today?

ESTHER

■ **The Book:** Esther

■ **The Author:** Unknown

■ **The Audience:** All future generations of the people of God

■ **The Setting:** Written in Persia, approximately 460 BC–430 BC

■ **The Story:** The book of Esther tells us how God watched over His people, even when they were living in exile. Esther was a young, orphaned Jewish girl who grew up to become the Queen of Persia. King Xerxes chose her as the winner of the most famous beauty pageant of all time!

More importantly, Esther was in the right place at the right time to save God's people from an evil plot to annihilate them.

■ **The Message:** In a fit of drunken rage, King Xerxes had banished his wife Vashti from the palace forever (1:1–20). His advisors suggest he conduct a nationwide search for a new queen. Xerxes chooses Hadassah: "This girl, who was also known as Esther, was lovely in form and features, and Mordecai [her cousin] had taken her as his own daughter when her father and mother died" (2:7). At Mordecai's insistence, Queen Esther keeps her Jewish heritage and family background a secret (2:10). Working in the palace, Mordecai offends one of the king's most powerful advisors by refusing to show him the deference due only to God. "When Haman saw that Mordecai would not kneel down or pay him honor, he was enraged. Yet having learned who Mordecai's people were, he scorned the idea of killing only Mordecai. Instead Haman looked for a way to destroy all Mordecai's people, the Jews, throughout the whole kingdom . . ." (3:5–6).

Mordecai asks Esther to plead with the king for mercy on behalf of her people. But Esther tells him the request could cost her her life. No one is allowed to approach the king without being summoned first, and it's been more than a month since he's asked for her (4:1–17). Mordecai insists Esther must rise to the occasion; perhaps this is why she has become queen—"for such a time as this" (4:14). So Esther bravely approaches the king and invites him to a series of banquets. Intrigued by her boldness, Xerxes presses her to reveal her agenda (5:1–7:2). Esther replies, "If I have found favor with you, O king, and if it pleases your majesty, grant me my life—this is my petition. And spare my people—this is my request. For I and my people have been sold for destruction and slaughter and annihilation . . ." (7:3–4). When the king discovers how Haman has deceived him, he orders his wicked advisor hung on the very gallows Haman had built for Mordecai (7:9–10). By law, the king's edict authorizing the slaughter of the Jews cannot be reversed or repealed, but at Mordecai's suggestion, a new decree is issued—giving the Jewish people permission to defend themselves and destroy any and all who attack them (8:11–12).

"In every province and in every city, wherever the edict of the king went, there was joy and gladness among the Jews . . ." (8:17).

Queen Esther calls for a feast to commemorate her people's deliverance. "These days should be remembered and observed in every generation by every family, and in every province and in every city. And these days of Purim should never cease to be celebrated by the Jews, nor should the memory of them die out among their descendants" (9:28).

Key Verse or Passage

"For if you remain silent at this time, relief and deliverance for the Jews will arise from another place, but you and your father's family will perish. And who knows but that you have come to royal position for such a time as this?" (Esther 4:14)

More on This Story in the Bible: To learn about the adventures of other "famous" exiles read Daniel 1–6 (there you'll find the stories of Shadrach, Meschach, and Abednego and Daniel in the lion's den). While Esther was exposing Haman's plot to destroy the Jews in Persia, the Jews who had returned to their homeland were struggling to rebuild the temple and the city of Jerusalem. Their story is told in Ezra and Nehemiah.

Words to Know:

citadel: a great fortress in or near a city.

sackcloth: a rough garment worn as a symbol of grief or remorse and repentance.

Did You Know? The first Feast of Purim described in Esther 9:18–22 was a two-day festival for giving thanks to God, honoring friends and family, and reaching out to the poor and needy. The name "Purim" comes from the word "pur"—which are "lots" or dice. Haman "cast lots" or "rolled the dice" to choose a day to kill all the Jews living in the Persian Empire. But God used Esther to put a stop to his evil plot! Jewish people today still celebrate God's deliverance with the Feast of Purim every spring.

■ **Think about It:** In the book of Esther, the name of God is never mentioned—not even once! But the whole story is a celebration of His sovereignty, His power to work in every situation and circumstance—even through what appear to be random "coincidences"—in order to accomplish His ultimate purpose.

■ **Making the Connection:** When Mordecai first calls on Esther to approach the king on behalf of her people, the young queen is flabbergasted at the thought—completely overwhelmed by the magnitude of the request, the risk involved in approaching her notoriously temperamental husband, and the doubtful outcome of such an enterprise. It could literally cost her her life. But Esther's cousin admonishes her to recognize the responsibility that comes with privilege. To whom much is given, much will be required (Luke 12:48). In Esther 4:14, Mordecai asks a pointed question: "Who knows but that you have come to royal position for such a time as this?" As the story unfolds, it becomes clear that Mordecai is right. God Himself has allowed Esther to become queen—placed her in the palace—for this very moment. He has a plan to deliver His people, and He will use Esther to accomplish it.

The Bible tells us that God has a plan and a purpose for each one of our lives. At times we may feel overwhelmed by the challenges we face. The task we've been given seems too hard, the cost too high. But we must remember that we've been blessed with the incredible privilege of being servants of the Most High. And God has put us where we are for a reason. When we look to Him, He will give us all the wisdom and strength we need to accomplish His purposes. For we, too, are called—for such a time as this.

JOB

■ **The Book:** Job

■ **The Author:** Unknown

■ **The Audience:** The people of God

■ **The Setting:** Uz (Mesopotamia—modern-day Jordan), sometime between 2000–1000 B.C.

■ **The Story:** Job was a man who loved God deeply and served him faith-fully—even when God allowed great suffering to come into his life. His story is one of the oldest in the Bible. (Job probably lived around the same time as Abraham, if not before.) But it still speaks to those who face hardship and suffering today.

■ **The Message:** "In the land of Uz there lived a man whose name was Job" (1:1). The story begins when God allows Satan to test Job, to see if his devotion is pure—or based on the abundant blessings he has been given (1:1–12). In one day, Job loses all of his herds and flocks—the source of his wealth. His camels, sheep, oxen, and donkeys are all stolen by raiders or destroyed by fire. At the same time, each one of Job's ten children is killed when the house they are staying in collapses on them. In spite of his gut-wrenching grief, Job determines to worship God anyway: "Naked I came from my mother's womb, and naked I will depart. The LORD gave and the LORD has taken away; may the name of the LORD be praised" (1:21). So Satan tries again, this time destroying Job's health in an attempt to break his spirit. But Job refuses to blame God and give in to the bitterness that his wife battles (2:1–10).

Job's friends, Eliphaz, Bildad, and Zophar, come to console him. However, they offer very little comfort and a whole lot of unsolicited advice—along with a generous serving of pious platitudes and worn-out clichés. They can't resist the urge to try to figure out where Job has gone wrong, what he might have done to bring this trouble on himself, and what he ought to do to fix it. Job is alternately anguished and outraged by the implications and accusations of his friends. Sometimes he expresses faith that God will vindicate him; other times he complains that he has not been informed of the charges against him and allowed to plead his case before the Judge. Around and around in circles they go, Job's friends trying to correct and instruct and inform him, and Job defending him-self and declaring his innocence (3:1–31:40). Late in the conversation, a young man named Elihu offers his observations on suffering and the sovereignty of God. But like the others, Elihu ultimately blames Job for what has happened to him (32:1–37:24).

Then all of a sudden God appears, interrupting the conversation. He will deal with Job's comforters in a moment, but first He wants to have a word with his servant, Job. Overall, Job is a righteous man who clearly did *not* bring his suffering on himself. But he has grown a little brash, a little arrogant in insisting that he deserves answers to all of his questions and complaints. God quickly puts him in his place. "Who is this that darkens my counsel with words without knowledge? Brace yourself like a man; I will question you, and you shall answer me. Where were you when I laid the earth's foundation? . . ." (38:2–4). God goes on to ask dozens of other questions that Job cannot answer, questions that reveal God's supreme power and authority, His majesty and glory (38:4–41:34). In the end, it's all Job can do to humbly reply: "Surely I spoke of things I did not understand, things too wonderful for me to know" (42:3). Job repents immediately and reaffirms his faith and trust in God.

Next, God soundly rebukes Job's friends for their foolishness and presumption. (They were not in a position to speak for God, and He hadn't asked them to!) And then He rewards His faithful servant. "The LORD blessed the latter part of Job's life more than the first" (42:12). God not only restores Job's health and wealth, He gives him ten more children to carry on his legacy of faith. "After this, Job lived a hundred and forty years; he saw his children and their children to the fourth generation. And so he died, old and full of years" (42:16–17).

Key Verse or Passage

"I know that my Redeemer lives, and that in the end he will stand upon the earth. And . . . in my flesh I will see God." (Job 19:25–26)

More on This Story in the Bible: Job's example of perseverance in suffering is mentioned in James 5:10–11, and Job's righteousness is held up as an example in Ezekiel 14:12–20. Other verses on patience and perseverance in times of suffering can be found in Romans 5:3–5; 8:17–18; 2 Corinthians 4:16–18; James 1:2–4; and 1 Peter 4:12–13.

Words to Know:

righteous: upright, moral, virtuous; often used in the "legal" sense of being in right standing (without guilt or sin) in the eyes of the Great Judge—God.

vindicate: to defend or justify someone; to clear a person of suspicion, accusation, or blame.

redeemer: one who frees or delivers another person from difficulty, danger, or bondage, usually by paying a ransom (in essence, "buying" the person back at a price).

Did You Know? Every culture in the world has stories and legends about dragons. There are many references to dragons in the Bible, some symbolically speaking of Satan and others referring specifically to real-life creatures who once roamed the earth. The book of Job mentions fire-breathing "leviathan" (Job 3:8; 41; see also Psalm 74:14; 104:26; Isaiah 27:1) and the mighty "behemoth" (Job 40:15–24) as evidence of God's power and glory revealed in His Creation. Early cultures often referred to these animals as "dragons" and "sea monsters." Creation scientists believe they were what we know as dinosaurs!

Think about It: Someone once said that the human heart is like a bucket. When it gets bumped, whatever's inside comes splashing out. In other words, our hearts are revealed by the way we respond to life's challenges. It's hard to imagine a better biblical example than the story of Job. God allowed Satan to bring calamity and disaster upon this righteous man to test him and prove his heart. As Job heard report after report of ruin and loss, the Bible says he fell to the ground in worship. Not in bitterness, not in rage, not in suicidal grief—in worship. He said, "The LORD gave and the LORD has taken away. May the name of the LORD be praised" (1:20–22). He did not sin by charging God with wrongdoing. Instead, he acknowledged God's sovereignty and affirmed his faith in Him. Job passed the test. Now, Job was human; he had his questions and frustrations. There were a few moments when—understandably—he lost perspective. But ultimately, his heart proved true. We can see that deep

down, Job's "bucket" was full of faith and trust and peace—a spirit of humble submission to the will of God.

What about us? When life bumps our bucket, what comes spilling out? When things don't go our way—when we're faced with an unexpected challenge or a difficult situation—how do we respond? Something to think about today.

PSALMS

■ **The Book:** Psalms

■ **The Author:** David, Moses, Asaph, Solomon, Ethan, Sons of Korah, and others

■ **The Audience:** The people of God

■ **The Setting:** Written in Israel, 1410 BC–430 BC

■ **The Story:** Psalms is a collection of 150 songs, poems, and prayers written over a period of hundreds of years by more than half a dozen different authors. Some are personal songs of praise and thanksgiving; others are hymns written for community worship. Some psalms preach and teach. Others cry out to God for mercy—or call for His justice. These heartfelt expressions of joy and sadness, hope and longing, courage and faith have brought comfort and strength to generations of God's people all over the world.

■ **The Message:** There are many, many familiar and beloved psalms. Here are excerpts from just a few: "Blessed is the man who does not walk in the counsel of the wicked or stand in the way of sinners or sit in the seat of mockers. But his delight is in the law of the LORD, and on his law he meditates day and night" (1:1–2). "I have hidden your word in my heart that I might not sin against you" (119:11). "Your word is a lamp to my feet and a light for my path" (Psalm 119:105).

"This is the day the LORD has made; let us rejoice and be glad in it" (118:24). "Make a joyful noise to the LORD, all the earth!" (100:1, ESV). "Let everything that has breath praise the LORD . . ." (150:6). "Give thanks to the LORD, for he is good. His love endures forever" (136:1).

"Taste and see that the LORD is good; blessed is the man who takes refuge in him" (34:8).

"Oh come, let us worship and bow down; let us kneel before the LORD, our Maker! For he is our God, and we are the people of his pasture, and the sheep of his hand . . ." (95:6–7, ESV). "The LORD is my shepherd; I shall not want. He makes me lie down in green pastures. He leads me beside still waters. He restores my soul . . ." (23:1–3, ESV).

"You created my inmost being; you knit me together in my mother's womb. I praise you because I am fearfully and wonderfully made. . . . My frame was not hidden from you when I was made in the secret place . . . your eyes saw my unformed body. All the days ordained for me were written in your book before one of them came to be" (139:13–16). "Delight yourself in the LORD and he will give you the desires of your heart" (37:4).

"Be still, and know that I am God; I will be exalted among the nations, I will be exalted in the earth" (46:10). "Blessed is the nation whose God is the LORD. . ." (33:12).

"God is our refuge and strength, an ever-present help in trouble. Therefore we will not fear, though the earth give way and the mountains fall into the heart of the sea" (46:1–2). "The LORD is my rock, my fortress and my deliverer; my God is my rock, in whom I take refuge . . ." (18:2). "My soul finds rest in God alone; my salvation comes from him" (62:1). "My flesh and my heart may fail, but God is the strength of my heart and my portion forever" (73:26).

"Cast your cares on the LORD and he will sustain you; he will never let the righteous fall" (55:22). "The angel of the LORD encamps around those who fear him, and he delivers them" (34:7). "I lift up my eyes to the hills—where does my help come from? My help comes from the LORD, the Maker of heaven and earth" (121:1–2). "I sought the LORD, and he answered me; he delivered me from all my fears. Those who look to him are radiant; their faces are never covered with shame" (34:4–5).

"As the deer pants for streams of water, so my soul pants for you, O God. My soul thirsts for God, for the living God . . ." (42:1–2). "O God, you are my God, earnestly I seek you; my soul thirsts for you, my body longs for you, in a dry and weary land . . ." (63:1). "How lovely is your dwelling place, O LORD Almighty! My soul yearns, even faints, for the courts of the LORD; my heart and my flesh cry out for the living God. . . . Better is one day in your courts than a thousand elsewhere . . ." (84:1–2, 10).

"He who dwells in the shelter of the Most High will rest in the shadow of the Almighty. I will say of the LORD, 'He is my refuge and my fortress, my God, in whom I trust.' . . . He will cover you with his feathers, and under his wings you will find refuge; his faithfulness will be your shield and rampart. You will not fear the terror of night, nor the arrow that flies by day. . . . A thousand may fall at your side, ten thousand at your right hand, but it will not come near you. . . . If you make the Most High your dwelling—even the LORD, who is my refuge—then no harm will befall you, no disaster will come near your tent. For he will command his angels concerning you to guard you in all your ways" (91:1–11).

"The LORD is compassionate and gracious, slow to anger, abounding in love. He will not always accuse, nor will he harbor his anger forever; he does not treat us as our sins deserve or repay us according to our iniquities. For as high as the heavens are above the earth, so great is his love for those who fear him; as far as the east is from the west, so far has he removed our transgressions from us" (103:8–12).

"Create in me a pure heart, O God, and renew a steadfast spirit within me. Do not cast me from your presence or take your Holy Spirit from me. Restore to me the joy of your salvation and grant me a willing spirit, to sustain me" (51:10–12).

"I waited patiently for the LORD; he turned to me and heard my cry. He lifted me out of the slimy pit, out of the mud and mire; he set my feet on a rock and gave me a firm place to stand. He put a new song in my mouth, a hymn of praise to our God. Many will see and fear and put their trust in the LORD" (40:1–3).

Key Verse or Passage

"May the words of my mouth and the meditation of my heart be pleasing in your sight, O LORD, my Rock and my Redeemer." (Psalm 19:14)

More on This Story in the Bible: Many of the psalms include references to the specific events in Israel's history that inspired them. A study Bible or a concordance can help you find these stories in the historical books of the Old Testament. King David wrote seventy-three of the psalms— more than any other author. His stories are found in 1 Samuel 16–31, 2 Samuel, and 1 Chronicles.

Words to Know:

> **exalt:** to lift up, to raise high, to honor with praise.
>
> **extol:** to praise highly.
>
> **meditate:** to reflect, to think deeply, to focus one's thoughts.
>
> **selah:** a musical notation; some scholars believe it may mean "pause" or "rest."
>
> **the fear of the Lord:** in Scripture, to "fear God" is to approach Him with a sense of awe and wonder, reverence and respect.

Did You Know? Psalm 119 has been called "a passionate love poem" celebrating God's Word. "I rejoice in following your statutes. . . . I meditate on your precepts. . . . I delight in your decrees!" (119:14–16). At 176 verses, it is the longest chapter in the book of Psalms—and the entire Bible. Psalm 119 is also an acrostic. There are twenty-two stanzas, one for each letter of the Hebrew alphabet. And (in the original Hebrew) each of the eight lines within a stanza start with the same alphabet letter.

Making the Connection: We don't usually think of the songs and poems and prayers that make up the book of Psalms as prophecies—but as it turns out, many of them are. Bible scholars tell us that Psalms 2, 45, 69, 72, and 110 point to the coming of the Messiah—Israel's eternal prophet, priest, and king. During His earthly ministry, Jesus frequently quoted the psalms. As He was dying on the cross, He cried out the words of Psalm 22:1: "My God, My God, why have you forsaken me? . . ." Further on, the psalmist says, "All who see me mock me; they hurl insults, shaking their heads: 'He trusts in the LORD; let the LORD rescue him. Let him deliver him, since he delights in him'" (22:7–8). This is exactly how the chief priests and teachers of the law taunted Jesus (see Matthew 27:41–44). And Psalm 22:16–18 says, "A band of evil men has encircled me, they have pierced my hands and my feet. I can count all my bones; people stare and gloat over me. They divide my garments among them and cast lots for my clothing." All of these things took place during Jesus' crucifixion (see Luke 23:32–35). The New Testament writers tell us that many other psalms were speaking prophetically of Jesus, including Psalms 2:6; 8:1b–2, 6; 16:10; 40:7–8; 41:9; 45:6; 69:9; 110:4; and 118:22, 26.

PROVERBS

■ **The Book:** Proverbs

■ **The Author:** Solomon, Agur, Lemuel, and others

■ **The Audience:** The people of God

■ **The Setting:** Written in Israel, 950 BC–686 BC

■ **The Story:** Proverbs is a book of wise sayings—profound observation and insights—collected by King Solomon and others for the purpose of guiding God's people in the way of wisdom.

■ **The Message:** The book of Proverbs begins by urging the reader to embrace wisdom and receive all of its benefits (1:1–4:27). The words in this book are meant to guide the simple (those who lack understanding) and instruct the young (those who lack experience). Those who already have wisdom can gain even more (1:1–7). True wisdom begins with the fear of the Lord, "for the LORD gives wisdom and from his mouth come knowledge and understanding . . ." (2:6; see also 1:7; 9:10). Those who reject wisdom will suffer for it (1:20–32). Wisdom protects and provides for those who are guided by it (2:1–3:35). "Hold on to instruction, do not let it go. . . . Above all else, guard your heart, for it is the wellspring of life" (4:13, 23).

A wise father warns his son about the absolute devastation and destruction that results from adultery and sexual immorality. If he values his life, he must avoid it at all costs (5:1–23; 6:20–35; 7:1–27). Laziness, too, is a trap—a snare (6:1–11; 21:25; 24:33–34). So are dishonest or deceitful companions (6:12–19; 12:26). Wisdom is personified as a woman who calls out to all who have ears to hear: "Listen, for I have worthy things to say. . . . Choose my instruction instead of silver, knowledge rather than choice gold, for wisdom is more precious than rubies, and nothing you desire can compare with her" (8:6, 10–11).

Here are some words of wisdom from the book of Proverbs:

"When words are many, sin is not absent, but he who holds his tongue is wise." (10:19)

"Reckless words pierce like a sword, but the tongue of the wise brings healing." (12:18)

"A gentle answer turns away wrath, but a harsh word stirs up anger." (15:1)

"An anxious heart weighs a man down, but a kind word cheers him up." (12:25)

"A friend loves at all times, and a brother is born for adversity." (17:17)

"A man's wisdom gives him patience; it is to his glory to overlook an offense." (19:11)

"Pride goes before destruction, a haughty spirit before a fall." (16:18)

"Whoever loves discipline loves knowledge, but he who hates correction is stupid." (12:1)

"Plans fail for lack of counsel, but with many advisers they succeed." (15:22)

"As iron sharpens iron, so one man sharpens another." (27:17)

"Many are the plans in a man's heart, but it is the LORD's purpose that prevails." (19:21)

"He who conceals his sins does not prosper, but whoever confesses and renounces them finds mercy." (28:13)

"The name of the LORD is a strong tower; the righteous run to it and are safe." (18:10)

"He is a shield to those whose walk is blameless, for he guards the course of the just and protects the way of his faithful ones." (2:7–8)

The book of Proverbs ends with a beautiful tribute to "a wife of noble character." She is praised for her virtue, her wisdom, her discipline, and her integrity (31:10–31). A wise man searches for a wife like this, and when he finds her, he treasures her. "Charm is deceptive, and beauty is fleeting; but a woman who fears the LORD is to be praised" (31:30).

Key Verse or Passage

"Trust in the LORD with all your heart and lean not on your own understanding; in all your ways acknowledge him, and he will make your paths straight." *(Proverbs 3:5–6)*

More on This Story in the Bible: Other writings by King Solomon include Psalms 72 and 127, the book of Ecclesiastes, and Song of Songs. The events of Solomon's reign are described in 1 Kings 2:1–11:43 and 2 Chronicles 1:1–9:31.

Words to Know:

wisdom: knowledge of what is right or true; sound judgment, insight, and discernment.

folly: foolish thinking or behavior; stupidity.

discipline: training that corrects, molds, or perfects a person's moral character.

rebuke: stern, sharply worded correction.

the fear of the Lord: in Scripture, to "fear God" is to approach Him with a sense of awe and wonder, reverence and respect.

Did You Know? To truly understand and appreciate the book of Proverbs, it's important to remember that proverbs are profound insights and observations of life principles that are *generally* true. Proverbs are *not* promises, commandments, or absolute-without-exception rules. Sometimes they may seem to contradict each other, when actually they are offering "both sides of the coin"—different truths that apply to different situations. All together, they help us see the big picture and guide us in the way of wisdom.

Think about It: Proverbs has a lot to say about family relationships—including the relationships between parents and their children. Many people are familiar with the old adage "spare the rod, spoil the child." It comes from Proverbs 13:24: "He who spares the rod hates his son, but he who loves him is careful to discipline him." In our culture today, corporal punishment is the subject of heated debate. Those who oppose it often associate it with child abuse—which, biblically speaking, is an entirely different and totally unacceptable scenario. (Nowhere does the Bible advocate bullying, terrorizing, or tormenting anyone—least of all children, who are especially precious to God.) The kind of discipline that Proverbs refers to is a response to deliberate disobedience, defiance, and rebellion. Whatever the form of punishment—whether a spanking or the suspension of video game privileges—the goal is ultimately to protect children from the kind of pain that lying, cheating, stealing, and other bad behavior will cause them later in life. "Discipline your son, for in that there is hope; do not be a willing party to his death" (19:18; see also 22:6, 15; 23:13–14; 29:17).

Simply put, the Bible says that if you care about your children—if you really love them—you will discipline them and teach them right from wrong. God, our heavenly Father, sets the example for all parents in the way that He relates to us, His children. He is patient and kind, merciful and compassionate and understanding. But He knows that our sinful behavior can lead to painful consequences—for us and for others. So He holds us accountable for our actions. He disciplines us. He teaches us to take responsibility and learn from our mistakes. Proverbs 3:11–12 says, "My son, do not despise the Lord's discipline and do not resent his rebuke, because the Lord disciplines those he loves, as a father the son he delights in." For more on God's loving discipline, see Lamentations 3:22–33 and Hebrews 12:7–11.

ECCLESIASTES

The Book: Ecclesiastes

The Author: Solomon

The Audience: The people of God

The Setting: Written in Jerusalem, 935 BC

The Story: Following the book of Proverbs, Ecclesiastes (meaning "the preacher" or "teacher") contains more of King Solomon's words of wisdom and the story of his search for the meaning of life. Fame and fortune, "wine, women, and song"—at one time or another, Solomon had it all. He found it empty and meaningless. In the end, he concluded that the only thing that really matters is to fear God and keep His commandments.

The Message: "Meaningless! Meaningless! . . . Everything is meaningless" (1:2). The Teacher observes that human beings in their own efforts, striving in their own strength, cannot achieve anything of any lasting significance (1:1–15; 2:17–26; 4:1–8; 9:2–10). "What has been will be again, what has been done will be done again; there is nothing new under the sun" (1:9). The Teacher (Solomon) says he has diligently applied himself to discovering the purpose or meaning of life, only to conclude: "I have seen all the things that are done under the sun; all of them are meaningless, a chasing after the wind" (1:14).

Hard work, accomplishment, and success don't satisfy the longings of the human heart. Neither does pleasure or self-indulgence (2:1–11). "Whoever loves money never has money enough; whoever loves wealth is never satisfied with his income . . ." (5:10). Riches don't bring lasting happiness, for as the Teacher points out, "Naked a man comes from his mother's womb, and as he comes, so he departs" (5:15). In other words, "You can't take it with you!"

Wisdom has great value—and yet there are questions it can't answer, mysteries it can't solve. God has "set eternity in the hearts of men; yet they cannot fathom what God has done from beginning to end" (3:11). Wisdom in and of itself—knowledge for the sake of knowledge—doesn't bring fulfillment or satisfaction (1:12–18; 2:12–16; 7:1–24; 8:16–17; 9:13–18). "Of making many books there is no end, and much study wearies the body" (12:12).

Often, life isn't fair. The Teacher has seen "righteous men who get what the wicked deserve, and wicked men who get what the righteous deserve . . ." (8:14). He notes: "The race is not to the swift or the battle to the strong, nor does food come to the wise or wealth to the brilliant or favor to the learned; but time and chance happen to them all" (9:11). But ultimately, God is in control, and He watches over those who fear Him and obey His commandments (12:13). "Although a wicked man commits a hundred crimes and still lives a long time, I know that it will go better with God-fearing men, who are reverent before God. . . . For God will bring every deed into judgment, including every hidden thing, whether it is good or evil" (8:12; 12:14).

Key Verse or Passage

"Fear God and keep his commandments, for this is the whole duty of man. For God will bring every deed into judgment, including every hidden thing, whether it is good or evil." (Ecclesiastes 12:13–14)

More on This Story in the Bible: Other writings by King Solomon include Psalms 72 and 127, the book of Proverbs, and Song of Songs. The events of Solomon's reign are described in 1 Kings 2:1–11:43 and 2 Chronicles 1:1–9:31.

Words to Know:

the fear of the Lord: in Scripture, to "fear God" is to approach Him with a sense of awe and wonder, reverence and respect.

wisdom: knowledge of what is right or true; sound judgment, insight, and discernment.

folly: foolish thinking or behavior; stupidity.

toil: hard work, exhausting labor or effort.

▩ **Making the Connection:** Many people know the words of Ecclesiastes 3:1–8 as the lyrics to a chart-topping folk song from the 1960s: "For everything there is a season, and a time for every matter under heaven: a time to be born, and a time to die; a time to plant, and a time to pluck up what is planted; a time to kill, and a time to heal; a time to break down, and a time to build up; a time to weep, and a time to laugh; a time to mourn, and a time to dance; a time to cast away stones, and a time to gather stones together; a time to embrace, and a time to refrain from embracing; a time to seek, and a time to lose; a time to keep, and a time to cast away; a time to tear, and a time to sew; a time to keep silence, and a time to speak; a time to love, and a time to hate; a time for war, and a time for peace" (ESV). The Bible tells us that God has created and ordained or established all of these things—and that He makes all things beautiful "in its time" (3:11).

▩ **Think about It:** The Teacher of Ecclesiastes finds that many things in life are "meaningless"—yet he notes that there are some things that do have great value. Like the power of friendship and the strength that comes from unity: "Two are better than one, because they have a good return for their work: If one falls down, his friend can help him up. But pity the man who falls and has no one to help him up! Also, if two lie down together, they will keep warm. But how can one keep warm alone? Though one may be overpowered, two can defend themselves. A cord of three strands is not quickly broken" (4:9–12).

SONG OF SONGS

▩ **The Book:** Song of Songs (also known as the Song of Solomon)

▩ **The Author:** King Solomon

▩ **The Audience:** The court of King Solomon

▩ **The Setting:** Written in Jerusalem, 965 BC

▦ **The Story:** This "greatest of all songs" is a lyric poem that celebrates "the agony and the ecstasy" of the love between a man (the Lover) and a woman (the Beloved) through their courtship and marriage. This is human love the way God meant for it to be, intensely thrilling, passionate, and—because it takes place in the context of marriage—holy and pure.

▦ **The Message:** The Beloved is enraptured with her one true love: "Let him kiss me with the kisses of his mouth—for your love is more delightful than wine" (1:2). Her Lover is equally intoxicated: "How beautiful you are, my darling! Oh, how beautiful! . . . Like a lily among thorns is my darling among the maidens" (1:15; 2:1). The couple's friends rejoice with them in the love that they have found (1:4; 5:1). Both the Lover and the Beloved express their delight in each other's physical beauty and look forward to the consummation of their love (2:1–6; 4:1–16; 5:10–7:13). The Lover exclaims, "All beautiful you are, my darling; there is no flaw in you. . . . You have stolen my heart, my sister, my bride; you have stolen my heart with one glance of your eyes . . ." (4:7, 9).

When the couple is separated, the longing they feel for each other is intense. The Beloved cries, "All night long on my bed I looked for the one my heart loves; I looked for him but did not find him. . . . The watchmen found me as they made their rounds in the city. 'Have you seen the one my heart loves?' . . . If you find my lover, what will you tell him? Tell him I am faint with love" (3:1, 3; 5:8). So great is their passion, the Beloved admits she wishes they could ignore society's standards of propriety and openly embrace one another, displaying their affection in public (8:1–3). From her own experience through the ups and downs of courtship, the Beloved has come to realize that love and passion are much too powerful for anyone to treat lightly. She warns her friends: "Daughters of Jerusalem, I charge you: Do not arouse or awaken love until it so desires" (8:4). The Lover calls to his bride, "Let me hear your voice!" (8:13) And she answers by inviting him to a private celebration of their love: "Come away, my lover, and be like a gazelle or like a young stag on the spice-laden mountains" (8:14).

Key Verse or Passage

"For love is as strong as death, its jealousy unyielding as the grave. It burns like blazing fire, like a mighty flame. Many waters cannot quench love; rivers cannot wash it away. . . ." (Song of Songs 8:6–7)

More on This Story in the Bible: Other writings by King Solomon include Psalms 72 and 127, the book of Proverbs, and Ecclesiastes. Solomon's reign is described in 1 Kings 2:1–11:43 and 2 Chronicles 1:1–9:31.

Words to Know:

myrrh: a fragrant perfume.

garden or vineyard: the word "garden" is often used in Scripture as a metaphor for the heart; in Song of Songs, it refers specifically to the Beloved's body—as well as the purity and exclusivity of the intimate relationship between her and her Lover.

jealous: vigilant or watchful in guarding something; wanting something all to one's self.

Making the Connection: Although Song of Songs is primarily a celebration of God-ordained human love, it can also be understood as an allegory—one that reflects God's love for Israel or Christ's love for the church. This theme of a "divine romance" between the Creator and His creation appears throughout the Scriptures.

Did You Know? The children's song "His Banner over Me Is Love" comes from an allegorical reading of Song of Songs, especially 2:4 and 2:16. Other hymns and choruses often describe Jesus as "the Lily of the Valley" and "the Rose of Sharon" (Song of Songs 2:1). In context, these are names that the Beloved actually uses to refer to herself, as she celebrates how beautiful her Lover makes her feel. At first it seems the hymn writers must have made a mistake in applying them to Jesus. (It might make more sense if the names described the Bridegroom—the Lover!) But perhaps the idea is that these terms of endearment suggest that the Person they refer to is the ultimate picture of beauty and perfection. In that case, they're not so inappropriate after all!

Think about It: If you've ever done much gardening, you know that in addition to choosing what to plant and when—aside from nurturing new growth and providing adequate water and sunlight—one of the most critical tasks is to keep the pests away. You've got to protect the tender plant—the new fruit—from being trampled or eaten by its enemies, be they bug or bird or beast. The same is also true for the garden of our hearts. In John 15:5, Jesus said, "I am the vine; you are the branches. If a man remains in me and I in him, he will bear much fruit. . . ." Further on, He said again, "I chose you and appointed you to go and bear fruit—fruit that will last." If we abide in the vine, He will provide all the nutrients, all the nurturing, we need. But it's our job to keep away the pests.

Song of Songs 2:15 says, "Catch for us the foxes, the little foxes that ruin the vineyards, our vineyards that are in bloom." Apparently these "little foxes" threatened the relationship between the Lover and the Beloved, and they can threaten our relationship with God today. "Little foxes" might be inappropriate thoughts that have gone unchecked, bad habits that have taken root, or small sins we secretly make allowance for. The trouble with "little foxes" is that they don't look dangerous from the outset. But these pesky critters nibble at the vine and destroy our life-giving connection to God. They quickly devour the fruit He has so patiently labored to produce in our lives. The guilt and hypocrisy alone is enough to cripple us and keep us from experiencing meaningful fellowship with the Lord. If you see any "little foxes" in the garden of your heart, don't be deceived by their harmless appearance. Catch them now before they grow into monsters. Protect that precious fruit.

ISAIAH

The Book: Isaiah

The Author: Isaiah

The Audience: The people of Judah

The Setting: The kingdom of Judah, between 740 BC and 680 BC

▪ The Story: The prophet Isaiah answered God's call to warn Judah that their enemies would soon conquer them. They had rebelled against God and disobeyed Him and they would pay the price. But God promised He would heal them and restore them. He would bring them back to their homeland and back into a right relationship with Him. He would also send them His Servant, the Messiah, their true King to set things right forever and ever.

▪ The Message: Isaiah says, "In the year that King Uzziah died, I saw the Lord seated on a throne, high and exalted, and the train of his robe filled the temple" (6:1). The cherubim and seraphim gathered around the throne cry, "Holy, holy, holy is the LORD Almighty; the whole earth is full of his glory" (6:3). Through this startling vision, God calls Isaiah to be His voice and speak His words to the people of Judah. Isaiah warns the people that God is about to judge them for their disobedience and rebellion against Him (22:1–25; 28:1–29; 29:1–31:9; 32:9–14; 48:1–22; 51:17–52:12). He exposes their hypocrisy: "Woe to those who call evil good and good evil. . . . These people come near to me with their mouth and honor me with their lips, but their hearts are far from me. Their worship of me is made up only of rules taught by men. . . . This is what the Sovereign LORD, the Holy One of Israel, says: 'In repentance and rest is your salvation, in quietness and trust is your strength, but you would have none of it'" (5:20; 29:13; 30:15). Isaiah urges the people to truly repent and sincerely serve God—not just with their lips, but with their lives (58:1–14). Isaiah says God will also judge the wicked nations that surround Judah—the people of Babylon, Assyria, Philistia, Moab, Damascus, Egypt, and Cush, Edom, Arabia, and Tyre (10:5–19; 13:1–21:17; 23:1–24:23; 33:1–34:17; 47:1–15).

Isaiah intersperses his prophecies with hymns of praise (12:1–6; 25:1–26:21; 42:10–17). He also includes an account of a time when Sennacherib of Assyria threatened the city of Jerusalem. Isaiah brings King Hezekiah the Word of the Lord—that God will intervene on His people's behalf and defeat the Assyrians with His own mighty hand (37:1–38). Later, when King Hezekiah falls ill, Isaiah intercedes on his behalf. God agrees to add fifteen more years to the king's life (38:1–22).

In addition to words of instruction and correction and rebuke, God gives Isaiah words of comfort and encouragement for His people—whom He still loves dearly. "'Come now, let us reason together,' says the Lord. 'Though your sins are like scarlet, they shall be as white as snow; though they are red as crimson, they shall be like wool'" (1:18; also 40:1–3; 49:8–26; 57:14–21). He promises to preserve a remnant of His people whom He will watch over and protect—and one day restore to their former glory (10:20–34; 35:1–10; 41:1–21; 45:1–25; 51:1–16; 54:1–17). God says He will give them the strength to endure: "Do you not know? Have you not heard? The LORD is the everlasting God, the Creator of the ends of the earth. He will not grow tired or weary, and his understanding no one can fathom. He gives strength to the weary and increases the power of the weak. Even youths grow tired and weary, and young men stumble and fall; but those who hope in the LORD will renew their strength. They will soar on wings like eagles; they will run and not grow weary, they will walk and not be faint" (40:28–31). He will never abandon His own: "This is what the LORD says—he who created you, O Jacob, he who formed you, O Israel: 'Fear not, for I have redeemed you; I have summoned you by name; you are mine. When you pass through the waters, I will be with you; and when you pass through the rivers, they will not sweep over you. When you walk through the fire, you will not be burned; the flames will not set you ablaze. For I am the LORD, your God, the Holy One of Israel, your Savior . . ." (43:1–3). To those who are thirsty, He offers living water—with the promise they will thirst no more (55:1–13).

God says He will send His people a Messiah, a Deliverer. "The Lord himself will give you a sign: The virgin will be with child and will give birth to a son, and will call him Immanuel [God with Us]" (7:14; also 9:1–7; 11:1–16; 32:1–8; 42:1–9; 49:1–7; 50:1–11). This Servant of the Lord will save His people by ransoming them—laying down His life for them, suffering and dying in their place (52:13–53:12). They will not recognize Him at first, but looking back they will realize: "He was pierced for our transgressions, he was crushed for our iniquities; the punishment that brought us peace was upon him, and by his wounds we are healed" (53:5).

Isaiah looks forward to the day God has promised to create a new heavens and a new earth. In that day, the pain and suffering of this life won't even be a memory; there will be no more sorrow or sadness, only peace and joy for the people of God (65:17–66:13). "He will swallow up death forever" (25:8). The Sovereign Lord will wipe every tear from their eyes.

Key Verse or Passage

"How beautiful on the mountains are the feet of those who bring good news, who proclaim peace, who bring good tidings, who proclaim salvation, who say to Zion, 'Your God reigns!'" (Isaiah 52:7)

More on This Story in the Bible: Isaiah prophesied at the same time as Amos, Hosea, and Micah, and during the reigns of four kings, including King Uzziah (2 Chronicles 26:1–23) and King Hezekiah (2 Kings 19:1–20:21; 2 Chronicles 32:1–33). In the New Testament, Jesus began His earthly ministry by quoting Isaiah 61:1–3 and identifying Himself as the one the prophet was speaking of (see Luke 4:16–21). Jesus also identified John the Baptist as the one Isaiah described as "a voice crying in the wilderness" (see Isaiah 40:3 and Matthew 3:3). When Philip encountered an Ethiopian official on the road to Jerusalem, the man was reading from Isaiah 53:7–8 (see Acts 8:26–40).

Words to Know:

woe: great sadness or sorrow.

remnant: something left over; a small surviving group of people.

Zion: the name "Zion" first referred to a specific hillside community King David conquered on the outskirts of Jerusalem, "the city of David." Over time, "Zion" came to refer to the nearby temple and then the city of Jerusalem itself, "the city of God." Isaiah uses "Zion" to mean the entire nation of Israel, God's kingdom here on earth. In the New Testament, the name "Zion" refers to God's heavenly and eternal kingdom, filled with people from every tribe and nation who faithfully love and serve Him.

also wanted His people to know that one day, He would heal them and restore them. He would bring them back into their homeland and back into a right relationship with Him.

■ **The Message:** Jeremiah begins by describing how God called him to his prophetic ministry while he was still a teenager—or even earlier! "The word of the LORD came to me, saying, 'Before I formed you in the womb I knew you, before you were born I set you apart; I appointed you as a prophet to the nations" (1:4–5). It would not be easy. The message God gave him to deliver was a hard one. Jeremiah had to confront God's people with their disobedience and sin, their wickedness and rebellion against Him. In graphic terms Jeremiah describes the people's spiritual adultery—how they have forsaken their heavenly husband (God) to run after other lovers (idols) (2:1–4:4). Through Jeremiah, God—the heart-broken husband—pleads with His bride: "Return, faithless Israel. . . . I will frown on you no longer, for I am merciful. . . . I will not be angry forever. Only acknowledge your guilt . . ." (3:12–13). If they do not repent, terrible punishment awaits them. They will be attacked by their enemies and betrayed by those they have trusted in and turned to instead of God. Their kingdom will be destroyed (4:5–6:30).

Jeremiah reminds the people how much God detests hypocrisy (7:1–9:26). He points out the futility of worshiping idols they have made with their own hands. He repeatedly exposes and denounces the corrupt government officials and religious leaders of the day. He rebukes the false prophets who keep assuring the people that all is well, promising peace and prosperity that will not come (23:9–40; 28:1–29:32). This does not make Jeremiah a very popular man. In fact, throughout his ministry, he will be mocked and ridiculed, isolated and ignored, and imprisoned—thrown into chains, thrown into the stocks, thrown into wells! His messages will be burned as rubbish (26:1–24; 32:2; 36:1–32; 37:1–21; 38:1–13).

Still, the prophet stands firm. Jeremiah continues to warn the people of the destruction coming their way (10:1–25). They have broken their vows—their sacred covenant with God (11:1–17). But the people refuse to listen, and at last the day comes when God says enough is enough. He tells Jeremiah not to bother praying for the people any more (7:16; 11:14;

14:11). It's too late. They have rejected God, and He has rejected them. For seventy years, they will be captives and exiles in Babylon (25:1–14). God tells Jeremiah not to marry and have children or attend feasts and celebrations or even funerals. All of these "normal" everyday activities are inappropriate and irrelevant in light of the day of disaster that is coming (16:1–21).

Yet in the midst of all the doom and gloom, God still has words of comfort and encouragement for the few who are faithful to Him. He will not forget His promises to the generations of His people who have come before. "Blessed is the man who trusts in the LORD, whose confidence is in him. He will be like a tree planted by the water that sends out its roots by the stream. It does not fear when heat comes; its leaves are always green. It has no worries in a year of drought and never fails to bear fruit" (17:7–8).

To the righteous remnant, God says, "I have loved you with an everlasting love; I have drawn you with loving-kindness. I will build you up again and you will be rebuilt. . . . So there is hope for your future. . . . Your children will return to their own land" (31:3–4, 17). Even as the city is beginning to fall, God tells Jeremiah to purchase a piece of property as a symbol of his faith that one day God will bring His people back to their homeland again (32:1–33:26). God also promises to raise up a righteous branch from King David's family tree, a Good Shepherd, a leader of integrity, "a King who will reign wisely and do what is just and right in the land" (23:5). This Messiah will be the mediator of a new covenant: "It will not be like the covenant I made with their forefathers. . . . I will put my law in their minds and write it on their hearts. I will be their God, and they will be my people. . . . They will all know me, from the least of them to the greatest. . . . For I will forgive their wickedness and will remember their sins no more" (31:32–34).

Jeremiah prophesies God's judgment against Judah's enemies—Egypt, Philistia, Moab, Ammon, Edom, Damascus, Kedar and Hazor, Elam, and Babylon (46:1–51:64). Although God has used these nations to discipline His people, ultimately they will be punished for their own wickedness. When Jeremiah's prophecy of Judah's destruction begins to come true, the people repent and beg Jeremiah for his advice. At first they promise to do what ever he says, but when they don't like what they hear, they throw him back in prison again (42:1–43:13).

The Babylonians attack Judah several times; brief periods of submission and surrender are followed by rebellion and uprising. Finally the Babylonians decide to end it once and for all. They capture the city of Jerusalem and destroy it utterly and completely. Solomon's magnificent temple is reduced to rubble, and the few remaining survivors are carried off into captivity and exile—just as Jeremiah said they would be (52:1–34). As for Jeremiah, it turns out the Babylonians have far more respect for the man of God than the people of Judah do. The Babylonians see clearly that everything Jeremiah has prophesied has come true. When they conquer the city, they make a point of rescuing Jeremiah from his imprisonment and setting him free (39:11–40:6). However, Jeremiah does not rejoice in his freedom or his vindication. The "weeping prophet" is too heartbroken over the pain and agony God's people are suffering.

Key Verse or Passage

"For I know the plans I have for you,' declares the LORD, 'plans to prosper you and not to harm you, plans to give you hope and a future.'" (Jeremiah 29:11)

■ **More on This Story in the Bible:** To learn more about Jeremiah's prophetic ministry and how his prophecies were fulfilled, read 2 Chronicles 35:25–36:22 and 2 Kings 25. Jeremiah also wrote Lamentations, a collection of songs mourning the destruction of the southern kingdom. The restoration of God's people that both books—Jeremiah and Lamentations—look forward to is described in Ezra and Nehemiah.

■ **Words to Know:**

sackcloth: a rough garment worn as a symbol of grief or remorse and repentance.

lament: a dirge; a poem or song of sadness and mourning often sung at a funeral.

repent: to make a change for the better as a result of feeling sorrow or regret or remorse over one's sins.

remnant: something left over; a small surviving group of people.

Did You Know? Many of the messages God gave His prophets were fulfilled in more ways than one. For instance, Jeremiah spoke of the day Judah would be utterly destroyed: "A voice is heard in Ramah, mourning and great weeping, Rachel weeping for her children and refusing to be comforted, because her children are no more" (Jeremiah 31:15). Rachel, Jacob's wife (Genesis 29–35), symbolized all of the mothers in Israel and the grief and heartbreak they were about to experience—losing their children to war, famine, and disease. But the Bible tells us that—whether he realized it or not—Jeremiah was also speaking of another day hundreds of years later when mothers of Israel would mourn. On that day, King Herod would try to kill the Christ child by ordering the slaughter of every baby boy in Bethlehem under the age of two (Matthew 2:18). Later, Jesus reminded His disciples that God's Word can be trusted because—for better or worse—it always comes true: "Until heaven and earth disappear, not the smallest letter, not the least stroke of a pen, will by any means disappear from the Law until everything is accomplished" (Matthew 5:18).

Making the Connection: Do you ever feel like you've made a mess of your life? You've made too many mistakes and bad choices. Yes, you've repented and asked God for forgiveness. But deep down inside you feel a sense of hopelessness and despair. Your life is ruined beyond repair. It's too late. God could never use you. "This is the word that came to Jeremiah from the Lord: 'Go down to the potter's house and there I will give you my message.'" Jeremiah says, "'I went down to the potter's house, and I saw him working at the wheel. But the pot he was shaping from the clay was marred in his hands; so the potter formed it into another pot, shaping it as it seemed best to him. Then the word of the Lord came to me: 'O house of Israel, can I not do with you as this potter does?' declares the Lord. 'Like clay in the hand of the potter, so are you in my hand . . .'" (Jeremiah 18:1–6).

The Bible tells us God is so merciful. Regardless of our past failures, in spite of our present weakness, He can and will use us for His glory—as long as we're fully surrendered to Him. He is the potter and we are the clay. We just have to be careful not to get impatient and start climbing off the wheel. Trust Him to complete the work that He's begun in your life. He makes all things beautiful in His time (Ecclesiastes 3:11).

LAMENTATIONS

The Book: Lamentations

The Author: Jeremiah

The Audience: The people of God living in the ruins of Jerusalem and in captivity in Babylon

The Setting: Written approximately 586 BC–584 BC

The Story: The people of God living in Judah (the southern kingdom) had not repented of their sins against Him, even after they saw the destruction of their brothers and sisters in Israel (the northern kingdom) and despite the warnings of the prophets God sent to them. So God had allowed the Babylonians to conquer them. The great temple of Solomon and the city of Jerusalem itself lay in ruins. Most of the people were killed or carried off as slaves. A handful were left in the wreckage. On behalf of the survivors, the prophet Jeremiah pours out his heart to God in a series of songs or "laments."

The Message: Jeremiah expresses his horror at what has come to pass: "How deserted lies the city, once so full of people! How like a widow is she, who once was great among the nations! She who was queen among the provinces has now become a slave" (1:1). The prophet acknowledges that this is God's doing; He has allowed the Babylonians to carry out His punishment on the people—just as He warned them He would. As awful as it is, the people have no one to blame but themselves. Their own wickedness and rebellion and disobedience is the cause of their suffering (1:14, 18; 2:1–17). "My eyes fail from weeping, I am in torment within, my heart is poured out on the ground because my people are destroyed

131

. . ." (2:11). Everywhere he looks, the prophet sees devastation, starvation, disease.

But even in the midst of unspeakable suffering, Jeremiah says there is hope. God is loving and merciful and compassionate. He is faithful even when we are not (3:21–23). "The LORD is good to those whose hope is in him, to the one who seeks him; it is good to wait quietly for the salvation of the LORD. It is good for a man to bear the yoke while he is young. Let him sit alone in silence, for the LORD has laid it on him. Let him bury his face in the dust—there may yet be hope" (3:25–29). As painful as it is, discipline has a purpose. It can humble us and teach us and ultimately restore us. "Let us examine our ways and test them, and let us return to the LORD. Let us lift up our hearts and our hands to God in heaven . . ." (3:40–41).

What God's people have experienced is brutal, but it will come to an end. The enemies who have carried out God's punishment will themselves be punished for their own wickedness and sin (3:46–4:22). Jeremiah concludes with a heartfelt prayer: "Remember, O LORD, what has happened to us; look, and see our disgrace. . . . Restore us to yourself, O LORD, that we may return; renew our days as of old" (5:1, 21).

Key Verse or Passage

"Yet this I call to mind and therefore I have hope: Because of the LORD's great love we are not consumed, for his compassions never fail. They are new every morning; great is your faithfulness." (Lamentations 3:21–23)

■ More on This Story in the Bible: You can learn more about "the weeping prophet's" life and ministry in the book of Jeremiah. For more on how Judah was conquered and the temple destroyed, see 2 Kings 25. The eventual restoration of God's people that the book of Lamentations looks forward to is described in Ezra and Nehemiah.

■ Words to Know:

lament: a dirge; a poem or song of sadness and mourning often sung at a funeral.

affliction: pain and suffering, grief and misery.

sackcloth: a rough garment worn as a symbol of grief or remorse and repentance.

iniquities: sins, wickedness, injustice.

Making the Connection: Jeremiah is often called "the weeping prophet," because in this book of laments (songs of mourning) he so movingly expresses his grief and heartache over the destruction of Judah, crying out to God for mercy and forgiveness.

Did You Know? Every one of the five chapters of Lamentations is an acrostic, with a verse or group of verses starting with each of the twenty-two letters in the Hebrew alphabet.

Think about It: Did you ever hear the expression uttered by a parent about to discipline a child: "This is going to hurt me a lot more than it hurts you." When you're a child, that statement seems ludicrous! But when you become an adult, you begin to understand just how difficult and unpleasant—even painful—it can be to have to inflict discipline on those precious little ones in your care. It's awful to see them suffer. How deeply you wish you didn't have to go through with it. If only they would obey!

The Bible tells us there are times when our heavenly Father has to discipline us—times when He must allow us to suffer the painful consequences of our disobedience—so that we'll have the opportunity to learn from our mistakes. "Though he brings grief, he will show compassion, so great is his unfailing love. For he does not willingly bring affliction or grief to the children of men" (Lamentations 3:32–33).

As a loving parent, God is never gleeful about disciplining us. It doesn't amuse Him to see us grapple with pain and heartbreak. On the contrary, it grieves Him deeply. But He loves us so much that He's willing to allow us to hurt so that we'll learn and grow, so that we'll be motivated to make a change, so that the next time, we'll obey. Then we won't have to suffer the pain of disobedience—or discipline—at all.

EZEKIEL

The Book: Ezekiel

The Author: Ezekiel

The Audience: The people of Judah living in exile

The Setting: Written from Babylon, between 593 BC and 571 BC

The Story: The kingdom of Judah was conquered by the Babylonians in steps and stages. Those who had already been taken captive hoped desperately that God would intervene, supernaturally enabling or empowering their countrymen to rise up against Babylon and come to their rescue. But Ezekiel warned the people that there would be no miraculous deliverance this time. Because of their rebellion and disobedience, Jerusalem would be completely and utterly destroyed. Still, God would be with them in their darkest days, and one day He would bring them home again.

The Message: "In the thirtieth year, in the fourth month on the fifth day, while I was among the exiles by the Kebar River, the heavens were opened and I saw visions of God" (1:1). Ezekiel sees four fantastic living creatures—seraphim and cherubim—who symbolically represent all of God's creation and reflect His radiance and glory (1:4–28). God tells Ezekiel, "Son of man, I am sending you to the Israelites, to a rebellious nation. . . . You must speak my words to them, whether they listen or fail to listen. . . . I have made you a watchman for the house of Israel; so hear the word I speak and give them warning from me" (2:3, 7; 3:17). Ezekiel calls God's people to repent of their sins, to turn from their wicked ways and return to Him. Already they have begun to experience the painful consequences of their disobedience. Things will get much worse before they get better (3:16–24:27).

God calls Ezekiel to go beyond dramatic imagery and literally, physically, and symbolically act out his prophecies in the sight of all the people. At God's direction, the prophet shuts himself in his house, tied up with ropes, unable to open his mouth. If the people won't listen, why should God speak (3:22–27)? Ezekiel enacts the future siege of the city of Jerusalem, lying first on his left side for 390 days and then on his right for forty days. Each day represents a year that the northern kingdom (Israel) and then the southern kingdom (Judah) have walked in rebellion and sin (4:1–17). God says, "I will make you a ruin and a reproach among the nations around you. . . . You will be a reproach and a taunt, a warning and an object of horror . . ." (5:14–15). When Ezekiel's wife dies, the prophet is not allowed to go through the traditional rituals of mourning. God says His people are about to experience such heartache and loss that they will not even be able to express it (24:15–27).

The people's wickedness and idolatry is more than God can bear. He cannot hold back His judgment any longer (6:1–8:18). Ezekiel looks up and sees God's glory—His presence—depart from the temple. God will no longer live among His people there (10:1–22). God compares Jerusalem to an abandoned baby that He rescued and adopted and lavished with love and affection, only to see her grow up to be a shameless prostitute, a brazenly adulterous wife (16:1–63). In the most shocking and graphic terms, God compares the people's unfaithfulness to Him to the most disgusting immorality imaginable (23:1–49). Still, they do not take His correction or rebuke seriously.

God's people are not the only ones who will suffer His wrath. Ezekiel prophesies God's judgment against the wicked people of Ammon, Moab, Edom, Philistia, Tyre, Sidon, and Egypt (25:1–32:32). The destruction and devastation will be great.

When Ezekiel hears that the city of Jerusalem has fallen at last, he reminds the people that this is exactly what God said would happen (33:21–29). He rebukes "the shepherds of Israel"—the leaders and teachers and prophets and priests—who have failed to care for their flock: "You have not strengthened the weak or healed the sick or bound up the injured. You have not brought back the strays or searched for the lost. You have ruled them harshly and brutally" (34:4). God says He will hold them accountable and remove them from positions of influence. "This is what the Sovereign LORD says: I myself will search for my sheep and look after them. . . . I will rescue them from all the places where they were scattered on a day of clouds and darkness. I will bring them out from the nations and gather them from the countries, and I will bring them into their own land. I will pasture them on the mountains of Israel . . . the mountain heights of Israel will be their grazing land . . ." (34:11–14). After He has disciplined His people, God will show mercy and have compassion. He will make a new covenant with them, a "covenant of peace" (34:25).

In a vision, God shows Ezekiel a valley full of dry bones and asks him if it's possible for those bones to come to life again:

> I said, "O Sovereign LORD, you alone know."
>
> Then he said to me, "Prophesy to these bones and say to them, 'Dry bones, hear the word of the LORD! . . . I will make breath enter you, and you will come to life.'". . . So I prophesied as he commanded me, and breath entered them; they came to life and stood up on their feet—a vast army. . . .
>
> Then he said to me: "Son of man, these bones are the whole house of Israel. They say, 'Our bones are dried up and our hope is gone; we are cut off.' . . . O my people, I am going to open your graves and bring you up from them; I will bring you back to the land of Israel. . . . I will put my Spirit in you and you will live, and I will settle you in your own land . . ." (37:3–14).

Next, God gives Ezekiel a wonderful vision of the future. There will come a day when the temple will be rebuilt with splendor and magnificence. The nation of Israel will be fully restored and the people of God will experience the glory of His presence as never before (40:1–48:35). The holy city of Jerusalem will also be rebuilt. "And the name of the city from that time on will be: the LORD is There" (48:35).

Key Verse or Passage

"I will give you a new heart and put a new spirit in you; I will remove from you your heart of stone and give you a heart of flesh." (Ezekiel 36:26)

▦ **More on This Story in the Bible:** Ezekiel and Jeremiah prophesied at the same time about the same thing: the destruction of Judah described in 2 Kings 25 and 2 Chronicles 36:15–21. Ezekiel prophesied to those who had already been taken captive and deported to Babylon in an earlier attack, while Jeremiah prophesied to those still living in Judah who were about to suffer the same fate. Other "famous" exiles living in Babylon at this time include Daniel and Esther. The promised restoration of God's people to their homeland is described in Ezra and Nehemiah.

▨ Words to Know:

lament: a dirge; a poem or song of sadness and mourning often sung at a funeral.

sovereign: the ultimate authority, the supreme power.

watchman: a person who watches over others, guards them, protects them, and warns them of danger; God called Ezekiel to be a watchman for His people.

▨ Did You Know?

Ezekiel had a startling, fantastic vision of the four living creatures who surround the throne of God and symbolically represent the power and majesty of His creation. (The lion is the mightiest of the wild animals, the ox the mightiest of domesticated animals, the eagle the mightiest of the birds, and God has made man ruler of all.) Elsewhere in Scripture, these creatures are identified as angels—"cherubim" and "seraphim"—fierce and magnificent and glorious, and nothing like the chubby winged babies in Renaissance paintings! One of the cherubim was stationed at the entrance to the garden of Eden to keep Adam and Eve out after they fell from grace (Genesis 3:24). God directed Moses and the children of Israel to decorate the tabernacle with artistic representations of these creatures, including the two that appeared on either end of the mercy seat above the ark of the covenant in the Holy of Holies (Exodus 25:17–22). Later, King Solomon created golden statues of the cherubim fifteen feet high to adorn the sanctuary in the temple. Isaiah had visions of these heavenly creatures, as did John the Apostle (Isaiah 6:1–7; Revelation 4:6–9). Ezekiel tells us that Satan himself was a cherub, until he rebelled against God and was cast out of heaven: "You were the model of perfection, full of wisdom and perfect in beauty. . . . Your heart became proud on account of your beauty and you corrupted your wisdom. . . . So I threw you to the earth" (Ezekiel 28:12, 17; see also Isaiah 14:12–14 and Luke 10:18).

DANIEL

■ **The Book:** Daniel

■ **The Author:** Daniel

■ **The Audience:** The people of God living in exile

■ **The Setting:** Written from Babylon, between 605 BC and 530 BC

■ **The Story:** The Babylonians had captured the best and brightest of God's people and carried them off into exile, including four young Hebrew boys—Daniel, Shadrach, Meshach, and Abednego. Living in a foreign country, far away from their friends and families—everything they knew—these young men stayed true to their faith in God, stood up for what they believed in, and set an example that inspired fear and awe in the hearts of Babylonian kings. Daniel, in particular, had the opportunity to display God's power and proclaim His truth in miraculous ways, time and time again.

■ **The Message:** Daniel and his friends Hananiah (Shadrach), Mishael (Meshach), and Azariah (Abednego) are taken to the palace in Babylon, where they are given new names, trained in the language and literature of the Babylonians, and prepared to enter the king's service. From the start, they find themselves forced to decide whether or not they will serve God in Babylon as they did in Judah. At the risk of their lives, they refuse to accept the food given to them from the king's table, realizing it would require them to violate God's commandments and eat meat that has been sacrificed to idols. A palace official decides to allow them to eat only the foods God has permitted during a trial period. "At the end of the ten days they looked healthier and better nourished than any of the young men who ate the royal food" (1:15). God honors His servants for their faithfulness to Him. "To these four young men God gave knowledge and understanding of all kinds of literature and learning. And Daniel could understand visions and dreams of all kinds" (1:17). When their training came to an end, "the king talked with them, and he found none equal to Daniel, Hananiah, Mishael and Azariah; so they entered the king's service. In every matter of wisdom and understanding about which the king questioned them, he found them ten times better than all the magicians and enchanters in his whole kingdom" (1:19–20).

Later, Nebuchadnezzar builds a gold statue ninety feet high and demands that everyone in the kingdom bow down and worship it—or be thrown into a fiery furnace. Shadrach, Meshach, and Abednego refuse to obey the king's decree. "If we are thrown into the blazing furnace, the God we serve is able to save us from it, and he will rescue us from your hand. . . . But even if he does not, we want you to know, O king, that we will not serve your gods or worship the image of gold you have set up" (3:17–18). Angrily, the king orders his favorite advisors thrown into the furnace—only to exclaim moments later: "Weren't there three men that we tied up and threw into the fire? . . . Look! I see four men walking around in the fire, unbound and unharmed, and the fourth looks like a son of the gods" (3:24–25). When the three men emerge from the furnace unharmed, the king cries out: "Praise be to the God of Shadrach, Meshach and Abednego, who has sent his angel and rescued his servants! They trusted in him and defied the king's command and were willing to give up their lives rather than serve or worship any god except their own God" (3:28).

Nebuchadnezzar's respect for the Most High God is short-lived. God sends him a dream to warn him about his pride and arrogance, and Daniel is called upon to give the interpretation. Daniel tells Nebuchadnezzar that one day he will not only lose his kingdom, but his sanity. For seven years, he will live in the fields like a wild animal until he finally, humbly acknowledges his Creator. Nebuchadnezzar's dream comes true exactly as Daniel says it will (4:1–37). Nebuchadnezzar's successor, King Belshazzar, calls for Daniel when, in the midst of his drunken revelry, he sees the hand of God writing on the palace wall: "Mene, mene, tekel, parsin." Daniel explains to the king that God is saying his days are numbered. Belshazzar has been weighed in the balance and found wanting. That very night, his kingdom will be conquered and divided by the Medes and Persians. Darius the Mede will take his throne (5:1–31).

Daniel soon becomes the new king's closest and most trusted advisor. Jealous, other advisors trick Darius into outlawing prayer to any other "god" but himself. Daniel not only defies this decree, he does so openly and in full view of his enemies and the entire kingdom. When the other advisors insist that Daniel be thrown in the lion's den, Darius realizes his mistake—but he has to honor his word. The king prays that God will somehow rescue Daniel and is thrilled beyond belief to find the prophet alive and well the next morning. Daniel tells Darius, "My God sent his angel, and he shut the mouths of the lions. They have not hurt me, because I was found innocent in his sight . . ." (6:22). It is Daniel's accusers who are devoured instead (6:24). "So Daniel prospered during the reign of Darius and the reign of Cyrus . . ." (6:28).

God begins to give Daniel startling and miraculous visions of the destiny of Israel, the rise and fall and final judgment of the nations of the earth, and things that will take place in the last days (7:1–12:13). "There will be a time of distress such as has not happened from the beginning of nations until then. But at that time your people—everyone whose name is found written in the book—will be delivered. Multitudes who sleep in the dust of the earth will awake: some to everlasting life, others to shame and everlasting contempt. Those who are wise will shine like the brightness of the heavens, and those who lead many to righteousness, like the stars for ever and ever" (12:1–3). Daniel doesn't understand everything that God has revealed to him; many of the things he has seen will not take place for thousands of years. But God assures him that one day it will all become clear. After his death, he will live again—and at that time, he will see that everything God told him has come true (12:13).

Key Verse or Passage

"Praise be to the name of God for ever and ever; wisdom and power are his. He changes times and seasons; he sets up kings and deposes them. He gives wisdom to the wise and knowledge to the discerning. He reveals deep and hidden things; he knows what lies in darkness, and light dwells with him." (Daniel 2:20–22)

More on This Story in the Bible: Daniel lived during the same time as Ezekiel. (They were taken captive at different times and exiled to different regions of the Babylonian Empire.) While Ezekiel proclaimed

God's truth to the people of Judah, Daniel revealed God's power to their Babylonian captors. The description of the "Ancient of Days" in Daniel 7:1–14 matches John's description of Jesus in Revelation 1:9–18, and the king who exalts himself in Daniel 11:36–45 sounds remarkably like John's vision of the Antichrist. A study Bible can help you compare these two prophetic books and explore their symbolism in greater detail.

■ Words to Know:

sovereign: the ultimate authority, the supreme power.

defile: to make "unclean" or impure, to contaminate something once pure and holy.

Ancient of Days: the name Daniel uses to refer to the eternal and everlasting God who judges the nations, kingdoms, and empires whose power and glory is only temporary. They rise and fall and then disappear from memory, but the Ancient of Days reigns over all the earth forever and ever.

■ Did You Know?

Daniel 10:1–14 gives us an amazing behind-the-scenes look at what goes on in the spirit world when we pray—and why sometimes the answers take so long to come our way. For three weeks Daniel had been fasting and praying, urgently seeking a Word from the Lord. It was one of those critical situations where time is of the essence. Why was there no answer?

Suddenly an angel appeared, saying, "Do not be afraid, Daniel. Since the first day that you set your mind to gain understanding and to humble yourself before your God, your words were heard, and I have come in response to them" (10:12). The reason for the delay? "For twenty-one days the spirit prince of the kingdom of Persia blocked my way. Then Michael, one of the archangels, came to help me . . ." (10:13, NLT). Now that the messenger was free, Daniel would finally receive the answer he had been waiting for.

In Ephesians 6:10–18, the apostle Paul reminds us that there are spiritual forces at work in the heavenly realms, an unseen battle going on all around us. We can't be fainthearted or easily discouraged when we don't see instant results. We may be right on the verge of a breakthrough—if

141

we press on and persevere in prayer. It may be that the answer is already on the way.

■ **Making the Connection**: When people can tell that something bad is going to happen, they often speak of "seeing" or "reading" the "writing on the wall." This expression comes from Daniel 5:1–30, where King Belshazzar quite literally sees the handwriting on the wall that spells his doom!

■ **Think about It**: The book of Daniel tells the story of a young man kidnapped from his home as a teenager and raised in a foreign land, in a culture that was not only different, but hostile to his own. Far away from his parents' watchful eyes, apart from the influence of respected religious leaders, and without the support of a like-minded community, Daniel stayed true to his faith in God and kept the Word of the Lord, no matter what it cost him. He stood up under tremendous pressure to adopt the lifestyle and customs of his new country. He refused to eat meat that had been sacrificed to idols. He wouldn't worship false gods. He continued to pray openly, even when a law was passed that made his prayers punishable by death. Daniel had the same faith as the psalmist who wrote, "You are my refuge and my shield; I have put my hope in your word. Away from me, you evildoers, that I may keep the commands of my God!" (Psalm 119:114–115).

Like Daniel, we live in a culture that is openly hostile to our faith. Unfortunately, many of us have been assimilated into that culture. We have adopted its lifestyle and values. But as Christians, we are called to a higher standard. We need to pray daily for the wisdom and strength and courage to be true to our God, no matter what the cost. Just like Daniel.

HOSEA

■ **The Book**: Hosea

■ **The Author**: Hosea, son of Beeri

■ **The Audience**: The people of Israel

■ **The Setting:** The land of Israel, between 755 BC and 710 BC

■ **The Story:** The prophet Hosea was called to be a living object lesson. God told him to marry Gomer—an adulterous wife—to show the Israelites how they had been unfaithful to Him. Although God's heart was broken, and in spite of the grief and heartache His people caused Him, Hosea prophesied that ultimately, God would forgive them and take them back.

■ **The Message:** When God first called Hosea to be His prophet, He gave him a startling assignment: "Go, take to yourself an adulterous wife and children of unfaithfulness, because the land is guilty of the vilest adultery in departing from the LORD" (1:2). Hosea did as God asked. During their marriage, Gomer gave birth to three children, whom Hosea named Jezreel ("God Scatters"), Lo-Ruhamah ("Not Loved"), and Lo-Ammi ("Not My People"). God had stern words for Israel, His wayward bride: "Rebuke your mother, rebuke her, for she is not my wife, and I am not her husband. . . . I will not show my love to her children, because they are the children of adultery" (2:2, 4).

God's people have cheated on Him and betrayed Him by chasing after other "lovers"—worshiping false gods and material possessions. God says He will expose Israel's shame and disgrace. He will punish her for her sin. And when she has been confronted and forced to face her own unworthiness, when she is heartbroken and embarrassed and ashamed, He will woo her again and win her heart back. God will gather her people, whom He has scattered: "I will plant her for myself in the land; I will show my love to the one I called 'Not my loved one.' I will say to those called 'Not my people,' 'You are my people'; and they will say, 'You are my God'" (2:23).

God directs Hosea to demonstrate this in his own life. "Go, show your love to your wife again, though she is loved by another and is an adulteress. Love her as the LORD loves the Israelites . . ." (3:1). Hosea speaks again on behalf of God, detailing the sins the people have committed. "There is no faithfulness, no love, no acknowledgment of God in the land" (4:1). God must deal with His people severely, "until they admit their guilt." Then, "in their misery they will earnestly seek me" (5:15). Hosea calls to the people: "Come, let us return to the LORD. He has torn us to pieces but he will heal us; he has injured us but he will bind up our wounds" (6:1). Otherwise, they will reap what they have sowed (8:1–10:15).

Though Israel is fickle, God's love is faithful (11:1–4). He dreams of the day their love relationship will be restored (14:4).

Key Verse or Passage

"Therefore I am now going to allure her; I will lead her into the desert and speak tenderly to her. There I will give her back her vineyards, and will make the Valley of Achor [trouble] a door of hope. There she will sing as in the days of her youth, as in the day she came up out of Egypt." (Hosea 2:14–15)

■ **More on This Story in the Bible:** Hosea is the first of the twelve "minor" (briefer, not lesser) prophets. These words were written at about the same time—and to the same people—as the book of Amos. Hosea includes many references to Israel's history, from Jacob and Esau in Genesis to the exodus out of Egypt to the time of the kings. A study Bible can help you identify and look up each of these references individually.

■ **Words to Know:**

adulterous: unfaithful, disloyal.

allure: to attract someone, to charm them.

prostitute: a person who sells his or her body to others for money.

compassion: feeling what others feel, showing them kindness and mercy and love.

■ **Making the Connection:** Throughout the Scriptures, the marriage relationship between a husband and a wife is used as an analogy—an example or illustration—of the kind of loving, committed relationship God longs to have with each one of us individually and with humanity as a whole. He designed marriage for that very purpose. In the New Testament, the church—which is made up of individual believers—is often referred to collectively as "the bride of Christ." Jesus is pictured as the passionate

Bridegroom who would do anything—even lay down His life—for His one true love.

Hosea helps us understand why God takes it so personally when we ignore Him, reject Him, or abandon Him to run after "other lovers"— giving our hearts to earthly things. Like a jealous husband (in the best sense of the word), God is not satisfied with our half-hearted, on again– off again affection. He wants us to love Him the way He loves us: passionately, wholeheartedly, exclusively.

JOEL

■ **The Book:** Joel

■ **The Author:** Joel, son of Pethuel

■ **The Audience:** The people of Judah

■ **The Setting:** The land of Judah, between 600 BC and 400 BC

■ **The Story:** A plague of locusts devastated the land of Judah. But according to the prophet Joel, the suffering and hardship that the people had experienced was nothing compared to what was coming—if they did not repent and turn away from their sins. "The day of the Lord," the day of God's judgment, would be far worse.

■ **The Message:** Joel begins by drawing attention to the significance of the plague that has overcome Judah: "Hear this, you elders; listen, all who live in the land. Has anything like this ever happened in your days or in the days of your forefathers? Tell it to your children, and let your children tell it to their children . . ." (Joel 1:2–3). Describing the devastation that has taken place, Joel says that this is a time for mourning. "Surely the joy of mankind is withered away" (1:12).

But there is something the people of God can do—something they must do! "Declare a holy fast; call a sacred assembly. Summon the elders and all who live in the land to the house of the LORD your God, and cry out to the LORD" (1:14). Otherwise, Joel warns that another army of "locusts" is coming to devour the land, the army of the Lord. "His forces are beyond number and mighty are those who obey his command . . ." (2:11).

God calls to His people; there is still time for them to repent of their sins and return to Him. They need to show that they are truly sorry for what they have done—not just on the outside, but on the inside (2:12–13). If the people return to God, He will have compassion on them and protect them and provide for them abundantly once more (2:1–24). "I will repay you for the years the locusts have eaten . . ." (2:25).

Afterward, God will pour out His Spirit on all people: "Your sons and daughters will prophesy, your old men will dream dreams, your young men will see visions" (2:28). Then He will judge the nations once and for all, according to what they have done. "The LORD will roar from Zion and thunder from Jerusalem; the earth and the sky will tremble. But the LORD will be a refuge for his people, a stronghold for the people of Israel" (3:16).

Key Verse or Passage

"'Even now,' declares the LORD, 'return to me with all your heart, with fasting and weeping and mourning.' Rend your heart and not your garments. Return to the LORD your God, for he is gracious and compassionate, slow to anger and abounding in love, and he relents from sending calamity." (Joel 2:12–13)

More on This Story in the Bible: Joel's prophecy is quoted by the apostle Peter in Acts 2:16. Joel's message is very similar to that of other prophets, including Amos, Micah, Zephaniah, Jeremiah, and Ezekiel.

Words to Know:

locusts: literally a plague of countless destructive insects; also used by Joel to refer to innumerable armies.

sackcloth: a rough garment worn as a symbol of grief or remorse and repentance.

fasting: giving up eating for a time; ignoring one's physical hunger to focus on one's spiritual hunger; often a sign of sorrow or repentance.

mourning: sadness and grieving.

"the day of the Lord": this phrase can refer to specific and individual days or times when God powerfully (and unmistakably) intervenes in human history; it can also mean the final "day of the Lord," in which God judges all the peoples of the earth, destroys the wicked, and rescues or rewards the righteous.

rend: to tear; in Bible times, it was customary for people to tear their clothing as an outward sign of grief and sadness.

Making the Connection: In the first message that the apostle Peter preached after the death and resurrection of Jesus, he quoted the words of the prophet Joel to explain the coming of the Holy Spirit as described in Acts 2:1–41. "In the last days, God says, I will pour out my Spirit on all people . . ." (Acts 2:17). In the past, God's Spirit came upon only a handful of men and women who were specially chosen by Him to accomplish a specific task. But today, says Peter, God's Spirit lives in and through all believers, empowering them to live lives that honor Him.

AMOS

The Book: Amos

The Author: Amos, a shepherd of Tekoa

The Audience: The people of Israel

The Setting: The kingdoms of Israel and Judah, between 760 BC and 750 BC

The Story: God called Amos to bring words of warning and rebuke to the rebellious people living in Israel. A farmer and a shepherd, Amos used many different images and examples from nature in his messages. After warning the people about the punishment God had in store for them, Amos spoke of a day to come when God would heal and forgive.

The Message: Amos first has some fiery words for the wicked nations that surround Israel: Aram, Philistia, Phoenecia, Edom, Ammon, Moab, and Judah. God is about to pour out His wrath on them. Then Amos turns to Israel. They have ignored the signs of the times, the words of the prophets. "When disaster comes to a city, has not the LORD caused it?" (3:6). God has done everything He can to get their attention. He has sent plagues, withheld rain, struck down their crops, and allowed their armies to be defeated in battle. "Yet you have not returned to me . . ." (4:11).

The prophet rebukes the people for their hypocrisy: "Seek good, not evil, that you may live. Then the LORD God Almighty will be with you, just as you say he is" (5:14). Amos says that God is angry with the people for their pride and arrogance, their complacency—especially in light of the judgment they have witnessed being carried out on the people around them (6:1–14). God has been merciful time and time again, relenting from sending more severe plagues and inflicting more damage and destruction. But no longer. He has measured Israel with a plumb line and found them crooked beyond repair (7:1–9). God shows Amos a basket of fruit and says the time is ripe for Israel's judgment (8:1–2).

In the midst of all this, Amos has a confrontation with a priest named Amaziah. The priest tries to silence the prophet; he tells Amos to take his negative message somewhere else. But Amos insists that, like it or not, he's only being obedient to deliver the words God gave him (7:10–17).

"'The days are coming,' declares the Sovereign LORD, 'when I will send a famine through the land—not a famine of food or a thirst for water, but a famine of hearing the words of the LORD. Men will stagger from sea to sea and wander from north to east, searching for the word of the LORD, but they will not find it" (8:11–12).

Almost in the same breath as he describes the destruction of Israel, Amos shares God's promise that one day He will heal and forgive. "I will restore David's fallen tent. I will repair its broken places, restore its ruins, and build it as it used to be" (9:11). For all their sin and rebellion, God's people still have a place in his heart. Ultimately one day, he says, "I will plant Israel in their own land" (9:15), never to be uprooted again.

Key Verse or Passage

"Seek good, not evil, that you may live. Then the LORD God Almighty will be with you, just as you say he is." (Amos 5:14)

■ More on This Story in the Bible: The book of Amos was written at about the same time—and to the same people—as the book of Hosea. The destruction that Amos prophesied is described in 2 Kings 17.

■ Words to Know:

wrath: anger or fury.

consume: to destroy, as in a fire.

oppress: to treat people in a harsh, cruel, and unjust way.

plumb line: a measuring tool in which a weight is suspended from a cord and used to determine height or depth. If something is "out of plumb," it is crooked—it doesn't line up the way it is supposed to.

■ Did You Know? Amos warned that a new and different kind of "famine" was coming, a famine for the Word of the Lord. This was a time when God would be silent. His people would be sorry that they rejected the prophets (the messengers) He sent to them and that they didn't listen to His words. In those days, God's people would be desperate to hear from Him, but He would not speak to them.

There was a "famine" just like the one Amos described, a few centuries later. Between the Old and New Testaments, from Malachi to Matthew, there is a four-hundred-year silence—a time when God said nothing. And then all of a sudden, on an ordinary day, the angel Gabriel appeared to a young woman named Mary: "When the time had fully come, God sent his Son . . ." (Galatians 4:4).

OBADIAH

■ The Book: Obadiah

■ The Author: Obadiah, "the servant of the Lord"

■ The Audience: The people of Edom

■ The Setting: Written from the land of Judah, 586 BC

The Story: The wicked people of Edom (descendants of Jacob's twin brother, Esau) had gloated over the destruction of Israel and Judah. But the prophet Obadiah warned the Edomites that God would also allow *their* enemies to triumph over *them*. In fact, Edom would be destroyed utterly and completely—whereas one day Israel would be restored.

The Message: The people of Edom took advantage of the Babylonian destruction of Jerusalem as an opportunity to wage their own war on the people of Judah. High up in their own mountain fortresses, they felt safe and secure. But Obadiah says that their arrogance will lead to their downfall: "The pride of your heart has deceived you, you who live in the clefts of the rocks and make your home on the heights, you who say to yourself, 'Who can bring me down to the ground?'" (v. 3). Even if they could soar like an eagle or make their nest in the stars, they would not be beyond God's reach (v. 4). He *can* bring them down—and He will!

"But how Esau will be ransacked, his hidden treasures pillaged! All your allies will force you to the border; your friends will deceive and overpower you; those who eat your bread will set a trap for you, but you will not detect it" (vv. 6–7).

Obadiah says God is disgusted that the people of Edom stood there and watched while their own flesh and blood (the people of Judah) were attacked and destroyed. They did nothing to help. In fact, they joined the enemy! God says to Edom, "You should not look down on your brother in the day of his misfortune, nor rejoice over the people of Judah in the day of their destruction, nor boast so much in the day of their trouble. You should not march through the gates of my people in the day of their disaster, nor look down on them in their calamity . . . nor seize their wealth. . . . You should not wait at the crossroads to cut down their fugitives, nor hand over their survivors in the day of their trouble. The day of the LORD is near for all nations. As you have done, it will be done to you; your deeds will return upon your own head" (vv. 12–15).

Because of their sin against Israel, the Edomites will themselves be destroyed. While God will one day forgive and restore His people, "there will be no survivors from the house of Esau . . ." (v. 18).

Key Verse or Passage

"Because of the violence against your brother Jacob, you will be covered with shame; you will be destroyed forever." (Obadiah 1:10)

More on This Story in the Bible: For more on the history of the relationship between the descendants of Jacob and Esau, see Genesis 25:19–34; 27:1–41; 32–33; Numbers 20:14–21; and Deuteronomy 2:1–6; 23:7–8. The destruction of Judah is described in 2 Kings 25. The shortest book in the Old Testament, Obadiah was written at about the same time—and around the same historical events —as Jeremiah and Lamentations.

Words to Know:

sovereign: the ultimate authority, the supreme power.

envoy: a messenger from one government to another.

pillaged: having destroyed a city or country and carried off all of its valuables.

fugitives: people who are trying to escape.

Did You Know? Obadiah's prophecy came true. By AD 70, the Edomites had ceased to exist. Edom was conquered first by Arab warriors in the fifth century BC and then again by the Nabataeans in the third century BC. The Nabataeans carved a great city into the rock cliffs of Edom. That city—Petra (in Jordan)—remains one of the most fascinating "monuments of the world." It was featured as the site of the holy grail in the movie *Indiana Jones and the Last Crusade* and as a refuge for Christians during the end times in the *Left Behind* series.

JONAH

The Book: Jonah

The Author: Jonah

The Audience: The people of Ninevah

The Setting: Written from Israel, between 800 BC and 750 BC

■ **The Story:** The prophet Jonah tried to run from God rather than deliver His warning to the people of Ninevah, but three days in the belly of a great fish changed his heart and his mind.

■ **The Message:** God calls the prophet Jonah: "Go to the great city of Nineveh and preach against it, because its wickedness has come up before me" (1:2). But Jonah would rather not. Instead, he takes a ship headed in the opposite direction. "Then the LORD sent a great wind on the sea, and such a violent storm arose that the ship threatened to break up" (1:4).

Jonah realizes that he can't hide or escape from God. He tells the frightened sailors, "It is my fault that this great storm has come upon you" (1:12). Jonah urges them to save themselves by throwing him overboard. "But the LORD provided a great fish to swallow Jonah, and Jonah was inside the fish three days and three nights" (1:17).

Inside the fish, Jonah is humble and repentant. He asks God to forgive him: "The engulfing waters threatened me, the deep surrounded me; seaweed was wrapped around my head. To the roots of the mountains I sank down; the earth beneath barred me in forever. But you brought my life up from the pit, O LORD my God. When my life was ebbing away, I remembered you, LORD, and my prayer rose to you, to your holy temple" (2:5–7). God hears Jonah's prayer. "And the LORD commanded the fish, and it vomited Jonah onto dry land" (2:10).

When God calls Jonah a second time, the prophet is ready to obey. Jonah goes straight to Ninevah, where he warns the people of the city that God is going to destroy them because of their wickedness. The people listen to Jonah's words—they respond by calling for a citywide fast. Everyone, "from the greatest to the least," repents of their sin and asks God to forgive them. "When God saw what they did and how they turned from their evil ways, he had compassion and did not bring upon them the destruction he had threatened" (3:10).

Outside the city, Jonah sits waiting to see Ninevah destroyed—and he is actually disappointed when it doesn't happen! But God reminds him of his own need for mercy and grace and urges him to have compassion—to be glad for the Ninevites' sakes—for the more than 120,000 people who have been spared (4:1–11).

Key Verse or Passage

"Those who cling to worthless idols forfeit the grace that could be theirs. But I, with a song of thanksgiving, will sacrifice to you. What I have vowed I will make good. Salvation comes from the Lord." (Jonah 2:8–9)

■ **More on This Story in the Bible:** The story of Jonah is also mentioned in 2 Kings 14:25; Matthew 12:38–41; 16:4; and Luke 11:29–32.

■ **Words to Know:**

calamity: a terrible disaster.

compassion: feeling what others feel, showing them kindness and mercy and love.

■ **Did You Know?** Over the years many people have wondered how anyone could survive three days in the belly of a fish. Is that scientifically possible? Of course, the answer from the scientific community is a resounding, "No!" So how did Jonah do it? There are several answers to that question. First of all, this was clearly a supernatural event. If we believe that God is powerful enough to suspend the laws of nature when it suits His purposes, then there's no question He could have done so with Jonah. While it may not be possible for us to survive being swallowed by a "great fish" today, it was possible for Jonah because God "prepared a fish" specifically for that purpose. It's also possible that Jonah did not "survive" in the traditional sense—that he actually died inside the fish and was then raised from the dead when the fish spit him out. Jesus told His disciples that the sign that He was the Messiah was "the sign of Jonah": "For as Jonah was three days and three nights in the belly of a huge fish, so the Son of Man will be three days and three nights in the heart of the earth." And of course, on the third day, Jesus was raised from the dead (see Matthew 12:38–40).

■ **Making the Connection:** Compared to the others, Jonah was one of the most successful prophets in the Bible. Once he got to Ninevah and preached the word God gave him, he was a huge success. The people actually listened to him—instead of stoning him to death or sawing him in half. Not only that, they repented of their sins and asked for God's forgiveness. You would think Jonah would be thrilled with the results.

But instead, Jonah was angry with God for forgiving them. He complained about God being so "gracious and compassionate . . . slow to anger and abounding in love" (4:2). "I knew this would happen," he said. Jonah really wanted God to destroy the city. He wanted to see those wicked people get what they deserved. It seems he forgot that if God had taken that attitude with him, he'd still be at the bottom of the ocean! God forgave him when he repented. But Jonah was annoyed when God gave the people of Ninevah a second chance.

Jonah's story reminds us that having experienced God's mercy and grace in our own lives, we should be quick to rejoice when He offers it to others.

MICAH

The Book: Micah

The Author: Micah

The Audience: The people of Israel and Judah

The Setting: Written in Judah, between 735 BC and 700 BC

The Story: The prophet Micah warned the people of Judah and Israel against listening to false prophets who told them only what they wanted to hear. Micah told them that "the day of the Lord" was coming soon—a day of judgment and deliverance.

The Message: Micah begins with words of warning: God is coming to punish the wicked. His judgment will be swift—and devastating. "The LORD says: 'I am planning disaster against this people, from which you cannot save yourselves . . .'" (2:3).

The people have practiced witchcraft and worshiped other gods. They have committed every imaginable sin against each other. Furthermore, their leaders and prophets have led them astray, promising them peace and prosperity—a message that has not come from God.

"But as for me," Micah says, "I am filled with power, with the Spirit of the LORD, and with justice and might, to declare to Jacob his transgression, to Israel his sin" (3:8). He will expose what the people have done—how they have failed to observe God's commandments and live up to His standards.

Micah urges God's people to repent and return to Him. The prophet looks forward to the day when people from all nations will say, "Come let us go up to the mountain of the Lord. . . . He will teach us his ways so that we may walk in his paths . . ." (4:2).

In the middle of a series of warnings, words of correction, and rebuke, Micah stops to speak of something incredible—amazing—wonderful—that will happen almost a thousand years in the future: "But you, Bethlehem Ephrathah, though you are small among the clans of Judah, out of you will come for me one who will be ruler over Israel, whose origins are from of old, from ancient times" (5:2).

Then Micah goes back to warning the people: God says that Israel is guilty of many grievous sins, and its people will be severely punished as a result (5:6–7). "I will give you over to ruin and your people to derision; you will bear the scorn of nations (6:16).

Still, Micah says, there is hope. "Who is a God like you, who pardons sin and forgives the transgression of the remnant of his inheritance? You do not stay angry forever but delight to show mercy. You will again have compassion on us; you will tread our sins underfoot and hurl all our iniquities into the depths of the sea" (7:18–19).

Micah is confident that God will not forget His promises. He will rescue and restore His people once again (7:20).

Key Verse or Passage

"He has showed you, O man, what is good. And what does the LORD require of you? To act justly and to love mercy and to walk humbly with your God." (Micah 6:8)

More on This Story in the Bible: Micah is mentioned in Jeremiah 26:18. He prophesied during the reign of King Hezekiah, which is described in 2 Kings 18–20 and Isaiah 36–38.

■ Words to Know:

sovereign: the ultimate authority, the supreme power.

transgressions: sins or offenses committed in violation of the law.

iniquities: immorality, sins.

divination: predicting the future through the supernatural practices of sorcery and/or witchcraft.

remnant: something left over; a small surviving group of people.

■ Making the Connection:
Christian author and speaker (and Nazi Holocaust survivor) Corrie Ten Boom was fond of quoting Micah 7:19 as she talked about the power of forgiveness. The verse says that God has "cast all of our sins into the depths of the sea." Corrie would add: "And He has put up a sign that reads 'NO FISHING.'"

The teaching of Scripture is clear: When we ask God to forgive us, He does so fully and completely. He doesn't hold our sins over our heads or continue to count them against us. They're gone—forgotten—buried at the bottom of the sea. We're the ones who keep fishing them up again, reliving the embarrassment, the humiliation, the horror—over and over again. But the truth is that we don't have to live burdened by guilt and shame. God has already set us free. If He doesn't go fishing, why should we?

NAHUM

■ The Book: Nahum

■ The Author: Nahum

■ The Audience: The people of Judah and Ninevah

■ The Setting: Written in Judah, between 664 BC and 612 BC

■ The Story:
Ninevah was the capital city of Assyria—the kingdom that had conquered Israel years earlier. God sent the prophet Nahum to warn the people of Ninevah that He would destroy the wicked nation for its sins, while protecting and preserving the people of Judah who put their faith in Him.

■ **The Message:** Nahum begins with a bold pronouncement: "The LORD is a jealous and avenging God. . . . The LORD takes vengeance on his foes . . ." (1:2). He will not leave the guilty unpunished (1:3). God's power is absolutely terrifying: "The mountains quake before him and the hills melt away. The earth trembles at his presence, the world and all who live in it. Who can withstand his indignation? Who can endure his fierce anger? . . ." (1:5–6). Those who love God and trust Him and turn to Him in times of trouble will find comfort. "But with an overwhelming flood he will make an end of Nineveh; he will pursue his foes into darkness" (1:8).

For a time, God has allowed the people of Judah to suffer for their sins at the hands of their enemies in Ninevah—but no more. "Although I have afflicted you, O Judah, I will afflict you no more. Now I will break their yoke from your neck and tear your shackles away" (1:12–13). God will raise up an army against the wicked city and she will be utterly destroyed: "She is pillaged, plundered, stripped! Hearts melt, knees give way, bodies tremble, every face grows pale" (2:10).

Speaking on behalf of God, Nahum describes the sins the people of Ninevah have committed. They are known for their cruelty and blood-shed; they are "never without victims," whose bodies they display as trophies in the city streets (3:1–3). They are also known for their lust, greed, prostitution, sorcery, and witchcraft (3:4). "'I am against you,' declares the LORD Almighty. . . . 'I will treat you with contempt and make you a spectacle'" (3:5–6). With the same brutality the kings of Assyria have treated the nations they conquered, they themselves will be treated (3:8–18). For God is a God of justice, and He has decided to make an end to Assyria once and for all. "Nothing can heal your wound; your injury is fatal. Everyone who hears the news about you claps his hands at your fall, for who has not felt your endless cruelty?" (3:19).

Key Verse or Passage

"The LORD is good, a refuge in times of trouble. He cares for those who trust in him." (Nahum 1:7)

■ **More on This Story in the Bible:** The people of Ninevah were known for their cruelty and immorality and wickedness. A hundred years before

Nahum pronounced judgment on this evil nation, God had given its people a chance to repent and turn from their wicked ways. This story is told in the book of Jonah.

Words to Know:

jealous: when this word is used to describe God, it means "jealous" as in intensely guarding or watching over something, such as His people, protecting them and preserving them for Himself; it also means not tolerating any unfaithfulness or any rivals.

vengeance: punishment or revenge; to harm a person who has harmed others.

splendor: magnificent beauty.

plunder: things stolen or captured in battle; to take everything of value from one's enemy.

Making the Connection: In spite of the thousands of years of "civilization" since the days of the Bible, there is still great wickedness, great cruelty and bloodshed taking place all around the world today. The headlines are full of the horror of it all. Nahum reminds us that sin will not go unpunished. Those who truly repent find God's mercy and grace. But the wicked cannot escape God's justice. Though sometimes it seems that evil people get away with the bad things they do, sooner or later, God will hold them accountable—either in this life or the life to come! And God's wrath—His judgment and punishment—isn't something to take lightly. He promises to settle the score, once and for all.

HABAKKUK

The Book: Habakkuk

The Author: Habakkuk

The Audience: The people of Judah

The Setting: Written in Judah, between 609 BC and 597 BC

The Story: The nation of Babylon was about to attack and destroy the kingdom of Judah. The prophet Habakkuk had a lengthy conversation

with God about the injustice he saw all around him—the prosperity of the wicked and the suffering of the righteous. Habakkuk asked God just when and how He would deal with the wicked—and God answered him!

The Message: Habakkuk begins with a complaint: "How long, O LORD, must I call for help, but you do not listen? . . ." (1:2). He wants to know why God seems to tolerate wrong, why He allows the people of Judah to get away with sin. Everywhere he looks, Habakkuk sees destruction and violence, strife, conflict, and injustice (1:3–4). God replies: "Look at the nations and watch—and be utterly amazed. For I am going to do something in your days that you would not believe, even if you were told" (1:5). He tells the prophet that He is going to raise up the ruthless Babylonians—"a feared and dreaded people"—to execute His judgment on the wicked people of Judah (1:6–11).

God's answer leads to Habakkuk's second complaint: Yes, the wicked people of Judah need to be punished, but how can God allow an even more wicked people to triumph over them? How is that fair (1:1–14)? God answers Habakkuk again: "Then the LORD replied: 'Write down the revelation and make it plain on tablets so that a herald may run with it. For the revelation awaits an appointed time; it speaks of the end and will not prove false. Though it linger, wait for it; it will certainly come and will not delay'" (2:2–3). Babylon will not escape God's judgment and wrath. "The cup from the Lord's right hand is coming around to you, and disgrace will cover your glory" (2:16). One day, God will destroy the wicked people of Babylon utterly and completely, while His own people He will forgive and heal and restore.

Habakkuk responds with a beautiful hymn of praise to God. "Lord, I have heard of Your fame; I stand in awe of your deeds, O Lord. Renew them in our day, in our time make them known; in wrath remember mercy." In the days of suffering that lie ahead for Judah, Habakkuk says He will trust God to carry out His justice in the end. "I will wait patiently for the day of calamity to come on the nation invading us. Though the fig tree does not bud and there are no grapes on the vines, though the olive crop fails and the fields produce no food, though there are no sheep in the pen and no cattle in the stalls, yet I will rejoice in the LORD, I will be joyful in God my Savior" (3:16–18).

Key Verse or Passage

"The Sovereign LORD is my strength; he makes my feet like the feet of a deer, he enables me to go on the heights." (Habakkuk 3:19)

More on This Story in the Bible: Habakkuk prophesied at the same time as Jeremiah. Read the story of how Babylon did conquer Judah—just as Habakkuk and Jeremiah prophesied—in 2 Kings 25 and 2 Chronicles 36. The story of how Babylon itself was conquered can be found in Daniel 5.

Words to Know:

injustice: something that is not right or just or fair.

revelation: something secret or hidden that is suddenly made known.

appointed: determined or chosen or arranged ahead of time.

sovereign: the ultimate authority, the supreme power.

Did You Know? Habakkuk 3:19 is the inspiration for one of the most famous Christian novels of all time. The verse reads, "The Sovereign LORD is my strength; he makes my feet like the feet of a deer [or hind], he enables me to go on the heights." In *Hinds' Feet on High Places*, author Hannah Hurnard tells the story of a young woman named Much-Afraid who follows the Good Shepherd on a difficult journey through the mountains and up to the High Places. Her companions are Sorrow and Suffering; it is through hardship that she develops "hinds' feet"—the grace and strength to travel to new heights of love and joy and victory. It is, of course, an allegory describing the spiritual journey we all take as we follow Jesus—learning to trust Him in hard times, growing strong in the face of life's challenges, and ultimately resting in the love He has for us.

ZEPHANIAH

▓ **The Book:** Zephaniah

▓ **The Author:** Zephaniah

▓ **The Audience:** The people of Judah

▓ **The Setting:** Written in Judah, between 640 BC and 628 BC

▓ **The Story:** Zephaniah warned the people that the day of the Lord was coming, a day when God would judge the wicked in Judah and in all the nations of the earth. But as always, God would be merciful to those who put their trust in Him.

▓ **The Message:** Zephaniah begins with a warning to the wicked and the complacent: God's judgment is at hand. "The great day of the LORD is near—near and coming quickly. . . . That day will be a day of wrath, a day of distress and anguish, a day of trouble and ruin . . ." (1:14–15). Before that day comes, people who fear God should repent and return to Him. "Seek the LORD, all you humble of the land, you who do what he commands. Seek righteousness, seek humility; perhaps you will be sheltered on the day of the LORD's anger" (2:3).

God will deal with Judah's enemies—Philistia, Moab, Ammon, Cush, and Assyria. "The remnant of my people will plunder them; the survivors of my nation will inherit their land. This is what they will get in return for their pride, for insulting and mocking the people of the LORD Almighty. The LORD will be awesome to them when he destroys all the gods of the land. The nations on every shore will worship him, every one in its own land" (2:9–11).

Jerusalem will also be judged (3:1). Her officials, prophets, and priests have become corrupt, and God will cleanse the city of them (3:3–10). "But I will leave within you the meek and humble, who trust in the name of the LORD" (3:12). Looking ahead, Zephaniah concludes on a high note—with a song of rejoicing: "Sing, O Daughter of Zion; shout aloud, O Israel! Be glad and rejoice with all your heart, O Daughter of Jerusalem! The LORD has taken away your punishment, he has turned back your enemy. The LORD, the King of Israel, is with you; never again will you fear any harm" (3:14–16).

Key Verse or Passage

"The LORD your God is with you, he is mighty to save. He will take great delight in you, he will quiet you with his love, he will rejoice over you with singing." (Zephaniah 3:17)

More on This Story in the Bible: Zephaniah prophesied during the reign of King Josiah (2 Kings 22–23) and at the same time as Jeremiah, Nahum, and Habakkuk. In one sense, the destruction and restoration that Zephaniah describes took place when Judah was conquered by Babylon and then later freed by Cyrus of Persia (see 2 Kings 25, 2 Chronicles 36, and Ezra 1–3). However the ultimate and final "day of the Lord" is still to come. For more on this judgment day, see Revelation 19–22.

Words to Know:

"the day of the Lord": this phrase can refer to specific and individual days or times when God powerfully (and unmistakably) intervenes in human history; it can also mean the final "day of the Lord," in which God judges all the peoples of the earth, destroys the wicked, and rescues or rewards the righteous.

profane: unholy; to show disrespect or disregard for God and the things that are precious to Him.

desolate: sad and lonely; deserted.

Did You Know? There are verses in the Bible that tell us that God laughs and verses that tell us He weeps. But did you know that the God of the universe also sings? Zephaniah says, "The Lord your God is in the midst of you, a Mighty One, a Savior [Who saves]! He will rejoice over you with joy; He will rest [in silent satisfaction] and in His love He will be silent and make no mention [of past sins, or even recall them]; He will exult over you with singing" (Zephaniah 3:17, AMPLIFIED).

This verse tells us that God is in the midst of us; He is with us. He is mighty—powerful—and greater than all of our problems. He is a Savior who has rescued us from the bondage of sin. And He rejoices over us! The verse says God will be satisfied with the work He has done in us and through us. Because of His love for us, He will forgive us. He won't bring up the past or beat us over the head with our old sins. Not only will God not *mention* our sins, He won't even recall them! Finally, we read that God will exult over us; He is so excited about being reconciled to us that it makes Him burst into song!

The next time you feel discouraged or defeated, when guilt and despair threaten to weigh you down, remember this wonderful picture of God's love for you and rejoice. God does.

HAGGAI

The Book: Haggai

The Author: Haggai

The Audience: The Jewish people returned from exile

The Setting: The city of Jerusalem, 520 BC

The Story: After seventy years in captivity and exile, God's people were finally allowed to return to Israel, their homeland. The prophet Haggai urged the people not to get so busy rebuilding their own homes and lives that they neglected their most important task: to complete the rebuilding of God's house—the temple.

The Message: Haggai announces that God has a grievance against His people: they have focused all their energies on rebuilding their own homes and lives, while God's house—His temple—sits neglected and in ruins (1:1–4). The people don't seem to make the connection between their disobedience to God and all the hardships they have been experiencing lately. God has been trying to get their attention! "This is what the LORD Almighty says: 'Give careful thought to your ways. . . .

Go up into the mountains and bring down timber and build the house, so that I may take pleasure in it and be honored,' says the LORD" (1:5, 8). God is the One who has been frustrating their efforts so far. But if they will turn their attention to rebuilding His house, He will bless theirs (1:9–11).

The people respond to Haggai's message; they immediately repent and begin the reconstruction of the temple (1:12–15). God knows that they are overwhelmed by the enormity of the task and discouraged by the memory of the temple's former glory. How can they possibly recapture it? "'Be strong, all you people of the land,' declares the LORD, 'and work. For I am with you. . . . This is what I covenanted with you when you came out of Egypt. And my Spirit remains among you. Do not fear'" (2:4–5).

God also promises that one day He will send the Messiah to establish His kingdom on earth, filling God's house—His temple and His people—with glory: "'In a little while I will once more shake the heavens and the earth, the sea and the dry land. I will shake all nations, and the desired of all nations will come, and I will fill this house with glory,' says the LORD Almighty. . . . 'The glory of this present house will be greater than the glory of the former house. . . . And in this place I will grant peace . . .'" (2:6–9).

Through Haggai, God says that He has forgiven His people for the failures of the past. He is pleased with their obedience—with the renewed effort to rebuild the temple. God's discipline or punishment has come to an end. "From this day on I will bless you" (2:19).

Key Verse or Passage

"'The glory of this present house will be greater than the glory of the former house,' says the LORD Almighty. 'And in this place I will grant peace,' declares the LORD Almighty." (Haggai 2:9)

■ **More on This Story in the Bible:** Haggai is mentioned in Ezra's account of the return of God's people to Israel (see Ezra 1:1–6:14). He prophesied at the same time and to the same people as Zechariah. The New Testament book of Hebrews explains that Haggai 2:6–9 is a prophecy about the second coming of Christ (Hebrews 12:26–27).

Words to Know:

remnant: something left over; a small surviving group of people.

house: in the book of Haggai, the word "house" is most often used to refer to the temple in Jerusalem—God's "house," which lay in ruins and desperately needed repair, both literally and figuratively.

Think about It: Five times in the two short chapters that make up the book of Haggai, God says to His people: "Give careful thought . . ." (1:5, 7; 2:15, 18). In other words, "Think about it!" or "Pay attention!" Here, you can almost see God as a father cupping His child's face between His hands, tipping his or her chin upward, insisting on eye contact: "Listen to Me!"

Like the people of Judah, we sometimes get so busy and distracted with daily life that we lose perspective, get our priorities mixed up, and miss what God is trying to say to us. As a loving Father, He will do whatever it takes to get our attention—including discipline and correction, allowing us to suffer the natural consequences of our poor choices. How much better it is when we learn to listen—truly listen and think things through—the first time!

ZECHARIAH

The Book: Zechariah

The Author: Zechariah

The Audience: The Jewish people returned from exile

The Setting: The city of Jerusalem, 520 BC

The Story: After seventy years in captivity and exile, God's people were finally allowed to return to their homeland. As the people began to physically rebuild their lives, the prophet Zechariah reminded them to rebuild themselves spiritually—to return their *hearts* to God, as well. For one day soon, their deliverer would come: the Messiah, the eternal King.

The Message: "This is what the LORD Almighty says: 'Return to me,' declares the LORD Almighty, 'and I will return to you . . .'" (1:3). Zechariah begins by reminding the people of the sins of their parents and grandparents and great-grandparents, which led to their captivity and exile in the first place. He warns the people not to follow in their ancestors' footsteps, and they agree not to (1:1–6).

Zechariah then has a series of visions or dreams, some of which shed light on the past—and others that speak to the future: the man among the myrtle trees (1:7–17); four horns and four craftsmen (1:18–21); a man with a measuring line (2:1–13); clean garments for the high priest (3:1–10); the gold lampstand and the two olive trees (4:1–14); the flying scroll (5:1–4); the woman in the basket (5:5–11); four chariots (6:1–8); and two shepherds (11:4–17). With each vision, God (through Zechariah) gives His people words of warning or instruction or encouragement.

Next, Zechariah calls God's people to administer justice and show mercy and compassion as evidence of their spirituality, rather than going through the motions of empty religious rituals (7:1–14). To the few righteous left among His people, God promises He will bless and restore the city of Jerusalem (8:1–23). He will punish Israel's enemies (9:1–8). Her true, eternal King will come (9:9–17). God will have compassion on His people (10:1–12), and He will cleanse them from their sin (13:1). "I will refine them like silver and test them like gold. They will call on my name and I will answer them; I will say, 'They are my people,' and they will say, 'The LORD is our God'" (13:9). They will sparkle like jewels in a crown (9:16–17).

Zechariah warns that the day of the Lord will bring horrific judgment and destruction to His enemies. They will learn to fear and reverence (or respect) His name. "The LORD will be king over the whole earth. On that day there will be one LORD, and his name the only name" (14:9).

Key Verse or Passage

"Rejoice greatly, O Daughter of Zion! Shout, Daughter of Jerusalem! See, your king comes to you, righteous and having salvation, gentle and riding on a donkey, on a colt, the foal of a donkey." (Zechariah 9:9)

More on This Story in the Bible: Zechariah is mentioned in Ezra's account of the return of God's people to Israel (see Ezra 1:1–6:14). He prophesied at the same time and to the same people as Haggai. Many of Zechariah's visions are prophecies about the coming of the Messiah—Jesus. A study Bible can help you understand the symbolism and identify when and how many of these prophecies have been fulfilled—and which ones are yet to come.

Words to Know:

> **remnant:** something left over; a small surviving group of people.

> **jealous:** when this word is used to describe God, it means "jealous" as in intensely guarding or watching over something—such as His people, protecting them and preserving them for Himself; it also means not tolerating any unfaithfulness, any rivals.

Did You Know? Jesus did arrive in the city of Jerusalem riding on a colt (or donkey), just as Zechariah said He would (see Zechariah 9:9 and Mark 11:1–11). A ruler who entered a city on a colt or a donkey—as opposed to a chariot or warhorse—was coming in peace. "See, your king comes to you, righteous and having salvation, gentle and riding on a donkey. . . . He will proclaim peace to the nations. His rule will extend from sea to sea . . ." (Zechariah 9:9–10).

Think about It: In Zechariah 4:10, God warned His people not to "despise the day of small beginnings." The work they had done on the rebuilding of the temple might seem insignificant to them—but God was in it. He would give them the strength to finish the task. And one day, they would stand back in awe at all He had accomplished in them and through them.

It's an important reminder for us today.

Sometimes our own little efforts might not seem like much to us—our attempts at obedience and ministry and service and sacrifice. They pale in comparison to the achievements of others—the men and women of Scripture for instance, the great heroes of the faith throughout history. But God sees our hearts. He can bless and multiply our efforts in ways we can't even begin to imagine. As Hudson Taylor, a famous missionary to China, once observed, "A little thing is a little thing, but faithfulness in little things is a great thing." Perhaps one day, we, too, will stand back in awe at all that God has accomplished in us and through us!

MALACHI

■ **The Book:** Malachi

■ **The Author:** Malachi

■ **The Audience:** The Jewish people returned from exile

■ **The Setting:** The city of Jerusalem, between 430 BC and 400 BC

■ **The Story:** After years of captivity and exile, God's people have finally settled back into their homeland, Israel. As they've gotten comfortable, they have forgotten all the promises they made to God when they first returned; they have failed to obey His commandments. The prophet Malachi urges the people to repent and make things right, because the great King is coming. He will not only judge and rebuke, He will also heal and restore.

■ **The Message:** Speaking through Malachi, God begins by reminding His people of how He has loved them and chosen them and set them apart for Him (1:2–5). Yet they have disrespected and dishonored Him by giving Him less than their best. "'When you bring blind animals for sacrifice, is that not wrong? When you sacrifice crippled or diseased animals, is that not wrong? Try offering them to your governor! Would he be pleased with you? Would he accept you?' says the LORD Almighty" (1:8–9). The priests themselves have dishonored God, as well. "For the lips of a priest ought to preserve knowledge, and from his mouth men should seek instruction—because he is the messenger of the LORD Almighty. But you have turned from the way and by your teaching have caused many to stumble . . ." (2:7–8). Some of God's people have married outside the faith—something they know is forbidden—while others recklessly, carelessly destroy their families through divorce (2:11–16).

God says He will send His Messenger to hold them accountable: "But who can endure the day of His coming? Who can stand when he appears?

For He will be like a refiner's fire or a launderer's soap" (3:2–3). He will purify them and cleanse them from their sin.

God says His people have also been stealing from Him: "'Will a man rob God? Yet you rob me. But you ask, 'How do we rob you?' In tithes and offerings. . . . Bring the whole tithe into the storehouse, that there may be food in my house . . .'" (3:8–11). Some people have complained that it is too hard to serve God, that the wicked have a much easier life. But God says that is simply not true. One day the wicked will face His fierce judgment, while those who are faithful to Him will be blessed (3:13–4:2).

Key Verse or Passage

"But for you who revere my name, the sun of righteousness will rise with healing in its wings. . . ." (Malachi 4:2)

■ **More on This Story in the Bible:** Malachi prophesied after the return of God's people to Israel, described in the books of Ezra and Nehemiah—a few years after the ministries of the prophets Haggai and Zechariah. He was the last prophet of the Old Testament era. In his final words, Malachi predicted the coming of the next prophet—John the Baptist—who would prepare the way for the Messiah, Jesus (see Malachi 4:5, Luke 1:1–17, and Matthew 11:13–14).

■ **Words to Know:**

covenant: a promise, an agreement, a legally-binding contract.

profane: unholy; to show disrespect or disregard for God and the things that are precious to Him.

refiner's fire: heat used to purify precious metals and burn off their imperfections; the Messiah who will expose sin for the purpose of cleansing it; the trials and tests God uses to purify His people and bring out the best in them.

■ **Making the Connection:** In the Old Testament, Moses directed the children of Israel to acknowledge that everything they had came from God by giving at least a tenth of it back to Him. It was an act of worship, as well as obedience. Malachi compares withholding the tithe to stealing from God, and urges people to give generously in order to experience God's blessing. God promises that if we will honor Him with our finances—no matter how difficult it seems—He will honor us. He will provide for us in ways we can't even begin to imagine. "'Test me in this,' says the Lord Almighty, 'and see if I will not throw open the floodgates of heaven and pour out so much blessing that you will not have room enough for it'" (Malachi 3:8–10).

Think about It: In Malachi 2:16, God says, "I hate divorce." Sadly divorce has become all too common in our culture today. Many Christians have suffered its devastation and heartbreak. They can testify that it's a tragedy that takes a terrible toll on every member of the family—especially children. That's why the Bible repeatedly warns us to make vows cautiously and to enter marriage as a sacred covenant we have completely committed ourselves to. It's an obligation not only to our spouse or our children, but to God Himself.

Over the years, there's been a lot of controversy about how to interpret biblical teaching on the subject of divorce. Some seem to completely ignore the grace of God—and the wisdom and guidance of all the other Scriptures—for an extreme form of legalism. Others seem to go to great lengths to find ways to dismiss what the Bible teaches, as though it's no longer relevant. Either approach is dangerous.

According to the Scriptures, there are certain circumstances under which divorce is permitted and in which remarriage is not frowned upon (see Deuteronomy 24:1–4 and Matthew 19:3–12). From what we can tell, a lot depends on the circumstances and the attitudes of those involved. Ultimately, each one of us has to seek God, study the Scriptures, and make our own peace with the issue. Those of us who are married (or remarried) should do everything we can to make our present marriage what God intended it to be—at its best, a beautiful reflection of the sacrificial love Jesus has for His bride, the church (Ephesians 5:21–33).

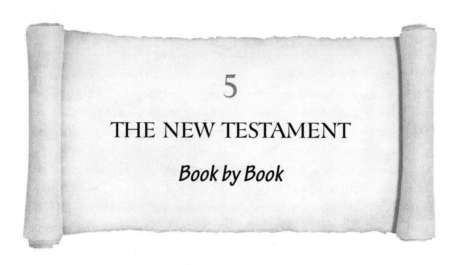

5

THE NEW TESTAMENT

Book by Book

MATTHEW

- **The Book**: Matthew
- **The Author**: Matthew (also called Levi)
- **The Audience**: The Jewish people
- **The Setting**: Written from Judea, between AD 50–100
- **The Story**: Matthew tells the story of Jesus from His birth to His death to His resurrection, showing how Jesus fulfilled every one of the prophecies written about Him in the Old Testament. Matthew wanted God's people to understand that Jesus truly was and is their Messiah, their long-awaited Deliverer, which makes their initial rejection of Him so heartbreaking. But many have since received and acknowledged Him—in part because of Matthew's testimony. And Jesus has called them to be His witnesses, to share this gospel, this "good news," with *everyone*.

- **The Message**: Matthew begins with the genealogy of Jesus, tracing His human ancestry all the way back to Abraham and noting: "There were fourteen generations in all from Abraham to David, fourteen from David to the exile to Babylon, and fourteen from the exile to the Christ" (1:17). When Jesus' mother, Mary, is found to be "with child," Joseph— her husband-to-be—considers calling off their marriage. But an angel appears to Joseph in a dream, saying: "Do not be afraid to take Mary home as your wife, because what is conceived in her is from the Holy Spirit. She will give birth to a son, and you are to give him the name Jesus, because he will save his people from their sins" (1:20–21). Not long after Jesus' birth, Magi (or wise men) arrive in Jerusalem, asking: "Where is the one who has been born king of the Jews? We saw his star in the east and have come to worship him" (2:2). Searching through the words of the ancient prophets, King Herod's advisors identify Bethlehem as the birthplace of the Messiah (2:1–6). Later, when the Magi fail to report back to Herod, he orders the slaughter of every male child in Bethlehem under age 2, in order to eliminate any threat to his throne. But Joseph and Mary and the infant Jesus escape, after being warned by an angel in a dream (2:13–23).

Matthew picks up the story nearly thirty years later, when John the Baptist appears preaching in the desert, preparing the way for the Lord (3:1–12). Jesus comes to John to be baptized, though John says it is Jesus who should baptize *him*. The Spirit of God descends on Jesus like a dove, and a voice from heaven says, "This is my Son, whom I love; with him I am well pleased" (3:17). Next Jesus is led by the Spirit into the wilderness to fast and pray for forty days. He resists the devil's efforts to tempt Him to rebel against God, and instead affirms His commitment to walk in obedience to all of God's commandments (4:1–11).

Jesus begins preaching and teaching, "Repent, for the kingdom of heaven is near" (4:17). By the sea, He calls His first disciples: "Come, follow me . . . and I will make you fishers of men" (4:19). "Jesus went throughout Galilee, teaching in their synagogues, preaching the good news of the kingdom, and healing every disease and sickness among the people" (4:23). Large crowds gather around Him. Jesus goes up on the side of a mountain, where everyone can see and hear Him. In His "Sermon on the Mount," He pronounces blessings on the poor in spirit, those who mourn, the meek, those who hunger and thirst for righteousness, the merciful, the pure in heart, the peacemakers, and those who are persecuted for His sake. He calls His followers to be salt (giving flavor) and light (shining His truth) to the world. He explains the purpose for the Law God gave Moses and the standards God has established for the behavior of His people, particularly regarding murder, adultery, divorce, making vows, taking vengeance, loving their enemies, giving to the needy, and communing with God in prayer. He urges the people to "store up treasures in heaven" rather than on earth, to trust God rather than worry, and to refrain from judging others—unless they want to be judged (5:1–7:27).

Jesus uses parables to teach "those who have ears to hear" about the kingdom of heaven, about truth, about faith, about obedience to God (7:24–27; 13:1–52; 16:1–12; 20:1–16; 21:28–22:14; 25:1–46). To demonstrate the power of God—and the love of God for His people—and to fulfill the words of the prophets, Jesus continues to heal the sick and cast out demons and raise the dead to life again (8:1–17; 9:1–8, 18–34; 15:21–28; 17:14–23; 20:29–34). He calms a storm by rebuking the wind and the waves and feeds more than five thousand people with two fish and five loaves of bread (8:23–27; 14:13–21). He walks on water (14:22–36). Jesus teaches His disciples that it will not be easy to follow in His footsteps and proclaim His truth (8:18–22). Yet the need is so very great. "When he saw the crowds, he had compassion on them, because they were harassed and helpless, like sheep without a shepherd. Then he said to his disciples, 'The harvest is plentiful but the workers are few. Ask the Lord of the harvest, therefore, to send out workers into his harvest field'" (9:36–38).

Jesus reveals Himself to His disciples in power and glory as the Messiah, the Deliverer, and the fulfillment of the Law and the Prophets when He appears talking with Moses and Elijah on a high mountain (17:1–13). Over and over, Jesus tells His disciples to love one another and serve one another and put each other first. He tells them to forgive those who have hurt and offended them, just as God has forgiven them. He reminds them to keep their hearts pure and innocent and to have childlike faith (18:1–19:30).

When Jesus enters the city of Jerusalem, the people welcome Him as a king (21:1–11). He drives out the moneychangers who have desecrated the temple—His "house," a place meant to be a "house of prayer" (21:12–17). Jesus confronts the Pharisees and Sadducees—the religious leaders of the day—and exposes their wickedness and hypocrisy (23:1–39). In response, they begin to plot to kill Him (26:3–4). Jesus tells His disciples that He will be leaving them soon. He gives them signs to watch for that will indicate that the world as they know it is coming to an end, and He urges them to be ready for His return (24:1–25:46). During the Passover meal, Jesus institutes a new feast—"the Lord's Supper"—that will one day commemorate His death on the cross. He tells His disciples that one of them (Judas) is about to betray Him (26:17–30). In fact, Jesus says, all of His disciples will soon fall away. Peter protests that even if everyone else does, he will never abandon Jesus. But Jesus tells him that this very night Peter will deny even knowing Him three times. In the garden of Gethsemane, the disciples sleep while Jesus prays to be delivered from the suffering that lies ahead—before ultimately surrendering Himself to the will of God (26:36–46). Judas brings soldiers to the garden to arrest Jesus, and Jesus is put on trial before the Sanhedrin (the chief priests, elders, and teachers of the law). Out in the courtyard, a terrified Peter repeatedly refuses to acknowledge that he is associated with Jesus: "I don't know the man." But when he realizes what he has done, he is heartbroken (26:47–75).

The Sanhedrin hand Jesus over to the Roman governor, Pontius Pilate. Pilate finds Him innocent of any crime, but gives in to pressure from the crowd crying, "Crucify Him!" Jesus is mocked and ridiculed, beaten and spat upon. The soldiers make this "King of the Jews" wear a "crown" of thorns, before nailing Him to the cross at Golgotha (27:11–44). At the moment of Jesus' death, the curtain in the temple that symbolically separates the people from the Most Holy Place—keeping them from entering the presence of God—is suddenly, miraculously torn in two, from the top to the bottom (27:45–56). Jesus is given a hasty burial just before sundown, when the Sabbath begins and no "work" can be done. After the Sabbath, a small group of women returns to the tomb to anoint His body with spices. They find the stone at the entrance rolled away—and the tomb itself empty. An angel tells them, "Do not be afraid . . . you are looking for Jesus, who was crucified. He is not here. He has risen, just as he said" (28:5–6). Then Jesus Himself appears to them, and to the other disciples—while the Roman soldiers conspire to a cover up and explain away the empty tomb (27:62–28:15). Before ascending into heaven, He tells His disciples to carry the good news of the gospel to the ends of the earth, sharing with others everything He has taught them.

Key Verse or Passage

"All authority in heaven and on earth has been given to me. Therefore go and make disciples of all nations, baptizing them in the name of the Father and of the Son and of the Holy Spirit, and teaching them to obey everything I have commanded you. And surely I am with you always, to the very end of the age." (Matthew 28:18–20)

More on This Story in the Bible: For more on the life and ministry, death and resurrection of Jesus Christ, see the Gospels of Mark, Luke, and John. Matthew was one of the twelve disciples called by Jesus to join Him in His ministry, and a founding member of the early church. He is mentioned in Matthew 9:9–13; 10:3; Mark 2:13–15; 3:18; Luke 5:27–30; 6:15; and Acts 1:13.

Words to Know:

beatitude: experiencing supreme blessedness or happiness; a declaration of blessing made by Jesus in the Sermon on the Mount (in Latin, each of His statements of blessing begins with the word *beatus*—"blessed").

synagogue: a local congregation of Jews gathered for worship and the study of the Scriptures. During Jesus' earthly ministry, synagogues could be found in nearly every town and village in the Roman Empire; sacrifices, however, could only be offered at the temple in Jerusalem.

disciple: a student, a follower, one who spreads the teachings of another; a follower of Jesus.

parable: a short, simple story used to communicate a powerful spiritual truth.

■ **Did You Know?** Although they all tell the story of Jesus, each of the four Gospels is unique—each one was written by a different author, with a different perspective and a different audience in mind. There are, of course, many similarities. In fact, Matthew, Mark, and Luke have so much in common that Bible scholars call these three the "synoptic Gospels"—meaning they "see together" and present the life and ministry of Jesus in much the same way. However, only Matthew and Luke include details of Jesus' birth and early childhood. And Matthew is the only one to mention the sudden appearance and gifts of the Magi.

■ **Making the Connection:** It's one of the most heartbreaking scenes in all of Scripture. Jesus has been preaching in the temple. He is the Messiah, the Anointed One, Israel's long-awaited Deliverer. He has come unto His own, but His own will not receive Him. They refuse Him and reject Him. They do not recognize Him (John 1:10–11).

Suddenly Jesus exclaims, "O Jerusalem, Jerusalem, you who kill the prophets and stone those sent to you, how often I have longed to gather your children together, as a hen gathers her chicks under her wings, but you were not willing" (Matthew 23:37). He wanted to embrace His people, to draw them tenderly to Himself—but they would not. What an indescribable tragedy.

Reading this verse, we can't help but be grieved—not only for the nation that missed their Messiah, but for the times when we ourselves have stubbornly refused to heed His call. Times when we have persisted in sin, ignored His counsel, denied our dependence on Him, rejected His love, and looked elsewhere for comfort in our pain. The suffering we experience as a result is entirely our own fault—and He would have spared us from it. In His love, He would have gathered us to Himself and kept us from harm's way. If only we had heeded His call. But we would not. His grief over it is even greater than our own, because His love for us is greater than our own. God forgive us! Help us to heed Your call today . . . and come running into Your arms of love!

MARK

■ **The Book:** Mark

■ **The Author:** John Mark

■ **The Audience:** Gentile (non-Jewish) believers living in Rome

■ **The Setting:** Written from Rome, between AD 50–70

■ **The Story:** In this brief, straight-to-the-point, action-packed account, Mark shares the gospel—the "good news"—of Jesus, tracing His earthly ministry from His baptism to His death and resurrection. These stories about Jesus would affirm and encourage the new believers in the church at Rome and teach them what it really means to be a disciple or follower of Jesus Christ. Jesus' teachings on servanthood and suffering and sacrifice seemed especially significant, as a time of great persecution appeared to be in store for the church.

■ **The Message:** Mark begins with the story of John the Baptist, the one whom Isaiah prophesied would "prepare the way for the Lord" (1:3). Jesus comes to John to be baptized in the Jordan river. As He emerges from the water, a voice from heaven says, "You are my Son, whom I love; with you I am well pleased" (1:11). For forty days, Jesus is tested in the wilderness, after which He begins His earthly ministry. "Jesus went into Galilee, proclaiming the good news of God. 'The time has come,' he said. 'The kingdom of God is near. Repent and believe . . .'" (1:14–15). By the sea, He calls His first disciples: "Come, follow me, and I will make you fishers of men" (1:17). He chooses twelve men to be His apostles: Simon Peter, James and John, Andrew, Philip, Bartholomew (Nathanael), Matthew (Levi), Thomas, James, Thaddaeus (Judas), Simon, and Judas Iscariot (3:13–19). Jesus begins driving out demons (evil spirits) and healing the sick (1:21–2:12). He teaches His disciples about true spirituality that goes beyond the slavish observance of empty rituals and strict adherence to the letter of the law, rather the intent behind it (2:18–3:6). Crowds soon gather everywhere that Jesus goes (3:7–12).

Jesus uses parables to teach "those who have ears to hear" about the kingdom of God, about truth, about faith. Often He explains the hidden meaning of His stories to His disciples afterward (4:1–34). On a boat in the middle of a lake, Jesus calms a storm by saying: "Quiet! Be still." His disciples are terrified: "Who is this? Even the wind and the waves obey him!" (4:35–41). Jesus casts a legion of demons out of a tormented man and into a herd of pigs (5:1–20). He raises a little girl from the dead and heals a woman who suffered twelve years from an incurable disease (5:21–43). In His own hometown, Jesus is greeted with derision and skepticism and is unable to do many miracles there, because of the people's lack of faith (6:1–6). He sends His twelve disciples to go out ahead of Him and preach the good news of the kingdom of God in the surrounding villages, preparing people's hearts to receive Him (6:7–13). Meanwhile, King Herod arrests and beheads John the Baptist (6:14–29).

With five loaves of bread and two fish, Jesus feeds five thousand people who had gathered around Him. "He had compassion on them, because they were like sheep without a shepherd. So he began teaching them many things" (6:34). That night, He sends His disciples ahead of Him across the lake and walks out on the water to meet them later (6:45–56). Jesus confronts the Pharisees—the Jewish religious leaders—with their hypocrisy and disobedience to God's law (7:1–23). He heals the daughter of a Syrophoenician woman and a deaf and mute man in Tyre (7:24–37). He feeds another four thousand people with seven loaves of bread and heals a blind man at Bethsaida (8:1–26). Peter recognizes that Jesus is the Messiah—the deliverer that God had promised to send His people since the garden of Eden (8:27–30). Jesus explains to His disciples that He "must suffer many things and be rejected by the elders, chief priests and teachers of the law, and that he must be killed and after three days rise again" (8:31). He adds, "If anyone would come after me, he must deny himself and take up his cross and follow me. For whoever wants to save his life will lose it, but whoever loses his life for me and for the gospel will save it" (8:34–35). Later, Jesus leads Peter, James, and John up on a high mountain, where He reveals His glory to them and appears with Moses and Elijah (9:2–13). Jesus heals a boy with an evil spirit and restores the sight of a blind man (9:14–32; 10:46–52). He rebukes His disciples for quarreling about which one of them has the most authority and power—the greatest position or rank—among His followers. "If anyone wants to be first, he must be the very last, and the servant of all" (9:35). Jesus teaches about resisting sin and temptation and, in response to a challenge put to Him by the Pharisees, God's view of divorce (9:38–10:12). The people bring their children to Jesus, and He holds them in His arms and blesses them (10:13–16). He urges a rich young man not to let his love for his material possessions keep him from entering the kingdom of God (10:17–31). Again He predicts His death, and rebukes His disciples for trying to position themselves next to Him—and ahead of each other—in God's kingdom (10:32–45). They have yet to understand what it truly means to follow in His footsteps: "Can you drink the cup I drink or be baptized with the baptism I am baptized with?" (10:38).

When Jesus enters the city of Jerusalem, the people welcome Him as a king (11:1–11). Entering the temple, He drives out the moneychangers who have desecrated what He calls His "house"—a place meant to be a "house of prayer" (11:12–17). "The chief priests and the teachers of the law heard this and began looking for a way to kill him, for they feared him, because the whole crowd was amazed at his teaching" (11:18). On the Mount of Olives, Jesus continues teaching His disciples about faith and forgiveness, respecting authority, the resurrection of the dead in heaven, the "greatest commandment," and what it means to give back to God (11:20–12:43). He tells them the signs to watch for that will signal the end of the world as we know it (13:1–37). In nearby Bethany, a woman anoints Jesus with a bottle of costly perfume (14:1–11).

Back in Jerusalem, during the Passover meal, Jesus institutes a new feast—"the Lord's Supper"—that will one day commemorate His death on the cross (14:12–26). Jesus tells His disciples that one of them (Judas) is about to betray Him. In fact, He says, all of His disciples will soon fall away. Peter protests that even if everyone else does, he will never abandon Jesus. But Jesus tells him that this very night, Peter will deny even knowing Him three times (14:27–31). In the garden of Gethsemane, the disciples sleep while Jesus prays to be delivered from the suffering that lies ahead—ultimately surrendering Himself to the will of God (14:32–42). Judas brings soldiers to the garden to arrest Jesus, and Jesus is put on trial before the Sanhedrin (the chief priests, elders, and teachers of the law). Out in the courtyard, a terrified Peter repeatedly refuses to acknowledge that he is associated with Jesus: "I don't know this man you're talking about." But when he realizes what he has done, he is heartbroken (14:43–72).

The Sanhedrin hands Jesus over to the Roman governor, Pontius Pilate. Pilate finds Him innocent of any crime, but gives in to pressure from the crowd crying, "Crucify Him!" Jesus is mocked and ridiculed, beaten and spat upon. The soldiers make this "King of the Jews" wear a "crown" of thorns before nailing Him to the cross at Golgotha (15:1–32). At the moment of Jesus' death, the curtain in the temple that symbolically separates the people from the Most Holy Place—keeping them from entering the presence of God—is suddenly, miraculously torn in two, from the top to the bottom (15:33–39). Jesus is given a hasty burial just before sundown, when the Sabbath begins and no "work" can be done. After the Sabbath, a small group of women return to the tomb to anoint His body with spices. They find the stone at the entrance rolled away—and the tomb itself empty (15:42–16:5). An angel tells them, "Don't be alarmed. . . . You are looking for Jesus the Nazarene, who was crucified. He has risen! He is not here. See the place where they laid him. But go, tell his disciples and Peter, 'He is going ahead of you into Galilee. There you will see him, just as he told you'" (16:6–7). Then Jesus Himself appears to Mary Magdalene, and to the other disciples on multiple occasions. He commissions them: "Go into all the world and preach the good news to all creation" (16:15). Afterward, He ascends into heaven and His disciples go forth to do all that He has commanded them (16:15–20).

Key Verse or Passage

"Whoever wants to become great among you must be your servant, and whoever wants to be first must be slave of all. For even the Son of Man did not come to be served, but to serve, and to give his life as a ransom for many." (Mark 10:43–45)

More on This Story in the Bible: For more on the life and death and resurrection of Jesus, see the Gospels of Matthew, Luke, and John. Although Mark was not one of the twelve disciples, as a teenager he was a part of the larger group of believers who followed Jesus during His earthly ministry. (Bible scholars believe the anonymous "young man" described in Mark 14:51 is actually Mark himself.) Later on, Mark served as Peter's ministry assistant and traveled with Paul and Barnabas on their missionary journeys. Mark is mentioned in Acts 12:12, 25; 13:5, 13; 15:36–39; Colossians 4:10; 2 Timothy 4:11; Philemon 24; and 1 Peter 5:13.

Words to Know:

baptize: to ceremonially wash with water, symbolizing an inner spiritual cleansing.

disciple: a student, a follower, one who spreads the teachings of another; a follower of Jesus.

parable: a short, simple story used to communicate a powerful spiritual truth.

apostle: a "messenger"; one who has been specially chosen by Jesus to be His messenger (as with the twelve disciples or "apostles"); a missionary; a leader in the church.

Did You Know?
Mark is the shortest of the four Gospels, and probably the first one to be written. Bible scholars believe that the book of Mark could also be thought of as "the Gospel of Peter," because as a young man, Mark was Peter's assistant and ministry partner. (Peter affectionately referred to Mark as his "son" in 1 Peter 5:13.) It is likely that many of the details in Mark's gospel actually came from Peter's eyewitness accounts, as well as his preaching and teaching.

Making the Connection:
Have you ever wistfully wondered if God would ever call you to some kind of major ministry? You feel so full of gratitude for all that He's done for you—you wish you could do great things for Him. You want to shout it from the mountaintops and tell the whole wide world about His amazing love. You'd be willing to make any sacrifice to demonstrate your love for Him. If only He would ask you. . . .

The Gospel of Mark tells us about a young man who felt this way. He had been possessed by a legion of evil spirits. "Night and day among the tombs and in the hills he would cry out and cut himself with stones" (5:5). Then Jesus came and set him free. In an instant the demons were gone. He was no longer tortured by their presence. The townspeople were amazed when they saw the young man clothed and in his right mind, sitting at Jesus' feet. No, more than amazed—they were terrified. They asked Jesus to go away and leave them alone. As Jesus got into the boat, the young man begged to be allowed to go with Him. He was eager to leave everything behind and follow Jesus (something some of the other disciples had been reluctant to do). But Jesus said no. He wouldn't let him. Instead, Jesus gave this young man a different assignment: "Go home to your family and tell them how much the Lord has done for you . . ." (5:19).

Some of us are called to the mission field overseas, and some of us are called to the mission field in our own families. After all, they're the ones who know us best; they're the ones who see the greatest change in our lives. And their salvation is no less important to Jesus than the millions we will never meet. Though it may have seemed like a small thing, the Scripture tells us the young man did just as Jesus asked. May we be willing to do the same.

LUKE

■ **The Book:** Luke

■ **The Author:** Luke, the physician

■ **The Audience:** Theophilus, a Roman governor

■ **The Setting:** Written from Caesarea and Rome, AD 60–62

■ **The Story:** "Many have undertaken to draw up an account of the things that have been fulfilled among us, just as they were handed down to us by those who from the first were eyewitnesses and servants of the word. Therefore, since I myself have carefully investigated everything from the beginning, it seemed good also to me to write an orderly account for you, most excellent Theophilus, so that you may know the certainty of the things you have been taught" (1:1–4). What Theophilus had been taught is the gospel—the "good news"—about Jesus. Tracing His earthly ministry from His birth to His death to His resurrection, Luke showed that Jesus Himself made it clear He had come to be the Savior not only of Israel, but the whole world.

The Message: Luke begins with the birth of John the Baptist—the prophet who will bring the people of Israel back to God and prepare them for the coming of the Lord. The same angel who heralded John's birth appears to a young woman named Mary. "You have found favor with God. You will be with child and give birth to a son, and you are to give him the name Jesus. He will be great and will be called the Son of the Most High. The Lord God will give him the throne of his father David, and he will reign over the house of Jacob forever; his kingdom will never end" (1:30–33). Mary and Joseph (her husband-to-be) travel to Bethlehem, where Mary gives birth to the infant Jesus in a stable because there is no room for them in the inn. Angels and shepherds rejoice (2:1–39). "And the child grew and became strong; he was filled with wisdom, and the grace of God was upon him" (2:40).

John the Baptist begins preaching in the desert, calling God's people to repentance: "I baptize you with water. But one more powerful than I will come, the thongs of whose sandals I am not worthy to untie. He will baptize you with the Holy Spirit . . ." (3:16). Jesus presents Himself to John to be baptized and then goes out into the wilderness to fast and pray for forty days in preparation for His earthly ministry (3:21–4:13). He begins in His own hometown of Nazareth, identifying Himself as the one the prophet Isaiah spoke of: "'The Spirit of the Lord is on me, because he has anointed me to preach good news to the poor. He has sent me to proclaim freedom for the prisoners and recovery of sight for the blind, to release the oppressed, to proclaim the year of the Lord's favor.' . . . Today this scripture is fulfilled in your hearing" (4:18–21). In a series of poignant encounters, Jesus heals the sick, drives out evil spirits, and raises the dead to life (4:31–44; 5:12–26; 7:1–17; 8:26–56; 9:37–45; 13:10–17; 17:11–19; 18:35–43). Regardless of their nationality or ethnicity or economic background, whether society considers them "sinners" or "saints," all who come to Him experience His mercy and compassion and love. To those who criticize Him for associating with people of poor reputation, Jesus replies, "It is not the healthy who need a doctor, but the sick" (5:31). And when a sinful woman anoints Jesus' feet with a costly perfume and washes them with her tears, Jesus tells the frowning Pharisees, "Her many sins have been forgiven—for she loved much. But he who has been forgiven little loves little" (7:47).

Jesus calls His followers—His disciples—to join Him in His ministry (5:1–11, 27–32; 9:1–9; 10:1–24). He chooses twelve of them to be apostles: "Simon (whom he named Peter), his brother Andrew, James, John, Philip, Bartholomew, Matthew, Thomas, James son of Alphaeus, Simon who was called the Zealot, Judas son of James, and Judas Iscariot . . ." (6:14–16). Jesus preaches and teaches many things, including the need for humility and repentance before God, patience and perseverance in times of suffering, forgiveness, and love—even for our enemies (6:17–45). He uses parables to teach "those who have ears to hear" about the kingdom of God, about truth, about faith. Often Jesus explains the hidden meaning of His stories to His disciples afterward (6:46–49; 8:1–18; 10:25–37; 11:29–36; 12:13–21, 35–48; 13:18–30; 14:1–16:31; 18:1–14; 19:11–27). Demonstrating the power and authority that has been given to Him as the Son of God, He calms a storm and feeds five thousand people with five loaves of bread and two fish (8:22–25; 9:10–17). He teaches His disciples how to pray in a way that pleases God (11:1–13). Jesus confronts the corrupt religious leaders of the day and exposes their wickedness and hypocrisy (11:37–54). He welcomes little children to come to Him "for the kingdom of God belongs to such as these" (18:16).

As Jesus enters the city of Jerusalem, the people welcome Him as a king (19:28–44). He drives out the moneychangers who have desecrated the temple: "'It is written,' he said to them, 'My house will be a house of prayer'; but you have made it a den of robbers.' Every day he was teaching at the temple. But the chief priests, the teachers of the law and the leaders among the people were trying to kill him. Yet they could not find any way to do it, because all the people hung on his words" (19:46–48). Jesus answers challenges from the Pharisees and Sadducees on complicated doctrinal issues, while warning His followers about the suffering and persecution that they will have to endure for His sake (20:1–38).

Celebrating the Passover with His disciples, Jesus institutes a new feast—"the Lord's Supper"—that will one day commemorate His death on the cross. "Do this in remembrance of me" (22:19). Jesus tells His disciples that one of them (Judas) is about to betray Him. In fact, He says all of His disciples will soon fall away. Peter protests that even if everyone else does, he will never abandon Jesus. But Jesus tells him that this very night, Peter will deny even knowing Him three times (22:7–38). In the garden of Gethsemane, the disciples sleep while Jesus earnestly prays to be delivered from the suffering that lies ahead—before ultimately surrendering Himself to the will of God (22:39–46). Judas brings soldiers to the garden to arrest Jesus, and Jesus is put on trial before the Sanhedrin, the chief priests, elders, and teachers of the law. Out in the courtyard, a terrified Peter repeatedly refuses to acknowledge that he is associated with Jesus: "The Lord turned and looked straight at Peter. Then Peter remembered the word the Lord had spoken to him . . . and he went outside and wept bitterly" (22:60–62).

The Sanhedrin hands Jesus over to the Roman governor, Pontius Pilate, who sends Him to King Herod, who sends Him back to Pilate. Like King Herod, Pilate finds Jesus innocent of any crime. But Pilate gives in to pressure from the Jewish leaders, who have already convinced the people to turn on Him and call for His execution. Jesus is crucified between two criminals, one of whom joins the crowd in mocking Him. The other rebukes him: "Don't you fear God? . . . We are punished justly, for we are getting what our deeds deserve. But this man has done nothing wrong. . . . Jesus, remember me when you come into your kingdom." Jesus answers, "I tell you the truth, today you will be with me in paradise" (23:41–43). Jesus is given a hasty burial just before sundown, when the Sabbath begins and no "work" can be done.

After the Sabbath, a small group of women return to the tomb to anoint His body with spices. They find the stone at the entrance rolled away—and the tomb itself empty. An angel asks them, "Why do you look for the living among the dead? He is not here; he has risen! . . ." (24:5–6). Then Jesus Himself appears to two of His disciples walking along the road to Emmaus (24:13–35). They rush back to Jerusalem to tell the other disciples what happened. Jesus then appears to all of them and reminds them of everything He has taught them. He tells them to wait until He sends the Holy Spirit to them. Then He wants them to be His witnesses and preach the gospel "to all nations" (24:36–49). Jesus leads His disciples outside the city, where He bids them farewell: "He lifted up his hands and blessed them. While he was blessing them, he left them and was taken up into heaven. Then they worshiped him and returned to Jerusalem with great joy" (24:50–52).

Key Verse or Passage

"For the Son of Man came to seek and to save what was lost." (Luke 19:10)

More on This Story in the Bible: For more on the life and death and resurrection of Jesus, see the Gospels of Matthew, Mark, and John. The book of Acts is the sequel to or second volume of the Gospel of Luke, carrying on the story of the early church after Jesus' ascension into heaven. Luke was a Gentile (non-Jewish) believer who often traveled with the apostle Paul during his missionary journeys. Luke is mentioned or referred to in Acts 16:10–17; 20:5–15; 21:1–8; 27:1–28:16; Colossians 4:14; Philemon 24; and 2 Timothy 4:11.

Words to Know:

magnificat: from the Latin, meaning "glorifies"; Mary's psalm or song or hymn of praise to God in Luke 1:46–56 is known as "The Magnificat."

baptize: to ceremonially wash with water, symbolizing an inner spiritual cleansing.

disciple: a student, a follower, one who spreads the teachings of another; a follower of Jesus.

parable: a short, simple story used to communicate a powerful spiritual truth.

apostle: a "messenger"; one who has been specially chosen by Jesus to be His messenger (as with the twelve disciples or "apostles"); a missionary; a leader in the church.

Did You Know? Bible scholars believe that the many details about Jesus' birth and early childhood that appear only in the Gospel of Luke probably came from his conversations with Mary, Jesus' mother. As Luke writes, "Mary treasured up all these things and pondered them in her heart" (Luke 2:19).

Making the Connection: Amazing. It's the only way to describe the incredible transformation that took place in the life of John Newton. A sailor in the 1700s, he lived a life of drunkenness, profanity, and immorality. He was a foul, ill-tempered man, despised by everyone who knew him. He cared for no one but himself and sought nothing but his own pleasure. When Newton became captain of his own slave trading ship, his hard heart grew even harder. Then one night, John was caught in a fierce storm. He came face-to-face with a gripping fear of death. An experienced sailor, he knew he had little chance of survival, and he was not ready to face eternity.

John tried to cry out to God for mercy, but he was stopped abruptly by the thought of how little he deserved it. During a harrowing night of soul-searching, he realized that he was a sinner in need of a Savior. He began to understand the meaning of God's grace. Newton survived the storm that night, but he was never the same again. He emerged from the experience a new man. At the age of 39, the former slave trader became a pastor. He dedicated the rest of his life to sharing with others the good news of the gospel: that Jesus Christ had come "to seek and to save the lost" (Luke 19:10). Reflecting on his experience that night in the storm— and the precious words of Scripture—he later penned words that have touched the hearts of millions: *Amazing Grace—how sweet the sound— that saved a wretch like me! I once was lost but now am found, was blind but now I see.* Praise God, the same grace that John Newton experienced is available to us today!

JOHN

The Book: John

The Author: John, the Beloved Disciple

■ **The Audience:** Those who have not yet come to know Jesus as the Son of God and their Savior

■ **The Setting:** Written from Asia Minor, between AD 70 and 95

■ **The Story:** John has written his own gospel—his own account of the "good news"—"that you may believe that Jesus is the Christ, the Son of God, and that by believing you may have life in his name" (20:31). The aspects of Jesus' earthly ministry that John chooses to highlight are presented as signs that point us to this life-changing, life-saving truth.

■ **The Message:** John begins his story at the very beginning—the beginning of time! He explains:

> In the beginning was the Word, and the Word was with God, and the Word was God. He was with God in the beginning. Through him all things were made; without him nothing was made that has been made. In him was life, and that life was the light of men. The light shines in the darkness, but the darkness has not understood it. . . . He was in the world, and though the world was made through him, the world did not recognize him. He came to that which was his own, but his own did not receive him. Yet to all who received him, to those who believed in his name, he gave the right to become children of God." (1:1–5, 10–12)

Continuing to speak of Jesus, John says, "The Word became flesh and made his dwelling among us. We have seen his glory, the glory of the One and Only, who came from the Father, full of grace and truth" (1:14).

John the Baptist is sent by God to call His people to repent and return to Him and prepare for the coming of His Son. "I baptize with water . . . but among you stands one you do not know. He is the one who comes after me, the thongs of whose sandals I am not worthy to untie" (1:26–27). When Jesus presents Himself to John to be baptized, John exclaims: "Look, the Lamb of God, who takes away the sin of the world! . . . I have seen and I testify that this is the Son of God" (1:29, 34).

After His baptism, Jesus begins preaching and teaching. He calls His followers—His disciples—to join Him in His ministry (1:35–50). Jesus reaches out to those who are hungry and thirsty for righteousness—those who long to know God in a deeper way and those who desperately need His forgiveness. He tells a Pharisee named Nicodemus, "No one can see the kingdom of God unless he is born again" (3:1–21). To the woman at the well, Jesus says, "Everyone who drinks this water will be thirsty again, but whoever drinks the water I give him will never thirst. Indeed, the water I give him will become in him a spring of water welling up to eternal life" (4:13–14). To the woman caught in adultery, He says simply: "Go now and leave your life of sin" (8:11).

Jesus turns water into wine, walks on water, casts out demons, heals the sick, and raises the dead. He feeds five thousand people with two fish and five loaves of bread (2:1–11; 4:43–5:15; 6:1–21; 9:1–41; 11:1–44). Each of the miracles—the "signs and wonders"—reveals something about who Jesus is. Afterward, He explains: "I am the bread of life" (6:35); "I am the light of the world" (8:12); "I am the good shepherd" (10:11); "I am the gate" (10:7); "I am the vine" (15:5); "I am the way and the truth and the life. No one comes to the Father except through me" (14:6). Jesus confronts the religious leaders of the day with their corruption and hypocrisy and stubborn unbelief (7:45–52; 8:12–59; 10:22–41). The Pharisees and Sadducees begin plotting to kill Him (11:45–57).

When Jesus enters the city of Jerusalem, crowds gather around Him, shouting, "Blessed is he who comes in the name of the Lord! Blessed is the King of Israel!" (12:13). During their Passover celebration, Jesus washes His disciples' feet, demonstrating the heart to serve others that He longs to see in them. He predicts His betrayal and death—and Peter's denial of Him (12:20–38). The disciples are distressed to learn that He will be leaving them soon. Jesus tells them, "Do not let your hearts be troubled. Trust in God; trust also in me. In my Father's house are many rooms; if it were not so, I would have told you. I am going there to prepare a place for you. And if I go and prepare a place for you, I will come back and take you to be with me that you also may be where I am" (14:1–3). He promises to send His Holy Spirit to lead them and guide them through all that lies ahead (14:1–16:33).

In the garden of Gethsemane, Jesus prays for Himself and for His disciples and for all who will one day believe in Him through their message (17:1–26). Judas brings soldiers to the garden to arrest Jesus, and Jesus is put on trial before the Sanhedrin, the chief priests, elders, and teachers of the law. Out in the courtyard, a terrified Peter repeatedly denies knowing Jesus, just as Jesus said he would. The Sanhedrin hands Jesus over to the Roman governor, Pontius Pilate. Pilate finds Jesus innocent of any crime, but he gives in to political pressure and orders His execution to appease Jewish leaders. "Then Pilate took Jesus and had him flogged. The soldiers twisted together a crown of thorns and put it on his head. They clothed him in a purple robe and went up to him again and again, saying, 'Hail, king of the Jews!' And they struck him in the face" (19:1–3).

Jesus is crucified beneath a sign that reads "Jesus of Nazareth, the King of the Jews." He is given a hasty burial just before sundown on the Sabbath, when no "work" can be done. After the Sabbath, Mary Magdalene discovers the tomb empty and alerts Peter and John; the disciples are troubled, thinking someone has stolen Jesus' body. "They still did not understand from Scripture that Jesus had to rise from the dead" (20:9). The resurrected Jesus appears first to Mary Magdalene and then to the other disciples. He shows Thomas the nail marks in His hands and the wound in His side as proof of who He is—that He who was crucified has been raised from the dead. Jesus says, "Because you have seen me, you have believed; blessed are those who have not seen and yet have believed" (20:29). Early one morning, Jesus again appears to His disciples by the sea and sends them a miraculous catch of fish. He gives Peter the opportunity to affirm his love for Him three times (just as Peter had denied Him three times) and reinstates him as one of the twelve disciples with this command: "Feed my sheep" (21:17).

John concludes: "Jesus did many other things as well. If every one of them were written down, I suppose that even the whole world would not have room for the books that would be written" (21:25).

Key Verse or Passage

"For God so loved the world that he gave his one and only Son, that whoever believes in him shall not perish but have eternal life. For God did not send his Son into the world to condemn the world, but to save the world through him." (John 3:16–17)

More on This Story in the Bible: For more on the life and ministry, death and resurrection of Jesus Christ, see the Gospels of Matthew, Mark, and Luke. Along with his brother James, John was one of the original twelve disciples called by Jesus to join Him in His ministry, and one of the founders of the early church. For more of John's writings, see 1 John, 2 John, 3 John, and Revelation.

Words to Know:

"the Word": the means by which God makes Himself known; the absolute, eternal, and ultimate being of Jesus Christ.

"I AM": in the Old Testament, God revealed to His people that His name is "I AM" or "I AM WHO I AM" (the Hebrew word is sometimes translated as "Yahweh" or "Jehovah" in English); Jesus identified Himself as God—the Son of God—whose name is "I AM" throughout the Gospel of John.

glory: beauty, power, or honor; a quality of God's character that emphasizes His greatness—His majesty and authority, His moral beauty and perfection.

sign: something that points to or represents something larger or more significant than itself; the deeper meaning of the "wonders" and "miracles" performed by Jesus.

Did You Know? John so clearly and concisely and convincingly makes the case for Christ that many pastors, evangelists, and Bible teachers recommend that people who are spiritually "seeking"—those who are undecided or who are new to the Christian faith—begin their study of the Bible with the Gospel of John.

Making the Connection: What's the difference between a Christian and a "born-again Christian"? Technically there shouldn't be any difference! The Scripture tells us that all who put their faith in Jesus—all true believers—are "born again" and made new in Christ (John 3:3; 2 Corinthians 5:17). The term "born-again Christian" became popular thirty or forty years ago, during a time of spiritual revival, as a way to distinguish between those who identify themselves as devout or enthusiastic Christians and those who are only nominally or culturally "Christian" (as opposed to being Jewish or Muslim). Though sometimes used disparagingly by unbelievers today, the phrase "born-again Christian" simply describes someone who has vital, living faith—a personal relationship with Jesus Christ.

Think about It: "He was in the world, and though the world was made through him, the world did not recognize him. He came to that which was his own, but his own did not receive him" (John 1:10–11). He was mocked and ridiculed. Spat upon. Beaten with fists—and with whips. A crown of thorns bruised His head. A sword pierced His side. He was nailed to the cross, condemned to a brutal and agonizing death.

"It was our weaknesses He carried; it was our sorrows that weighed Him down. And we thought His troubles were a punishment from God, a punishment for His own sins! But He was pierced for our rebellion, crushed for our sins. He was beaten so we could be whole. He was whipped so we could be healed. All of us, like sheep, have strayed away. We have left God's paths to follow our own. Yet the Lord laid on Him the sins of us all" (Isaiah 53:4–6, NLT).

The Bible tells us the blood of Jesus was shed for us. That day on the cross, He paid the penalty for our sin; He took the punishment in our place. Now, thanks to Jesus, we have been set free from the power of sin and death. We have been reconciled to God. We have been given eternal life. Tragedy was turned to triumph. A day of sorrow became a day of celebration.

ACTS

The Book: Acts

The Author: Luke, the Physician

The Audience: Theophilus, a Roman governor

The Setting: Written from Caesarea and Rome, AD 60–62

The Story: The book of Acts is the history of the early church. It tells what happened to those first disciples after Jesus rose from the dead and ascended into heaven. Sometimes known as "the Acts of the Apostles," it is perhaps more accurately described as "the Acts of the Holy Spirit"—as it was clearly the Spirit of God who empowered His church to spread the good news of the gospel far and wide and to work miracles in the lives of all they touched.

The Message: Jesus tells His disciples: "Do not leave Jerusalem, but wait for the gift my Father promised, which you have heard me speak about. For John baptized with water, but in a few days you will be baptized with the Holy Spirit. . . . You will receive power when the Holy Spirit comes on you; and you will be my witnesses in Jerusalem, and in all Judea and Samaria, and to the ends of the earth" (1:4–5, 8). On the day of Pentecost, all the disciples are together in one place. "Suddenly a sound like the blowing of a violent wind came from heaven and filled the whole house. . . . They saw what seemed to be tongues of fire that separated and came to rest on each of them. All of them were filled with the Holy Spirit and began to speak in other tongues as the Spirit enabled them" (2:2–4). The disciples go out into the streets of the city, preaching in languages they have never learned. "Now there were staying in Jerusalem God-fearing Jews from every nation under heaven. When they heard this sound, a crowd came together in bewilderment, because each one heard them speaking in his own language" (2:5–6). Peter gets up to address the crowd and explain what has happened. He calls to the people: "Repent and be baptized, every one of you, in the name of Jesus Christ for the forgiveness of your sins. And you will receive the gift of the Holy Spirit. The promise is for you and your children and for all who are far off—for all whom the Lord our God will call" (2:38–39). More than three thousand people respond to his message.

Empowered by the Holy Spirit, believers everywhere begin preaching and teaching, healing the sick, casting out demons, raising the dead— just as Jesus said they would (2:1–6:7). The gospel spreads like wildfire, much to the dismay of the religious leaders of the day. After healing a crippled beggar outside the temple, Peter and John are brought before the Sanhedrin (the Jewish council) to explain themselves. Peter boldly testifies, "It is by the name of Jesus Christ of Nazareth, whom you crucified but whom God raised from the dead, that this man stands before you healed. . . . Salvation is found in no one else, for there is no other name under heaven given to men by which we must be saved" (4:10, 12). Later, Philip encounters an Ethiopian official who is struggling to understand the Old Testament Scriptures. Philip explains how Jesus has fulfilled the word of the prophets, and the man is baptized on the spot—taking the good news with him back to his own country (8:26–40).

More and more people join the community of those who have put their faith in Christ. "All the believers were one in heart and mind. No one claimed that any of his possessions was his own, but they shared everything they had. With great power the apostles continued to testify to the resurrection of the Lord Jesus, and much grace was upon them all" (4:32–33). As the church grows, so does the hostility and opposition to it. Stephen becomes the first martyr when members of the Sanhedrin have him stoned to death for preaching the gospel (6:8 –7:60). "On that day a great persecution broke out against the church at Jerusalem, and all except the apostles were scattered throughout Judea and Samaria" (8:1). But the Holy Spirit has a purpose, even in this, for "those who had been scattered preached the word wherever they went" (8:4).

A zealous young Pharisee named Saul prepares to travel to Damascus where he intends to arrest and imprison believers there. Suddenly a blinding light knocks him to the ground. He hears a voice calling, "Saul, Saul, why do you persecute me?" Saul answers, "Who are you, Lord?" The voice replies, "I am Jesus, whom you are persecuting . . ." (9:4–6). In that moment, Saul becomes a believer himself. His name is changed to Paul. God reveals, "This man is my chosen instrument to carry my name before the Gentiles and their kings and before the people of Israel . . ." (9:15). Paul begins powerfully preaching and teaching the very gospel he once sought to destroy.

Meanwhile, Peter has a vision in which God reveals that all foods are now "clean." It is no longer necessary to live by the ceremonial rules and regulations set forth in the Law of Moses. At that moment, a Roman centurion—a God-fearing Gentile—sends for Peter. Because of his vision, Peter is not afraid to "defile" himself by entering a non-Jewish, ceremonially unclean home. When Peter shares the gospel with the centurion and his friends and family, these Gentiles immediately believe and are filled with the Holy Spirit, speaking in tongues just as the disciples had done (10:1–48). Stunned, Peter says, "I now realize how true it is that God does not show favoritism but accepts men from every nation who fear him and do what is right" (10:34–35). He later explains to the church council in Jerusalem. "God, who knows the heart, showed that he accepted them by giving the Holy Spirit to them, just as he did to us. He made no distinction between us and them, for he purified their hearts by faith" (15:8–9). From now on, the disciples decide to welcome Gentile believers as their brothers and sisters in Christ, without requiring them to observe Jewish laws and customs (11:1–18; 15:1–29).

Paul and Barnabas set out on a missionary journey to share the good news of the gospel with the people in Cyprus, Psidian Antioch, Iconium, Lystra, and Derbe (12:25–14:28). "The word of the Lord spread through the whole region" (13:49). On another journey Paul is joined by Silas and Timothy, who travel with him through Galatia to Philippi (16:1–40). In Philippi, Paul and Silas are arrested for causing an uproar in the city after casting a demon out of a fortune-telling slave girl. "About midnight Paul and Silas were praying and singing hymns to God, and the other prisoners were listening to them" (16:25). An earthquake causes the prison doors to fly open and the chains fall loose. Thinking the prisoners will have escaped, the jailer prepares to kill himself—but Paul and Silas stop him. Everyone is still there. In awe of their character and integrity—and the power of God displayed on their behalf—the jailer cries out, "Sirs, what must I do to be saved?" Paul and Silas reply, "Believe in the Lord Jesus, and you will be saved—you and your household" (16:30–31).

Paul and his companions travel to Thessalonica, Berea, Athens, Corinth, Ephesus, Macedonia, and Greece—preaching the good news of the gospel all along the way. At times they are welcomed with open arms; at times they are met with suspicion, hostility, and opposition (17:1–20:38). On his way back through Ephesus, Paul tells his dear friends there, "Now, compelled by the Spirit, I am going to Jerusalem, not knowing what will happen to me there. . . . In every city the Holy Spirit warns me that prison and hardships are facing me. However, I consider my life worth nothing to me, if only I may finish the race and complete the task the Lord Jesus has given me—the task of testifying to the gospel of God's grace" (20:22–24).

Almost immediately after he arrives in Jerusalem, Paul is arrested and put on trial before the Sanhedrin, Roman governors Felix and Festus, and King Herod Agrippa II (21:27–26:32). Ultimately, as a Roman citizen, Paul appeals his case to Caesar. He sets sail for Rome, where—after surviving a storm, a shipwreck, and a deadly snake bite—he lives under house arrest, awaiting trial (27:1–28:31). "For two whole years Paul . . . welcomed all who came to see him. Boldly and without hindrance he preached the kingdom of God and taught about the Lord Jesus Christ" (28:30–31).

Key Verse or Passage

"But you will receive power when the Holy Spirit comes on you; and you will be my witnesses in Jerusalem, and in all Judea and Samaria, and to the ends of the earth." (Acts 1:8)

More on This Story in the Bible: Acts is the sequel to or second volume of the Gospel of Luke. All four of the Gospels—Matthew, Mark, Luke, and John—provide the backstory of the people and events that take place in the book of Acts. Many of the letters that follow Acts in the New Testament were written *by* people and *for* people whose stories are told in this book. For instance, Acts introduces us to the apostle Paul. And Paul, in turn, mentions his dear friend Luke in Colossians 4:14, 2 Timothy 4:11, and Philemon 1:24.

Words to Know:

witness: someone who shares with others what they have seen and heard; one who testifies or gives evidence or proof.

church: the local assembly of believers, as well as all believers everywhere, for all time.

fellowship: friendship, companionship, communion; sharing things in common with others; a close-knit community of like-minded people. The phrase "the fellowship of believers" is sometimes used to refer to the gathering or congregation of Christians for worship, as in "church."

Pentecost: originally a term for the Jewish festival known as the Feast of Weeks or Feast of Harvest, the Day of the First Fruits; Christians use the word "Pentecost" to refer to the day when the Holy Spirit came upon the first disciples and filled them with His power. ("Pentecostal" Christians believe that the Holy Spirit still empowers believers the same way—with signs and wonders and speaking in tongues—today.)

persecute: to treat someone cruelly or unfairly because of their ideas or beliefs.

Think about It: Many of the first disciples were imprisoned, tortured, and executed for their faith. At one point, King Herod arrested Simon Peter, planning to bring him to trial after the Passover. Peter was guarded by a squad of sixteen men, chained between two of the soldiers around the clock. But regardless of Herod's plans, it wasn't Peter's time to go. God still had work for him to do. The night before the trial, "an angel of the Lord appeared and a light shone in the cell. He struck Peter on the side and woke him up. 'Quick, get up!' he said, and the chains fell off Peter's wrists" (Acts 12:7).

As you read that verse, did anything strike you as odd or unusual—aside from the angelic visitation? If you were in a prison cell, knowing you would likely be executed in the morning, what would you be doing? Anxiously pacing the floor? Wringing your hands? Crying out to God in fear and desperation? Or sleeping so soundly someone would have to hit you to wake you up? How did Peter do it? How could he sleep at a time like this? In a word, trust. Peter trusted God utterly and completely. He knew his life was in the hands of his heavenly Father. One way or another, things would turn out all right. If he lived, God would be with him. If He died, he'd be with God. Either way, it was okay with him. When you live with that perspective, you can sleep through anything!

Did You Know? The first believers were simply known as disciples or followers of Jesus Christ. (In the beginning, most of them were devout

Jews who recognized Jesus as their Messiah. They didn't think of themselves as belonging to a faith other than or apart from Judaism.) Over time, believers began referring to themselves and each other as followers of "the Way"—because Jesus had said, "I am the way, the truth, and the life" (see John 14:6; Acts 9:2; 19:9, 23; 22:4; and 24:14). The book of Acts explains that it was in the city of Antioch that those who belonged to Christ were first called "Christians" (Acts 11:26).

Making the Connection: Some of us have learned everything we know about our faith from someone else—we've never actually studied the Bible for ourselves. Unfortunately, a lack of firsthand experience with the Word of God can put us at a real disadvantage when it comes to living out the faith we profess. For one thing, we miss out on the joy of personal discovery—the thrill when, through the Scriptures, God speaks directly to us. We find we lack the confidence to share our beliefs and convictions because we can't back them up with Scripture. We're not *exactly* sure what the Bible says and where it says so. Worst of all, when we're content to take somebody else's word for it, we leave ourselves wide open to false doctrine—faulty or misleading teachings. Acts 17:11 tells us that the Berean people had a much different approach: When Paul came, preaching the gospel of Jesus Christ, they listened to his message with great eagerness. Then, they examined the Scriptures "to see if what Paul said was true." Because they studied the Word for themselves, they were able to recognize and discern the truth of the gospel message, and they received it with great joy. In their diligence, they set a great example for all of us who are believers today.

ROMANS

The Book: Romans

The Author: The apostle Paul

The Audience: Roman Christians, both Jewish and Gentile (non-Jewish) believers

The Setting: Written from Corinth, AD 57

The Story: For many years, the apostle Paul had wanted to visit the new believers living in Rome. The church there had not yet received any formal teaching or training. Paul was actually planning to travel to Rome in the near future; in the meantime, he wrote the believers a lengthy letter to explain to them more fully the basic teachings of the Christian faith. He wanted them to understand God's plan of salvation for both Jews and Gentiles—and how they should live differently, now that they were Christians.

The Message: After greeting the Romans warmly, Paul begins laying the foundation for faith in Christ. He explains how human beings have angered their Creator by rejecting Him and defying Him and ignoring Him (1:18–27). Since people are so intent on going their own way, God has allowed them to sink deeper and deeper into rebellion and sin (1:28–31). Paul says God has every right to judge humanity for its wickedness—and He will (2:1–16). He gave His own people the Law of Moses not only to teach them right from wrong, but to reveal to them the sinfulness of their own hearts—their unwillingness and inability to do as He asks (2:17–3:9). "There is no one righteous, not even one; there is no one who understands, no one who seeks God" (3:10–11). We are all guilty of breaking the Law and deserve the penalty—death.

Because God is a just Judge, He could not let sin go unpunished. So He sent His Son Jesus to take the penalty in our place (3:22–25). Paul says it is faith in Jesus that makes us "righteous," not our feeble attempts to keep the Law, just as it was faith—and not good deeds—that made Abraham righteous (3:27–4:25). "You see, at just the right time, when we were still powerless, Christ died for the ungodly. Very rarely will anyone die for a righteous man, though for a good man someone might possibly dare to die. But God demonstrates his own love for us in this: While we were still sinners, Christ died for us" (5:6–8). We came by our sinful nature honestly—we inherited it from our common ancestor, Adam. But in the same way that Adam's sin cursed all of mankind, Jesus' sacrifice saves all mankind. "Just as through the disobedience of the one man the many were made sinners, so also through the obedience of the one man the many will be made righteous" (5:19).

We are no longer "slaves to sin"—compelled by our nature to rebel and disobey. We have been set free and are now "slaves to righteousness"— earnestly desiring to love and serve (6:15–22). Not that it isn't a challenge to overcome the habits and behavior patterns of our past (7:7–25)! Though our salvation was accomplished with Jesus' death on the cross, we're not in heaven yet. We continue to battle temptation, and sometimes we do still fall into sin. But "there is now no condemnation for those who are in Christ Jesus" (8:1). We don't live in fear of God's judgment and wrath. He is our Father and we are His children whom He dearly loves (8:15). The suffering and hardship we face in this life will not last long (8:18–27). We will overcome them, for God has promised us victory: "In all these things we are more than conquerors through him who loved us" (8:37).

Paul longs for the Jewish people who have rejected Jesus to recognize Him as their Messiah and come to faith in Him. Together, Jewish believers and Gentile believers become the new "people of God"—Christians (9:30–11:32). Paul concludes his letter with detailed instructions on how Christians should live—in love and unity with one another, at peace with the community and those who rule over it (12:1–16:22). "May the God of hope fill you with all joy and peace as you trust in him, so that you may overflow with hope by the power of the Holy Spirit" (15:13).

Key Verse or Passage

"Therefore, I urge you, brothers, in view of God's mercy, to offer your bodies as living sacrifices, holy and pleasing to God—this is your spiritual act of worship. Do not conform any longer to the pattern of this world, but be transformed by the renewing of your mind. Then you will be able to test and approve what God's will is—his good, pleasing and perfect will." (Romans 12:1–2)

More on This Story in the Bible: You can learn more about the apostle Paul, his missionary journeys, and how he eventually ended up in Rome (and under what circumstances) by reading Acts 9, 13–28. The next twelve books of the Bible are also letters written by Paul; Galatians deals with many of the same themes. See pages 282–283 for a list of Scriptures from Romans that Bible scholars call the "Roman Road" to faith in Christ.

Words to Know:

apostle: a follower of Jesus specially chosen to share His message with the world.

righteous: upright, moral, virtuous; Paul often uses the word in the "legal" sense of being in right standing (without guilt or sin) in the eyes of the great Judge—God.

"the Law": God's rules for holy living, sometimes called the "Law of Moses" because God first gave these instructions to Moses to give to the people. This Law includes the Ten Commandments and the other rules and regulations found in Exodus, Leviticus, Numbers, and Deuteronomy.

condemnation: an expression of strong disapproval; the final judgment that one is guilty and deserving of punishment.

justified: made right.

"grafted in": something that happens when a bud or shoot is attached to an established plant, so that the two separate plants grow together into one new plant. Paul teaches that Gentiles who believe in Jesus are "grafted in" with the Jewish believers and together they make up God's new "chosen people."

sacrifice: something that is surrendered, given up, or offered to God as an act of worship.

Did You Know? Have you ever heard that God has a wonderful plan for your life? That He wants to fill you with love and joy and peace? He certainly does! But becoming a Christian doesn't mean you'll never have any problems or that bad things will never happen to you. We do still live in a fallen, sinful world—surrounded by fallen, sinful people. But Romans 8:28 tells us, "God causes everything to work together for the good of those who love God . . ." (NLT). The apostle Paul says God is so loving and so powerful that He can take even the worst things that happen to us and bring good out of them somehow.

Paul continues, "Can anything ever separate us from Christ's love? Does it mean he no longer loves us if we have trouble or calamity, or are persecuted, or hungry, or destitute, or in danger, or threatened with death? . . . No, despite all these things, overwhelming victory is ours through Christ, who loved us. And I am convinced that nothing can ever separate us from God's love. Neither death nor life, neither angels nor demons, neither our fears for today nor our worries about tomorrow—not even the powers of hell can separate us from God's love. No power in the sky above or in the earth below—indeed, nothing in all creation will ever be able to separate us from the love of God that is revealed in Christ Jesus our Lord" (Romans 8:35–39, NLT).

Making the Connection: For over a thousand years, there was only one Christian church or denomination—the catholic ("universal") church. But over time, church leaders lost their way. They began teaching things that contradicted the Scriptures—sometimes out of ignorance, sometimes as a result of greed and corruption. They held that salvation was only available to those who could *earn* it with their good deeds or those who could afford to *purchase* it from the church—paying a hefty fee for an "indulgence."

It was through his study of Romans 1:17 that a German monk named Martin Luther had a revelation: "For in the gospel a righteousness from God is revealed, a righteousness that is by *faith* from first to last, just as it is written: 'The righteous will live by *faith*.'" Luther confronted church leaders and called for reform in his "95 Theses," which he nailed to the door of the Wittenberg church in 1517. At the time, church leaders refused to address the corruption and false doctrine that had overtaken them—so Luther and others like him left the Catholic Church in protest. These "Protestants" created a new, "reformed" church they believed to be more faithful to the teachings of Scripture.

1 CORINTHIANS

The Book: 1 Corinthians

The Author: The apostle Paul

▪ The Audience: The church in Corinth

▪ The Setting: Written from Ephesus, AD 55

▪ The Story: The church Paul founded in Corinth was not doing well. Believers were behaving immaturely and irresponsibly—even immorally. They had embraced false doctrine. There were all kinds of division and strife and lawsuits between members of the church. Paul wrote to answer the church leaders' questions and teach them how to deal with these kinds of problems. He also urged the believers in Corinth to truly love and respect one another and to grow up and mature in their faith in Christ.

▪ The Message: Paul begins his letter with an appeal for unity among the believers in Corinth. He urges them to be humble, not proud: "Brothers, think of what you were when you were called. Not many of you were wise by human standards; not many were influential; not many were of noble birth. But God chose the foolish things of the world to shame the wise; God chose the weak things of the world to shame the strong" (1:26–27). Those who don't have the Spirit of God don't understand God's truth; it doesn't make any sense to them. But God has revealed His truth to us who believe (2:6–16). Paul rebukes the Corinthians for their "worldliness" and immaturity—the jealousy and quarreling among them (3:1–23; 6:1–8). He reminds them of how he and others have sacrificed to bring them the good news of the gospel and of the godly example that has been set for them (4:1–21; 9:1–23). Paul is grieved by reports that the Corinthians have allowed sexual immorality in the church in the name of "freedom" in Christ (5:1–13; 6:9–20). Just because God has saved us by His grace (rather than our own obedience to the Law) doesn't mean we can flout His commandments and go on living in willful and deliberate sin:

> Do you not know that the wicked will not inherit the kingdom of God? Do not be deceived: Neither the sexually immoral nor idolaters nor adulterers nor male prostitutes nor homosexual offenders nor thieves nor the greedy nor drunkards nor slanderers nor swindlers will inherit the kingdom of God. And that is what some of you were. But you were washed, you were sanctified, you were justified in the name of the Lord Jesus Christ and by the Spirit of our God. . . . Do you not know that your body is a temple of

the Holy Spirit, who is in you, whom you have received from God? You are not your own; you were bought at a price. Therefore honor God with your body. (6:9–11, 19–20)

In response to some specific questions, Paul offers the Corinthians instruction and advice on the subjects of marriage, divorce, and singleness (7:1–40). He says that for the mature believer, eating food that has been sacrificed to idols is a nonissue; however, we should be careful not to let the exercise of our freedom lead a less mature Christian to engage in behavior that will cause them to fall into sin and temptation (8:1–13). Paul encourages believers not to get distracted by all of these things, but to stay focused. He refers to our spiritual journey as a "race" of faith for which we should train like Olympic athletes: "Everyone who competes in the games goes into strict training. They do it to get a crown that will not last; but we do it to get a crown that will last forever" (9:25). Again, Paul says, we should be careful about our freedom in Christ. Some things are "permissible"—they are not sinful in and of themselves—but they are also not "beneficial." They don't help us or others live the kind of life that honors God (10:23–11:1). Instead, Paul urges the Corinthians to learn a lesson from Israel's history and exercise self-discipline and restraint (10:1–13). "No temptation has seized you except what is common to man. And God is faithful; he will not let you be tempted beyond what you can bear. But when you are tempted, he will also provide a way out so that you can stand up under it" (10:13).

When the Corinthians gather for worship, it should not be a raucous and chaotic affair (11:1–33; 14:1–40). "For God is not a God of disorder but of peace . . ." (14:33). Paul explains that the Holy Spirit has given all believers "spiritual gifts"—gifts of supernatural wisdom, knowledge, faith, healing, miracles, prophecy, discernment, and speaking in and interpreting unknown tongues (12:1–11). These gifts are meant to build up and strengthen the church. Just as the human body is made up of many different parts, so individual believers make up "the body of Christ." We have different gifts and different roles, but each one of us is dependent on all of the others; we need each other in order to function properly (12:12–31). The greatest gift of all, Paul says, is love (13:1–13).

Paul answers questions and corrects some misunderstandings about the resurrection of Jesus and what it means to our faith, as well as the future physical and spiritual resurrection of all who believe (15:1–58). Whether we have already died or are still living when Jesus comes again, we will all be given new and perfect sinless bodies. "Listen, I tell you a mystery: We will not all sleep, but we will all be changed—in a flash, in the twinkling of an eye, at the last trumpet. For the trumpet will sound, the dead will be raised imperishable, and we will be changed. . . . 'Where, O death, is your victory? Where, O death, is your sting?' The sting of death is sin, and the power of sin is the law. But thanks be to God! He gives us the victory through our Lord Jesus Christ" (15:51–52, 55–57). Paul concludes his letter to the Corinthians: "Be on your guard; stand firm in the faith; be men of courage; be strong. Do everything in love. . . . My love to all of you in Christ Jesus . . ." (16:13–14, 24).

Key Verse or Passage

"Love is patient, love is kind. It does not envy, it does not boast, it is not proud. It is not rude, it is not self-seeking, it is not easily angered, it keeps no record of wrongs. Love does not delight in evil but rejoices with the truth. It always protects, always trusts, always hopes, always perseveres. Love never fails. . . ." (1 Corinthians 13:4–8)

More on This Story in the Bible: To learn more about the apostle Paul and his life and ministry, read Acts 9:1–30; 13:1–28:31. His time in Corinth is described in Acts 18:1–28. You can read Paul's further instructions to this church in 2 Corinthians.

Words to Know:

"**yeast**": in the Scriptures, "yeast" (leaven) often symbolizes sin; even the smallest sin can grow and spread through an individual or community in the same way that a tiny amount of yeast will spread through a large batch of dough.

the Lord's Supper: a special ceremony instituted by Jesus, in which believers commemorate His death on the cross; also called "the Love Feast" or Holy Communion.

tongues: languages previously unknown to the speakers that are miraculously uttered by believers who have been filled with the Holy Spirit.

Did You Know? The city of Corinth was famous for its widespread sexual immorality, so much so that the Greek expression for practicing such behavior was "to corinthianize." No wonder the church struggled in this area! New believers often brought their old way of life into the church with them. Paul had to make it clear that any kind of sex outside of marriage—including premarital sex, adultery, homosexuality, incest, or prostitution—was inappropriate and unacceptable for God's people. The Bible tells us God intended for sex to be a sacred gift enjoyed by a man and a woman who have committed their lives to each other, the way God committed Himself to His people, the way Christ committed Himself to His bride, the church. Sex creates a powerful spiritual connection, a bond between participants. At its best, it is meant to be a representation of the kind of beautiful, intimate, exclusive union God longs to have with each one of us. Anything else—anything less—is an affront to God and His design and His plan for humankind (6:9–20). The good news for the people of Corinth—and for us today—is that regardless of our past, God can redeem our future. Whatever we may have done in ignorance or rebellion, if we repent and turn from our sin, God will forgive us and restore us to a right relationship with Him. Whatever may have been done *to* us, He can cleanse us and make us new.

Think about It: The Corinthians lived in a specific time and place, in a specific culture, with specific issues when it came to practically living out their faith on a daily basis. Paul answered their questions as best he could, with the wisdom God had given him. Ever since, Christians have debated whether instructions given centuries ago to one particular church or fellowship are binding for all believers, for all time—or whether there are more general principles that can be drawn from these teachings and then applied to our own culture, time, and place. For instance, are head coverings still necessary for women who don't live in a society where an uncovered head indicates loose morals? Or is the real issue modesty, whatever that looks like in our own culture? Is long hair on men always a "disgrace," a sign of rebellion or excessive vanity—or is the real issue not deliberately offending others with an unconventional appearance? Bible scholars remind us it's important to consider "the whole counsel of God"—everything that Scripture has to say on a particular subject—before we try to create a doctrine out of a single verse. Some things are moral issues, while others are cultural. On some things the Scripture is clear; others seem to be up to our own personal conviction and/or discretion (8:1–13). Paul says whatever we do—whatever we eat and drink, however we choose to dress—ultimately our goal is to conduct ourselves in a way that brings glory to God and others to greater faith in Him (8:9–13; 10:31).

2 CORINTHIANS

The Book: 2 Corinthians

The Author: The apostle Paul

The Audience: The church in Corinth

The Setting: Written from Philippi, AD 55–56

The Story: The church Paul founded in Corinth continued to struggle with some serious issues. False teachers had undermined the believers' faith in Christ and their confidence in Paul himself. The apostle returned to Corinth to try to straighten things out, but his visit did not go well. Afterward, he sent the Corinthians a severe letter—a sharply-worded rebuke. Now Paul writes to let them know how glad he is to hear that they have taken his words to heart and repented for their wrongdoing. It's time to move forward and continue growing in God's grace.

The Message: Paul greets the Corinthians warmly and tenderly. He knows they have been deeply wounded by all the things they have suffered. "Praise be to the God and Father of our Lord Jesus Christ, the

Father of compassion and the God of all comfort, who comforts us in all our troubles, so that we can comfort those in any trouble with the comfort we ourselves have received from God" (1:3–4). Because of his own experience with hardship and suffering, Paul can comfort the Corinthians—and one day they will be able to comfort others (1:5–11). The apostle explains why he felt compelled to rebuke them so sharply in his previous letter. "I wrote you out of great distress and anguish of heart and with many tears, not to grieve you but to let you know the depth of my love for you" (2:4). He urges the church to forgive and restore the person responsible for stirring up this latest trouble, now that the man has demonstrated genuine sorrow and repentance (2:5–11).

Paul rejoices in the ministry to which God has called all believers—to spread everywhere "the fragrance" of the knowledge of Christ (2:12–17). Unlike others, Paul and his companions "do not peddle the word of God for profit" (2:17). Their only goal is to lead people to Christ. Paul reminds the Corinthians of what a privilege it is to be members of the new covenant between God and His people (3:7–18). "For God, who said, 'Let light shine out of darkness,' made his light shine in our hearts to give us the light of the knowledge of the glory of God in the face of Christ. But we have this treasure in jars of clay to show that this all-surpassing power is from God and not from us" (4:6–7). In spite of all the difficulty they have encountered, the Corinthians must not lose heart (4:1–18). "We are hard pressed on every side, but not crushed; perplexed, but not in despair; persecuted, but not abandoned; struck down, but not destroyed" (4:8–9). Our suffering in this life will bring us an eternal reward. Remember, Paul says, believers are no longer "dead" in their sins, chained to their pasts. "If anyone is in Christ, he is a new creation; the old has gone, the new has come!" (5:17). God has reconciled us to Himself through Jesus—a message we are to share with others (5:11–21).

Paul warns the Corinthians: "Do not be yoked together with unbelievers. For what do righteousness and wickedness have in common? Or what fellowship can light have with darkness? . . . What does a believer have in common with an unbeliever?" (6:14–15). Closely joining themselves to others who don't share their faith can only lead to heartache and frustration.

Paul is glad that the church has responded to his correction exactly as he hoped they would—with "godly sorrow" that leads to repentance (7:1–16). He urges the Corinthians to follow the example of other churches and give generously to the work of the kingdom, supplying the needs of God's people (8:1–9:15). Again, Paul defends his ministry—his character and integrity—against the accusations leveled against him by false apostles. He reminds the Corinthians of how much he loves them, how much he has given to them, and how much he has suffered on their behalf (10:1–12:10). He speaks of the spiritual battle that they are engaged in: "The weapons we fight with are not the weapons of the world. On the contrary, they have divine power to demolish strongholds. We demolish arguments and every pretension that sets itself up against the knowledge of God, and we take captive every thought to make it obedient to Christ" (10:4–5). Paul tells the church not to be deceived by Satan, who masquerades as an "angel of light"—or by his followers, who masquerade as "servants of righteousness" (11:13–15).

Paul reiterates his love for the Corinthians and his desire to be a blessing, not a burden to them. Like an anxious parent, Paul worries that somehow they will fall right back into their old patterns of sinful behavior (12:11–21). With a few final warnings and words of encouragement, Paul says he is looking forward to his third visit. "Aim for perfection, listen to my appeal, be of one mind, live in peace. . . . May the grace of the Lord Jesus Christ, and the love of God, and the fellowship of the Holy Spirit be with you all" (13:11, 14).

Key Verse or Passage

"Therefore we do not lose heart. Though outwardly we are wasting away, yet inwardly we are being renewed day by day. For our light and momentary troubles are achieving for us an eternal glory that far outweighs them all. So we fix our eyes not on what is seen, but on what is unseen. For what is seen is temporary, but what is unseen is eternal." (2 Corinthians 4:16–18)

More on This Story in the Bible: To learn more about the apostle Paul and his life and ministry, read Acts 9:1–30; 13:1–28:31. His time in

Corinth is described in Acts 18:1–28. You can read Paul's earlier instructions to this church in 1 Corinthians.

▥ Words to Know:

reconciliation: bringing together friends after a separation because of a disagreement; through Jesus, God is reconciled to us, and we are reconciled to Him and to each other.

"tent": a word Paul used to refer to the earthly, physical bodies that temporarily house our eternal spirits.

"jars of clay": a phrase Paul used to refer to our weak, imperfect, all-too-human selves, through which God's power and glory are mightily displayed.

persecuted: treated cruelly or unfairly because of one's ideas or beliefs.

▥ Did You Know?

Some of Paul's letters to the Corinthians are missing! The one we call 1 Corinthians refers to an earlier letter that we have no record of (see 1 Corinthians 5:9). And then there is the severe letter, the rebuke Paul refers to in 2 Corinthians that prompted the church to repent. Some scholars think that 2 Corinthians 10–13 *is* actually the severe letter, that these four chapters originally stood on their own, but years later were incorporated into the letter we have now. (They note that the tone of these chapters is different from the rest.) Other scholars believe that the reason Paul suddenly goes back into "correction mode" is that while he was writing the letter, he received reports of further problems he wanted to address.

▥ Making the Connection:

There are times many of us feel like failures in our relationship with Christ. Perhaps there's a particular area of our lives where it seems that victory escapes us. We struggle and struggle to overcome that temptation or face that fear, but we keep falling on our faces. We've begged God to help us, but for some reason He has yet to deliver us. We wonder if we're doomed to lose this battle again and again. In 2 Corinthians 12:7–8, the apostle Paul talks about wrestling with a "thorn in his flesh." He says: "Three times I pleaded with the Lord about this, that it should leave me. But He said to me, 'My grace is sufficient for you, for my power is made perfect in weakness.'" Paul goes on to say, "Therefore I will boast all the more gladly of my weaknesses, so that the power of Christ may rest upon me. For the sake of Christ, then, I am content with weaknesses, insults, hardships, persecutions, and calamities. For when I am weak, then I am strong." Though we don't always understand the whys and wherefores, the Scripture promises us that God can and will use all of these things for His glory. Our struggles humble us and keep us daily on our knees. Our very human weakness is an opportunity for God's power to work in us and through us. So don't give up. Learn to rest in His mercy and grace. For when you're weak, He is strong.

GALATIANS

The Book: Galatians

The Author: The apostle Paul

The Audience: The churches in Galatia

The Setting: Written from Asia Minor, between AD 49 and 57

The Story: Paul wrote this letter to Jewish Christians in Galatia. Teachers had come after Paul, insisting that non-Jewish believers had to first convert to Judaism, submit to being circumcised, and follow the Law of Moses in order to become Christians and experience salvation. Paul vehemently denounced this teaching as false doctrine. In his most strongly-worded letter, he insisted that believers are saved only by God's grace, not by strict adherence to outdated rules and regulations.

The Message: After a few brief words of greeting, Paul immediately confronts the Galatians with the concern that has prompted his letter: "I am astonished that you are so quickly deserting the one who called you by the grace of Christ and are turning to a different gospel—which is really no gospel at all. Evidently some people are throwing you into confusion and are trying to pervert the gospel of Christ" (1: 6–7). Paul declares: "I want you to know, brothers, that the gospel I preached is not something that man made up" (1:11). He shares his personal testimony—how he received the gospel not from the preaching of the other apostles, but from Jesus Himself in a divine encounter on the road to Damascus (1:12–24).

Many years later, Paul met with the leaders of the church in Jerusalem—Peter, James, and John. Considering the evidence in Scripture and their own experience, they came to the conclusion that God clearly intended to save Gentiles, as well as Jews. Since salvation came through faith in Christ alone, there was no need for the Gentiles to observe the Law—though many Jewish Christians continued to do so, as a part of their culture. Paul wasn't afraid to confront the other apostles when he saw them sliding into hypocrisy, living one way in front of Jewish believers and another way with Gentiles (2:1–14). "We who are Jews by birth and not 'Gentile sinners' know that a man is not justified by observing the law, but by faith in Jesus Christ . . ." (2:15–16).

As further evidence of this truth, Paul points to Abraham, the one with whom God first established His covenant. Abraham couldn't follow the Law—he lived before its time! "He believed God, and it was credited to him as righteousness" (3:6). Again, Paul reminds the Galatians that no one can perfectly follow the Law, and that this was the whole point all along. The Law was given to show us how sinful we are—how unable we are to keep God's commandments and live up to His standards. The Law helps us understand our need for a Savior (3:10–25).

Paul goes back again to the story of Abraham to show that this has always been God's plan. Abraham's son Ishmael was born to the slave girl, Hagar, to represent the old covenant—and our slavery to the Law that could not save us. Abraham's son, Isaac, was born to his wife, Sarah. Isaac was the "child of the promise"—representing the new covenant, which is built on faith in Jesus, God's Son (4:21–31).

Paul warns the Galatians not to go back to trying to earn their salvation through careful observance of the Law. "It is for freedom that Christ has set us free. Stand firm, then, and do not let yourselves be burdened again by a yoke of slavery" (5:1). He concludes by challenging the Galatians to "live by the Spirit," not the Law. Of course, this does not mean casting off all moral restraint. If anything, believers are called to an even higher standard (5:16–6:6). Paul adds, "Do not be deceived: God cannot be mocked. A man reaps what he sows. The one who sows to please his sinful nature, from that nature will reap destruction; the one who sows to please the Spirit, from the Spirit will reap eternal life. Let us not become weary in doing good, for at the proper time we will reap a harvest if we do not give up" (6:7–9).

Key Verse or Passage

"The law was put in charge to lead us to Christ that we might be justified by faith. Now that faith has come, we are no longer under the supervision of the law." (Galatians 3:24–25)

More on This Story in the Bible: Paul uses several examples and illustrations from the life of Abraham, whose story is found in Genesis 12–22. To learn more about how Paul went from persecutor to preacher, see Acts 9. Paul's visit to the Roman province of Galatia is described in Acts 13–14; 16:6; and 18:23. Also Acts 15 includes an account of the church council Paul refers to, the meeting in which the circumcision of non-Jewish believers was discussed by the apostles. And just as he does in Galatians, Paul makes many of the same points about Christian freedom in his letter to the Romans.

Words to Know:

zealous: enthusiastic, eager.

persecute: to treat people cruelly or unfairly because of their ideas or beliefs.

revelation: something secret or hidden that is suddenly made known.

hypocrisy: doing one thing and saying another; pretending to be something you are not.

justified: made right.

Making the Connection: In John 15:16, Jesus told His disciples, "I chose you and appointed you to go and bear fruit—fruit that will last."

Fruit is the product of something, the result. In this case, it's the natural—or rather supernatural—evidence of God's Spirit working in us. In Galatians 5:22–23, Paul tells us what this looks like: "The fruit of the Spirit is love, joy, peace, patience, kindness, goodness, faithfulness, gentleness and self-control. . . ." We know we are "walking in the Spirit" when we see this fruit growing in our hearts and lives. If the fruit is missing, then something isn't right. We've got to do whatever it takes to reconnect with Jesus, the true Vine (John 15:1).

EPHESIANS

▪ **The Book:** Ephesians

▪ **The Author:** The apostle Paul

▪ **The Audience:** The church in Ephesus

▪ **The Setting:** Written from prison in Rome, AD 60

▪ **The Story:** Unlike most of the other letters in the New Testament, Ephesians wasn't written to combat error or expose false teachings or to clear up problems in the local church. Paul wrote simply to encourage the believers in Ephesus and teach them more about what it means to live as disciples of Jesus Christ.

▪ **The Message:** Paul begins his letter with a celebration of God's glorious plan of salvation, a plan established long before the beginning of time and accomplished through Christ's death on the cross. "In him we have redemption through his blood, the forgiveness of sins, in accordance with the riches of God's grace" (1:7). Paul says he thanks God for the Ephesians and prays for them often, that they will continue to grow and mature in their faith: "I keep asking that the God of our Lord Jesus Christ, the glorious Father, may give you the Spirit of wisdom and revelation, so that you may know him better" (1:17).

Paul goes on to speak of the unity that Jewish and Gentile believers now experience, a unity made possible because of what Jesus has done. "For he himself is our peace, who has made the two one and has destroyed the barrier, the dividing wall of hostility" (2:14). Then Paul stops to offer a beautiful prayer on behalf of the Ephesians, asking God to bless them and strengthen them. "And I pray that you, being rooted and established in love, may have power, together with all the saints, to grasp how wide and long and high and deep is the love of Christ" (3:17–18).

The apostle again encourages the Ephesians to live in unity with one another, recognizing that God has given them different gifts and callings so that they can help each other and build each other up (4:1–13). He reminds them that as they grow in their faith, they need to leave their sinful ways behind them—the wicked things they used to do when they lived in "darkness." Now they must learn to live as "children of the light" (4:14–32). He urges them to be kind and compassionate and forgiving of one another. "Do not let the sun go down while you are still angry" (4:26).

Paul warns the Ephesians explicitly about the kind of behavior that is inappropriate for believers and unacceptable to God (5:3–4). He wants them to set a good example as they witness to the world around them: "Be very careful, then, how you live—not as unwise but as wise, making the most of every opportunity, because the days are evil" (5:15–16). And as they minister to each other, they should "speak to one another with psalms, hymns and spiritual songs. Sing and make music in your heart to the Lord, always giving thanks to God the Father for everything, in the name of our Lord Jesus Christ" (5:19–20).

Paul gives some instruction on family relationships—particularly speaking to husbands and wives: "Submit to one another out of reverence for Christ" (5:21). He explains that the marriage relationship is meant to mirror a "profound mystery," to be a flesh-and-blood illustration of a spiritual reality, a reflection of the love between Christ and His bride, the church (5:22–33).

Paul closes by reminding the Ephesians of the spiritual battle that rages all around them. He urges them to stay alert and stand firm against the enemy of their souls (6:10–18). And he asks them to remember him in their prayers, "that whenever I open my mouth, words may be given me so that I will fearlessly make known the mystery of the gospel" (6:19).

Key Verse or Passage

"Be imitators of God, therefore, as dearly loved children and live a life of love, just as Christ loved us and gave himself up for us as a fragrant offering and sacrifice to God." (Ephesians 5:1–2)

More on This Story in the Bible: Paul spent almost three years in or around Ephesus. For more on his experiences there, see Acts 19 and 20:17–38. To learn what led to Paul's imprisonment at the time he wrote this letter, see the account of his arrest and trial in Acts 21–27 and his arrival in Rome in Acts 28:14–31. Other "prison letters" written at the same time include Philippians, Colossians, and Philemon.

Words to Know:

predestined: something that has been decided or determined (by God) in advance.

transgressions: sins or offenses committed in violation of the law.

revelation: something secret or hidden that is suddenly made known.

submit: to choose to obey someone or something.

Did You Know? The Bible tells us that there is a battle raging all around us—a spiritual battle between good and evil, between the armies of God and the forces of darkness (Ephesians 6:12). And whether we realize it or not, each one of us plays an important part.

We face a brutal opponent—the enemy of our souls—and he is determined to destroy us. But we're not defenseless against Satan's attacks. We have been given what Paul calls the "armor of God" to help us win the battle: "Be strong in the Lord and in his mighty power. Put on the full armor of God, so that you can take your stand against the devil's schemes" (6:10–11). That armor includes the "belt" of truth, the "breastplate" of righteousness, the "shoes" of readiness, the "helmet" of salvation, the "shield" of faith, and the "sword of the Spirit"—the Word of God (6:14–17). When we put on this armor, we will be able to stand firm against the enemy, fight the good fight, and experience victory through God's grace.

PHILIPPIANS

The Book: Philippians

The Author: The apostle Paul

The Audience: The church in Philippi

The Setting: Written from prison in Rome, AD 61

The Story: Paul wrote to the Christians in Philippi to thank them for their gift and to report on the progress of his ministry—a ministry he continued even under house arrest. Paul also wanted to encourage the Philippians to find joy and peace and contentment through their faith in Christ, no matter what their circumstances.

The Message: Paul can't thank the Philippians enough for their faithful friendship. He is thrilled to hear how they have grown in their faith and is confident that their progress will continue: "He who began a good work in you will carry it on to completion until the day of Christ Jesus" (1:6). Though Paul now finds himself in chains for the sake of the gospel, he knows his ministry goes on. Honestly, he doesn't know whether to hope that his imprisonment ends in his eventual release—or his execution! "I am torn between the two: I desire to depart and be with Christ, which is better by far; but it is more necessary for you that I remain in the body" (1:23–24). So as long as he has life and breath, he will do the work God has given him to do.

Paul encourages the Philippians to follow the example of Jesus—to imitate His gentleness, His humility, and His servant's heart. Paul notes that God has given Jesus "the name above all names." One day, every knee will bow and every tongue confess that Jesus is Lord (2:9–11).

Paul tells the Philippian believers not to argue or complain, but to set a good example by "shining like stars" in a dark world (2:12–16). He again reminds them that spiritual growth and maturity is a journey, a process. In fact, he himself is still a work in progress. "But this one thing I do: Forgetting what is behind and straining toward what is ahead, I press on toward the goal to win the prize for which God has called me heavenward in Christ Jesus" (3:13–14). He tells the believers to follow his example, too. He urges them to "rejoice in the Lord always"—no matter what challenges they face (4:4).

"Do not be anxious about anything, but in everything, by prayer and petition, with thanksgiving, present your requests to God. And the peace of God, which transcends all understanding, will guard your hearts and your minds in Christ Jesus" (4:6–7). Paul adds, "Whatever is true, whatever is noble, whatever is right, whatever is pure, whatever is lovely, whatever is admirable—if anything is excellent or praiseworthy—think about such things" (4:8).

Paul again thanks the Philippians for their love and support and tells them they will be blessed for their faithfulness: "My God will meet all your needs according to his glorious riches in Christ Jesus" (4:19).

Key Verse or Passage

"I want to know Christ and the power of his resurrection and the fellowship of sharing in his sufferings, becoming like him in his death, and so, somehow, to attain to the resurrection from the dead." (Philippians 3:10–11)

More on This Story in the Bible: To learn more about Paul's first visit to Philippi, read Acts 16:12–40. For more on what led to Paul's imprisonment at the time he wrote this letter, see the account of his arrest and trial in Acts 21–27 and his arrival in Rome in Acts 28:14–31. Other "prison letters" written at the same time include Ephesians, Colossians, and Philemon.

Words to Know:

contending: competing, arguing, fighting for, or defending.

humility: being humble and modest, not proud or full of oneself.

"mutilators of the flesh": false teachers who insisted that circumcision (a symbolic rite God required of His people under the old covenant) was still necessary for salvation.

content: happy and satisfied, having enough.

■ **Think about It:** "I can do everything through him who gives me strength" (Philippians 4:13) is a favorite verse of many Christians. For some, this verse has almost become a "mantra"—an affirmation—to be repeated over and over in order to achieve the kind of positive mental attitude that will guarantee success . . . in sports, in school, in business, and in life. The thought is that whatever it is we want to accomplish or achieve—if we believe—Jesus will give us the strength we need to make it happen.

But when we read the verse in context, we learn that's not really what Paul is talking about. He's speaking of finding peace and contentment, no matter what our circumstances. Paul had experienced moments of triumph and victory; he had seen thousands of people trust in Christ as a direct result of his ministry. He had been admired and respected by the community. He had been well-to-do. He'd also been despised and rejected, tortured and imprisoned for his faith. He had been poverty-stricken and destitute. So he could say with authority: "I have learned the secret of being content in any and every situation, whether well fed or hungry, whether living in plenty or in want. I can do everything through him who gives me strength" (4:12–13).

In Philippians 4:13, Paul says that whether we win or lose, whether we achieve success or experience failure, in good times and in bad, Jesus gives us the strength to be content, to trust Him, and to rest in the love He has for us.

COLOSSIANS

■ **The Book:** Colossians

■ **The Author:** The apostle Paul

■ **The Audience:** The church in Colossae

■ **The Setting:** Written from prison in Rome, AD 60

■ **The Story:** The Colossian believers were confused by false teachings they had received. Paul wrote to correct their misunderstandings, clear up the misinformation, refute the false doctrine, and instruct the church in the true teachings of the faith.

■ **The Message:** Paul thanks God for the believers in Colossae; he thinks of them and prays for them often (1:1–12). He wants them to fully understand what a privilege it is to be counted among the people of God. "For he has rescued us from the dominion of darkness and brought us into the kingdom of the Son he loves, in whom we have redemption, the forgiveness of sins" (1:13–14).

To those who have heard that Jesus is somehow less than God or not as important and powerful as the angels, Paul says: Jesus is everything! "For by him all things were created: things in heaven and on earth, visible and invisible, whether thrones or powers or rulers or authorities; all things were created by him and for him . . . in him all things hold together" (1:16–17). And He is the one through whom salvation comes.

Paul urges the Colossians not to be deceived by worldly wisdom— caught up by "hollow and deceptive philosophy" (2:8). Furthermore, believers are no longer bound to all the rules and regulations of the Law of Moses (such as the circumcision of the flesh) because Jesus has "canceled the written code . . . he took it away, nailing it to the cross" (2:14). These requirements were meant to be symbolic—"a shadow of the things that were to come; the reality is, however, found in Christ" (2:17).

Paul devotes the rest of his letter to providing the Colossians with some new "rules"—or guidelines—for living a life that pleases God: "Therefore, as God's chosen people, holy and dearly loved, clothe yourselves with compassion, kindness, humility, gentleness and patience. . . . Let the word of Christ dwell in you richly as you teach and admonish one another with all wisdom, and as you sing psalms, hymns and spiritual songs with gratitude in your hearts to God. And whatever you do, whether in word or deed, do it all in the name of the Lord Jesus, giving thanks to God the Father through him" (3:12, 16–17).

Key Verse or Passage

"So then, just as you received Christ Jesus as Lord, continue to live in him, rooted and built up in him, strengthened in the faith as you were taught, and overflowing with thankfulness. See to it that no one takes you captive through

hollow and deceptive philosophy, which depends on human tradition and the basic principles of this world rather than on Christ." (Colossians 2:6–8)

More on This Story in the Bible: Colossians is often referred to as one of the four "prison letters"—letters Paul wrote when he was under house arrest in Rome. (The others are Ephesians, Philippians, and Philemon.) Paul's imprisonment is described in Acts 28:16–31.

Words to Know:

supremacy: being the most powerful, the greatest, the best.

reconciled: brought back together as friends after a separation because of a disagreement.

admonish: to warn or advise someone about his or her faults.

humility: being humble and modest, not proud or full of oneself.

submit: to agree to obey someone or something.

Think about It: In his letter to the Colossians, Paul gives some important instructions to families. For instance, he says: "Children, obey your parents in everything, for this pleases the Lord" (3:20, ESV). It's vitally important for children to learn to respect and obey their earthly father and mother, because this teaches them how to respect and obey their heavenly Father, God.

But parents have responsibilities, too. Paul tells parents not to aggravate—some translations say "irritate" or "provoke"—their children (3:21). Parents provoke their children when they aren't clear about the rules and their consequences, when they make decisions that aren't fair, or when they wield their power and authority like a sledgehammer.

As a family, we are supposed to encourage one another, support one another, and strengthen one another. God has called us to live together in peace, in unity, and in love (3:14).

1 THESSALONIANS

The Book: 1 Thessalonians

The Author: The apostle Paul

The Audience: The church in Thessalonica

The Setting: Written from Corinth, AD 51

The Story: During his missionary journeys, Paul wasn't able to spend as much time at the church in Thessalonica as he would have liked. So after he left, he wrote a letter to the new believers there to teach them more about living to please God and to prepare them for the second coming of Christ.

The Message: Paul begins by thanking God for the Thessalonians' faith. He recalls how they first received the good news of the gospel so eagerly and how in their faith they have become role models for other believers (1:1–10). Paul reminds the Thessalonians that when he first came to them, he had no hidden agenda; his motives were pure. In spite of great opposition from unbelievers in neighboring communities, he and his companions continued to preach the gospel because they were "not trying to please men but God, who tests our hearts" (2:4). In spite of the persecution they faced, the apostles were happy to have the opportunity to live and work among the Thessalonians. "We loved you so much that we were delighted to share with you not only the gospel of God but our lives as well, because you had become so dear to us" (2:8).

Paul says he knows that the Thessalonian believers have since suffered for their faith in Christ (2:14–16). Timothy—whom Paul sent to strengthen and encourage them—has brought back a good report: they are standing firm. Paul is very pleased, and he prays that God will continue to bless them: "May he strengthen your hearts so that you will be blameless and holy in the presence of our God and Father when our Lord Jesus comes with all his holy ones" (3:13).

Until Paul can come and visit them again, he has a few words of instruction for the church. He reminds them of how important it is to live in a way that pleases God (4:1–12). He emphasizes the need for discipline and self-control (4:3–7; 5:7–8). Paul also addresses a question the Thessalonians have asked. They are eagerly awaiting the second coming of Christ. But what happens to believers who die before Jesus returns? Paul says that they will be raised from the dead just as Jesus was (He'll bring them back with Him when He comes), and the "dead in Christ" will join the living in heaven for all eternity (4:16–17).

Paul ends his letter by sharing a few more specific instructions about living the Christian life, encouraging the Thessalonians to continue to grow in Christian maturity while they wait for Jesus to return (5:12–24).

Key Verse or Passage

"Be joyful always; pray continually; give thanks in all circumstances, for this is God's will for you in Christ Jesus." (1 Thessalonians 5:16–18)

More on This Story in the Bible: To learn more about the founding of the church in Thessalonica—and Paul's experience there—read Acts 17:1–9 and 2 Thessalonians.

Words to Know:

endurance: the ability to put up with something or to last for a long time.

conviction: a strong belief in something.

opposition: people who are against someone or something.

ambition: something you strongly want to do.

"asleep": Jesus and His disciples often used the word "sleep" or "asleep" to mean death, because, thanks to Jesus, death is no longer something to fear. Everyone who trusts in Him and "falls asleep" will "awaken" to eternal life.

Did You Know? In his first letter to the Thessalonians, Paul writes that "the voice of the archangel" will signal the second coming of Christ (1 Thessalonians 4:16–17). Although there are religious traditions that identify as many as seven archangels, the Bible names only one—Michael

(Daniel 10:1–21; 12:1; and Jude 1:9). Michael is the warrior angel who watches over Israel.

Although the Scriptures tell us there are "hosts"—literally thousands and thousands—of angels in heaven, the only other one that we know by name is Gabriel, the messenger who appears in Daniel 8:16; 9:21; Luke 1:19; and 1:26.

Both angels' names are expressions of praise. In the Hebrew language, "el" is the word for "God." Michael's name means, "Who is like God?" and Gabriel's name means, "God is great!"

2 THESSALONIANS

The Book: 2 Thessalonians

The Author: The apostle Paul

The Audience: The church in Thessalonica

The Setting: Written from Corinth, AD 50–54

The Story: A few months after writing his first letter to the church at Thessalonica, Paul wrote another letter to encourage the believers facing persecution, to clear up a misunderstanding about the return of Christ, and to remind them to hold on to the truths they had been taught.

The Message: As in his first letter to the Thessalonians, Paul begins by telling the believers how proud he is of them. He thanks God "because your faith is growing more and more, and the love every one of you has for each other is increasing. Therefore, among God's churches we boast about your perseverance and faith in all the persecutions and trials you are enduring" (1:3–4). Paul promises that one day their suffering will come to an end: "God is just: He will pay back trouble to those who trouble you and give relief to you who are troubled, and to us as well . . ." (1:6–7).

The Thessalonians again have questions about the second coming of Christ. They've been hearing reports that Jesus has already come—and that they've somehow missed Him! But Paul tells the church not to be unsettled or alarmed or deceived by these reports. Jesus has not yet returned (2:1–2). There are still many things that have to happen first, including the coming of the "man of lawlessness"—the Antichrist. "He will oppose and will exalt himself over everything that is called God or is worshiped, so that he sets himself up in God's temple, proclaiming himself to be God" (2:4). Many people will fall for his counterfeit miracles, signs, and wonders. But ultimately, Paul says, this man will be overthrown by the Lord Jesus Himself (2:5–12).

"So then, brothers, stand firm and hold to the teachings we passed on to you, whether by word of mouth or by letter" (2:15). Paul asks the Thessalonians to pray for him and his ministry, just as he prays for them (3:1–5). He warns those in the church who have stopped working—and are now sitting around waiting for Jesus to return—to follow the example the apostles set for them: "We were not idle when we were with you. . . . On the contrary, we worked night and day, laboring and toiling so that we would not be a burden to any of you" (3:7–8). The "idle" believers in Thessalonica need to settle down and earn the bread they eat (3:13).

Paul concludes by sending his blessings and praying that the Thessalonians will experience God's peace. "The Lord be with all of you" (3:16).

Key Verse or Passage

"May our Lord Jesus Christ himself and God our Father, who loved us and by his grace gave us eternal encouragement and good hope, encourage your hearts and strengthen you in every good deed and word." (2 Thessalonians 2:16–17)

More on This Story in the Bible: To learn more about the founding of the church in Thessalonica—and Paul's experience there—read Acts 17:1–9 and 1 Thessalonians.

Words to Know:

persecution: cruel and unfair treatment because of one's ideas or beliefs.

"**counterfeit miracles**": miracles that encourage trust in the wrong people or things.

delusion: a false idea or hallucination.

idle: not active, not working.

▦ **Did You Know?** The Thessalonians wanted to know how they could be sure that the letter they received actually came from the apostle Paul. After all, there were some "fakes" going around (2:1–2). Paul usually dictated his letters to a secretary or assistant and then added a personal note himself at the very end. He points this out at the close of his second letter to the church at Thessalonica, when he says: "I, Paul, write this greeting in my own hand, which is the distinguishing mark in all my letters. This is how I write."

Whenever the Thessalonians saw his signature, they would know that the letter they were reading was the real deal.

1 TIMOTHY

▦ **The Book:** 1 Timothy

▦ **The Author:** The apostle Paul

▦ **The Audience:** Timothy

▦ **The Setting:** Written from Rome, AD 64

▦ **The Story:** Timothy was a young man Paul led to faith in Jesus. He often traveled with Paul as his assistant; a gifted preacher, he became an important part of Paul's ministry team. When Paul heard that the church in Ephesus was having trouble, he sent Timothy ahead of him to straighten things out. Later, Paul wrote Timothy a letter to warn him about the danger of false teachers infiltrating the church and to give the young pastor some instruction on what to preach and teach to various groups.

▦ **The Message:** Paul begins by reminding Timothy that as a pastor, he has the responsibility to protect the church from false teachers and to warn those who get caught up in myths and genealogies and controversies.

"They want to be teachers of the law, but they do not know what they are talking about or what they so confidently affirm" (1:6–7).

Paul explains why he is writing: "Timothy, my son, I give you this instruction in keeping with the prophecies once made about you, so that by following them you may fight the good fight, holding on to faith and a good conscience . . ." (1:18–19). Sadly, others have fallen away from the faith, and he doesn't want Timothy to do the same.

The apostle gives some practical instruction on worship and prayer (2:1–14). He advises Timothy on how to choose "overseers" or "deacons" to share the responsibility of leading the church. Paul says there are some very specific qualifications these leaders must meet, as they are to set an example for the rest of the church (3:1–13).

"The Spirit clearly says that in later times some will abandon the faith and follow deceiving spirits and things taught by demons" (4:1). Paul urges Timothy to stay on guard and not be drawn into their deception: "Have nothing to do with godless myths and old wives' tales; rather, train yourself to be godly. For physical training is of some value, but godliness has value for all things, holding promise for both the present life and the life to come" (4:7–8).

Part of Timothy's duties as pastor include making sure that the church cares for the elderly and the destitute. Paul has some advice on how to distinguish between those who are really in need and those who are taking advantage (5:1–16). Paul also talks about the importance of learning to be content with what we have, rather than chasing after riches, which can be a trap: "For the love of money is a root of all kinds of evil" (6:10).

Paul concludes by challenging Timothy: "But you, man of God, flee from all this, and pursue righteousness, godliness, faith, love, endurance and gentleness. Fight the good fight of the faith. Take hold of the eternal life to which you were called . . ." (6:11–12). He hopes to see him soon.

Key Verse or Passage

"Don't let anyone look down on you because you are young, but set an example for the believers in speech, in life, in love, in faith and in purity. Until I come,

devote yourself to the public reading of Scripture, to preaching and to teaching. Do not neglect your gift, which was given you. . . ." (1 Timothy 4:12–14)

▨ **More on This Story in the Bible:** Learn how Paul met Timothy and how they began working together in ministry by reading Acts 16:1–5; 17:13–15; 18:5; and 20:4. Timothy is also mentioned in Romans 16:21; 1 Corinthians 4:17; 16:10; 2 Corinthians 1:19; Philippians 1:1; 2:19, 22; 1 Thessalonians 1:1; 3:2, 5–6; 1 Thessalonians 1:1; Philemon 1:1; and Hebrews 13:23. To read another letter Paul wrote to the young pastor, see 2 Timothy.

▨ **Words to Know:**

conscience: an understanding of right and wrong that guides a person's actions.

intercession: pleading on behalf of someone else; praying to God for someone else.

mediator: an intercessor, a go-between; someone who connects two parties or individuals or groups.

ransom: the price that must be paid before a captive is set free.

propriety: concern for what is proper, appropriate.

temperate: moderate, controlled, restrained.

consecrated: set apart or dedicated to the service of God.

diligent: working hard and carefully.

▨ **Did You Know?** The apostle Paul was far from perfect, and he knew it. "Christ Jesus came into the world to save sinners—of whom I am the worst" (1 Timothy 1:15). He particularly regretted the dark days of his past, when (as an unbeliever) he had cruelly persecuted other Christians for their faith. But Paul saw that God could use his past to demonstrate the power of His saving grace. "Even though I was once a blasphemer and a persecutor and a violent man . . . I was shown mercy so that in me, the worst of sinners, Christ Jesus might display his unlimited patience as an example for those who would believe on him and receive eternal life" (1:13, 16). After all, if God could save Paul, He could save anyone! And that was a message Paul was happy to preach.

Think about It: In his instructions on worship, Paul writes, "A woman should learn in quietness and full submission. I do not permit a woman to teach or to have authority over a man; she must be silent" (2:11–12). Unfortunately, this verse has often been taken out of context—creating all kinds of controversy, leading to some serious misunderstandings.

It's true that God has given men and women different roles in the family, in society, and in the body of Christ. As someone once said, "The man is the 'head' of the home; the woman is the 'heart.'" Each one is incredibly and equally important. But the buck has to stop somewhere, and the Bible says it stops with the man—the husband or father or pastor—that God has put in charge in a given family or church. It's an enormous responsibility. The Bible says that these men will be held accountable for how they watch over and provide for and protect those God has put in their care (Ephesians 5:22–33).

But it's a mistake to conclude from this that the Bible teaches that women are somehow second-class citizens. On the contrary! As Paul himself pointed out, both men and women are created in the image of God and have equal standing before Him (Galatians 3:26–29). In both the Old Testament and the New Testament, women were prophets and judges and queens. Jesus Himself unfailingly treated women with compassion, kindness, and respect. They were among His most faithful disciples. Women stayed with Him to the bitter end; they alone stood at the foot of the cross. After His resurrection, Jesus appeared to them first. Clearly, women were involved in leadership of the early church. They are featured prominently in the book of Acts and mentioned repeatedly in most of the letters written by Paul and the other disciples. Mature Christian women were in fact *urged* to teach and train and mentor other women (Titus 2:3–5).

So what could Paul have meant in this passage? Reputable Bible scholars suggest that at a time and in a culture where women's rights were severely restricted, some women in the church were having trouble adjusting to their newfound freedom in Christ. Unlike their fathers and brothers and husbands, most of them would not have been taught the Scriptures from childhood—little girls didn't go to Hebrew school. But now they were eager to make their voices heard, even when they didn't know what they were talking about! Far from being helpful, their contribution to the worship service often ended up being disruptive and distracting. So, according to these scholars, Paul said that—generally speaking—it wasn't a good idea to have these women trying to teach and that Timothy should put a stop to it.

How does this apply us today? Men (who were even more often rebuked) *and* women who don't know the Scriptures shouldn't teach! They need to be humble and quiet and respectful of others while they grow in their understanding and learn all they can. However, both men and women who are mature in the faith are obligated to exercise their spiritual gifts and teach others in an appropriate biblical context what God has taught them, for the ultimate benefit of the body of Christ (Colossians 3:16).

2 TIMOTHY

The Book: 2 Timothy

The Author: The apostle Paul

The Audience: Timothy

The Setting: Written from prison in Rome, between AD 65 and AD 67

The Story: Once again, Paul had been imprisoned for preaching the gospel. But this time, instead of being under house arrest, he found himself chained in a cold, dark dungeon. He sensed that he was finally coming to the end of his life and ministry—he would soon be executed for his faith in Christ. Paul wrote to his "son in the faith"—Timothy—to ask him to come and visit him soon. He also wrote to give Timothy some further instruction and encouragement as the young pastor continued to care for the church at Ephesus.

The Message: Paul remembers how he first met Timothy and how Timothy came to believe in Jesus. He encourages Timothy to continue to develop the spiritual gifts God had given him and to be confident in his calling. "For God did not give us a spirit of timidity, but a spirit of power, of love and of self-discipline" (1:7). Although he himself has suffered greatly for the sake of the gospel, Paul says he is not ashamed to be known as a follower of Jesus Christ. "I know whom I have believed, and am convinced that he is able to guard what I have entrusted to him for that day" (1:12).

Because of the persecution the church is facing—and because of Paul's most recent arrest—some Christians have grown fearful. They no longer want to be associated with Paul and his ministry, so they have deserted him (1:15–18). Paul urges Timothy not to follow their example, but to remain strong and steadfast and carry on the work of the ministry (2:3). He wants Timothy to continue to study the Scriptures faithfully. "Do your best to present yourself to God as one approved, a workman who does not need to be ashamed and who correctly handles the word of truth" (2:15). Timothy should continue to honor God in his personal life, as well as his public ministry (2:22–26).

Paul says that wickedness and every kind of immorality will continue to increase in the world (3:1). That's why it's all the more important for Timothy to stay focused on the task at hand: "Preach the Word; be prepared in season and out of season; correct, rebuke and encourage—with great patience and careful instruction. For the time will come when men will not put up with sound doctrine. Instead, to suit their own desires, they will gather around them a great number of teachers to say what their itching ears want to hear. They will turn their ears away from the truth and turn aside to myths. But you, keep your head in all situations, endure hardship, do the work of an evangelist, discharge all the duties of your ministry" (4:2–3).

Paul ends by sharing with Timothy that he knows his days are numbered—his execution is imminent. But he's at peace, because he also knows that he has "fought the good fight" himself—he has done everything God has asked of him, and he is ready. "The Lord will rescue me from every evil attack and will bring me safely to his heavenly kingdom. To him be glory for ever and ever. Amen" (4:18).

Key Verse or Passage

"All Scripture is God-breathed and is useful for teaching, rebuking, correcting and training in righteousness, so that the man of God may be thoroughly equipped for every good work." (2 Timothy 3:16–17)

■ **More on This Story in the Bible:** Learn how Paul met Timothy and how they began working together in ministry by reading Acts 16:1–5; 17:13–15; 18:5; and 20:4. Timothy is also mentioned in Romans 16:21; 1 Corinthians 4:17; 16:10; 2 Corinthians 1:19; Philippians 1:1; 2:19, 22; 1 Thessalonians 1:1; 3:2, 5–6; 1 Thessalonians 1:1; Philemon 1:1; and Hebrews 13:23. To read another letter Paul wrote to the young pastor, see 1 Timothy.

■ **Words to Know:**

timidity: being shy and easily frightened.

ashamed: embarrassed.

deposit: something given as the first part of a payment—a down payment.

"sound doctrine": true, reliable teachings of the faith.

evangelist: a Christian missionary; a person who travels to share his or her faith with others.

■ **Did You Know?** There are many dramatic stories in the Bible of people who came to faith later in life—former thieves, prostitutes, murderers, adulterers, drunkards, the demon-possessed, even crooked politicians and corrupt religious leaders. And of course "ordinary people" who simply lived the kind of life a person lives when they have no particular moral code—when they don't have a faith that gives them guidelines to follow. Their stories are wonderful examples of the power of God to turn someone's world upside down, to change their hearts and lives miraculously and completely. It's something He still does today.

But Timothy had known the Scriptures "from infancy" (2 Timothy 3:15). He grew up in a household of faith, surrounded by godly influences (1:5). As a young man, he went right into a life of ministry and Christian service. Timothy's story is a wonderful example of the power of God at work in a different way—the power to get hold of a child's heart at a young age and to keep that child from ever wandering too far from the faith in the first place. It's something He still does today.

TITUS

The Book: Titus

The Author: The apostle Paul

The Audience: Titus

The Setting: Written from Rome, between AD 63 and AD 65

The Story: Titus was a Gentile (non-Jewish) Christian who traveled with Paul on his missionary journeys and assisted the apostle in his ministry. Titus hand-delivered many of Paul's other letters to the churches. This letter was written to him when he was "on assignment" in Crete. Paul had sent Titus there to straighten out some problems in the church and get things back on track.

The Message: Paul gives Titus instructions on restoring order to a disorderly congregation of believers. He reminds him of the proper qualifications of those Titus should put in positions of leadership (1:6–9) and warns him to get rid of those who are teaching false doctrine (1:10–16). Paul also offers guidance on what should be taught to various groups in the church—men, women, young people, servants or slaves—that they may lead exemplary lives that will set them apart from the unbelievers in their community (2:1–15). "At one time we too were foolish, disobedient, deceived and enslaved by all kinds of passions and pleasures. We lived in malice and envy, being hated and hating one another. But when the kindness and love of God our Savior appeared, he saved us, not because of righteous things we had done, but because of his mercy. He saved us through the washing of rebirth and renewal by the Holy Spirit, whom he poured out on us generously through Jesus Christ our Savior" (3:3–6). Things should be different, Paul says, now that we are

Christians. Our lives should reflect the change that God has brought about in our hearts.

In closing, Paul reminds Titus not to get drawn into foolish controversies and arguments that bring disunity in the church. "Warn a divisive person once, and then warn him a second time. After that, have nothing to do with him" (3:10). And once again, he urges the believers in Crete to devote themselves to doing good (3:14).

Key Verse or Passage

"For the grace of God that brings salvation has appeared to all men. It teaches us to say 'No' to ungodliness and worldly passions, and to live self-controlled, upright and godly lives in this present age, while we wait for the blessed hope—the glorious appearing of our great God and Savior, Jesus Christ." (Titus 2:11–13)

More on This Story in the Bible: Titus is mentioned in Galatians 2:1–5; 2 Corinthians 2:12–13; 7:6–7, 13–14; 8:6, 16–17; 8:23; and 2 Timothy 4:10. For a look at Paul's advice to another young pastor, see 1 and 2 Timothy.

Words to Know:

"the circumcision group": Jewish Christians who insisted that Gentiles had to be circumcised and observe Jewish law (in essence, converting to Judaism) in order to become Christians.

sound doctrine: religious teachings that are sensible, logical, reliable, true.

integrity: honest and true character.

slander: lies that damage another's reputation.

Making the Connection: In his letter to Titus, Paul gives a lot of instruction as to how Christians in different positions and walks of life should behave. He reminds them that one of the reasons they are to live a certain way is to set a good example to those around them—particularly unbelievers.

As Christians, the way we behave reflects on our faith. It says something not only about who we are, but about what we believe and who we believe in. In a very real sense, it's God's reputation that's at stake. If His children are unruly, rebellious, and out of control, it brings shame on Him (Titus 2:1, 6–15; 3:1). If His children are self-controlled, godly, upright people—"eager to do good"—they bring glory and honor to His name.

PHILEMON

■ **The Book**: Philemon

■ **The Author**: The apostle Paul

■ **The Audience**: Philemon, a Christian living in Colossae

■ **The Setting**: Written from prison in Rome, AD 60

■ **The Story**: One of Philemon's slaves, Onesimus, had stolen from him and run away. In the Roman Empire, this was a crime punishable by death. But on the run, Onesimus met the apostle Paul and became a Christian through his teachings. Now Onesimus wants to make things right. He is willing to return to his master, though he faces the possibility of harsh punishment or even death. With him, Onesimus carries a letter from Paul—who has become like a father to him and is pleading for mercy on his behalf.

■ **The Message**: Paul begins by greeting Philemon warmly, thanking God for the friend he has been in the past: "Your love has given me great joy and encouragement, because you, brother, have refreshed the hearts of the saints" (v. 7). Paul goes on to explain what has happened—how he has crossed paths with Philemon's runaway slave and how Onesimus has become a new man in Christ. Now that they are brothers in the faith, Paul urges Philemon to forgive Onesimus and show him mercy. As Philemon's former pastor and mentor—a father in the faith now to both men—Paul feels he could demand that Philemon comply. After all, Philemon owes him his very life (v. 19)! But instead, Paul says, he is asking him to forgive Onesimus as a personal favor: "I appeal to you on the basis of love . . .

welcome him as you would welcome me. If he has done you any wrong or owes you anything, charge it to me" (vv. 9, 17–18). Paul closes his letter confident that Philemon will do the right thing, and hopeful that he will be able to visit his dear friend again soon.

Key Verse or Passage

"Perhaps the reason he was separated from you for a little while was that you might have him back for good—no longer as a slave, but better than a slave, as a dear brother." (Philemon 15–16)

More on This Story in the Bible: For more of Paul's instructions how slaves or servants (employees) and their masters (employers) should relate to one another, see Ephesians 6:5–9; Colossians 3:22; 4:1; 1 Timothy 6:1–2; and Titus 2:9.

Words to Know:

appeal: to ask for something urgently.

refresh: to make someone feel fresh and new again, giving them new life and energy and strength.

spontaneous: something that happens by itself, without being forced.

Did You Know? The Bible does not specifically forbid slavery; it was a common practice in almost every culture at the time. Some slaves were prisoners of war; others sold themselves or their family members into slavery for a period of time in order to pay off debts. Scripture does forbid kidnapping and then making those kidnapped into slaves (Exodus 21:16; Deuteronomy 24:7). It also includes slave traders—those who sell other human beings without their consent—in a list of godless immoral people, such as liars, murderers, and adulterers (1 Timothy 1:9–10).

According to the Old Testament law, slaves were to be treated with dignity and respect. Provisions were made for them to earn or receive their freedom (Exodus 21:2–11; Leviticus 25:35–55; Deuteronomy 15:12–18). In the New Testament, the apostle Paul made it clear that slaves and slave owners had equal standing in the kingdom of God—as brothers and sisters in Christ (Galatians 3:28; Philemon 12–16; Ephesians 6:5–9).

HEBREWS

■ **The Book:** Hebrews

■ **The Author:** Uncertain—but probably the apostle Paul

■ **The Audience:** Hebrew (Jewish) Christians

■ **The Setting:** Between AD 60 and AD 69

■ **The Story:** A group of Jewish Christians were struggling to hold onto their faith in Jesus as the Messiah in the face of persecution from the Jewish community—their friends and neighbors, as well as the members of their own families. So great was the opposition that some of these believers were considering abandoning their Christian faith to return to their Jewish roots. The author of the book of Hebrews urges them not to turn back.

■ **The Message:** The book of Hebrews begins, "In the past God spoke to our forefathers through the prophets at many times and in various ways, but in these last days, he has spoken to us by his Son . . ." (1:1–2). The ways of the past are simply that—past! A new day has come. The writer of Hebrews insists that the old rituals and customs were only symbols, "copies" or "shadows," imperfect imitations of the real thing. So "let us hold firmly to the faith we profess" (4:14). Jesus is our "high priest" now—and we need no other, for He understands us perfectly and sympathizes with us completely. After all, He was "tempted in every way, just as we are—yet was without sin. Let us then approach the throne of grace with confidence, so that we may receive mercy and find grace to help us in our time of need" (4:15–16).

The writer of Hebrews goes on to explain how Jesus fulfilled every one of the prophecies made about Him in the Old Testament. He is the Promise kept. As the Lamb of God, Jesus was sacrificed on the cross. His blood was shed for the sins of the world. So there is no need to offer sacrifices on the altar at the temple any more. The penalty has been paid in full, once and for all (7:27). The new covenant God has established makes the old one "obsolete" (8:13). "Christ is the mediator of a new covenant, that those who are called may receive the promised eternal inheritance—now that he has died as a ransom to set them free from the sins committed under the first covenant" (9:15).

As Christians, the writer says, we must persevere in hard times, whenever we face trials and tribulations. For we're not alone. Men and women of God through the ages have always faced such persecution and opposition (as did Jesus Himself). Furthermore, God uses hard times to correct us and teach us. "No discipline seems pleasant at the time, but painful. Later on, however, it produces a harvest of righteousness and peace for those who have been trained by it" (12:11). The writer of Hebrews says the fact that God cares enough to take the time to discipline us should be a great encouragement to us. And so, we press on.

The writer of Hebrews concludes by reminding the Hebrew believers to continue to honor God in their everyday lives. "Do not forget to do good and to share with others, for with such sacrifices God is pleased" (13:16).

Key Verse or Passage

"Therefore, since we are surrounded by such a great cloud of witnesses, let us throw off everything that hinders and the sin that so easily entangles, and let us run with perseverance the race marked out for us. Let us fix our eyes on Jesus, the author and perfecter of our faith, who for the joy set before him endured the cross, scorning its shame, and sat down at the right hand of the throne of God. Consider him who endured such opposition from sinful men so that you will not grow weary and lose heart." (Hebrews 12:1–3)

More on This Story in the Bible: Hebrews is full of references to the Old Testament. It's a lesson taken from the history of God's people in centuries past. Most Bibles today include little alphabet letters at the end of certain words or phrases that will lead you to an index in a center column or at the bottom of the page. The index will give you the reference for similar verses that appear in other books of the Bible. When you study the book of Hebrews, use this feature to look up any Old Testament stories you're not familiar with. It will help you grasp the significance of the verse or chapter you're reading in the New Testament now.

Words to Know:

priest: a religious leader who conducts ceremonies and rituals; one who mediates between a people and their God.

mediator: an intercessor, a go-between; someone who connects two parties or individuals or groups.

covenant: a promise, an agreement, a legally-binding contract.

sacrifice: something that is surrendered, given up, or offered to God as an act of worship.

faith: trust, confidence, belief.

discipline: correction or training.

Making the Connection: Hebrews 11 is sometimes called the "Hall of Faith" chapter. It tells the stories of men and women of God down through the ages who put their faith in Him. It was by faith that they "conquered kingdoms, administered justice, and gained what was promised . . . shut the mouths of lions, quenched the fury of the flames, and escaped the edge of the sword." Their weakness was turned to strength; they became powerful in battle and routed foreign armies. "Women received back their dead, raised to life again. Others were tortured and refused to be released, so that they might gain a better resurrection. Some faced jeers and flogging, while still others were chained and put in prison. They were stoned; they were sawed in two; they were put to death by the sword. They went about . . . destitute, persecuted and mistreated—the world was not worthy of them . . ." (Hebrews 11:35–38).

The writer of Hebrews notes in this stirring and inspirational chapter that "all these people were still living by faith when they died. They did not receive the things promised; they only saw them and welcomed them from a distance . . ." (Hebrews 11:13). These heroes of the faith didn't get to witness the coming of Jesus, their Messiah, the Holy One of Israel. But we have. They didn't have the privilege of responding to the good news of the gospel, but we do. God "counted their faith as righteousness"—He gave them credit for believing everything He had revealed to them in their own time, and they are now in heaven—"a great cloud of witnesses"—cheering us on as we make the journey and run our own "race" of faith!

JAMES

The Book: James

The Author: James, the brother of Jesus

The Audience: Jewish Christians everywhere

The Setting: Written from Jerusalem, sometime between AD 40 and AD 60

The Story: James (the brother of Jesus) was one of the leaders of the church in Jerusalem. As the church experienced persecution, many of its new believers were scattered all across the Roman Empire. James wrote to give these young Christians some much-needed guidance and direction as they continued to grow in the faith they had been taught.

The Message: James begins with warm words of encouragement to those who are facing trials and temptations. Even in the midst of it all, there is joy to be found, "because you know that the testing of your faith develops perseverance" (1:3). He encourages believers to ask God for wisdom when they need it (1:5) and to continue resisting temptation (1:12–21).

James challenges Christians to live what they say they believe: "Do not merely listen to the word and so deceive yourselves. Do what it says" (1:22). James writes that the church should not show preference to its more wealthy or powerful members. There's no room for favoritism in the body of Christ (2:1–13). He also points out that faith and good deeds go hand in hand. Good deeds don't get us into heaven; faith does. But "faith by itself, if it is not accompanied by action, is dead" (2:17).

James uses powerful imagery from nature to explain how difficult—but necessary—it is to "tame the tongue" (3:1–12).

Believers must also learn to distinguish between worldly wisdom and the wisdom that comes from God (3:13–18). As Christians, we can't live with one foot in the world and one foot in the church—we have to choose where our hearts will call home (4:1–5). James concludes with further encouragement to the church to "be patient and stand firm, because the Lord's coming is near" (5:8).

Key Verse or Passage

"Consider it pure joy, my brothers, whenever you face trials of many kinds, because you know that the testing of your faith develops perseverance. Perseverance must finish its work so that you may be mature and complete, not lacking anything." (James 1:2–4)

More on This Story in the Bible: James is mentioned as one of Jesus' brothers and sisters in Matthew 13:55 and 6:3. You can find other references to James in Acts 12:17; 15:13; 21:18; Galatians 1:19; 2:9; and Jude 1:1.

Words to Know:

perseverance: not giving up; the courage to keep trying even in difficult circumstances.

wisdom: knowledge, experience, understanding, sound judgment.

favoritism: unfairly treating one person better than another.

submit: to agree to obey someone.

Making the Connection: A few years ago, Laura Joffe Numeroff wrote a best-selling children's book called *If You Give a Mouse a Cookie*. In the story, an adorable mouse shows up at the home of a small boy, asking for a cookie. As soon as he gets his cookie, the mouse has another request: he'd like a glass of milk. Then he needs a straw, and then a napkin . . . and on and on it goes. By the end of the book, this cute little critter has completely taken over the house. His young host has spent the entire day accommodating the mouse's ever-growing list of demands—and cleaning up after the mess that results. The moral of the story is clear: If you give a mouse a cookie, you'll get more than you ever bargained for!

James says the power of sin works the same way. At one time or another, we've all had an "unexpected visitor" show up at our door. We've all been tempted to make room in our hearts for a "little" sin. Nothing major, of course. No big deal. At first, its demands are few. But the longer we entertain that "little" sin, the bigger—and more demanding—it grows. Before we know it, it's taken over our lives in ways we never dreamed of. "Each one is tempted when, by his own evil desire, he is dragged away and enticed. Then, after desire has conceived, it gives birth to sin; and sin, when it is full-grown, gives birth to death" (James 1:14–15).

James reminds us that as Christians, we already have a heavenly House Guest who has made our hearts His home. We can't afford to make room for anything that will keep us from loving and serving Him.

1 PETER

The Book: 1 Peter

The Author: The apostle Peter

The Audience: Christian believers everywhere

The Setting: Written from Rome, between AD 64 and AD 65

The Story: The first Christians often faced tremendous persecution. They were disowned by their families and driven from their homes and communities. Some were beaten and thrown into prison. Others were executed for their faith. The apostle Peter (who himself would die a martyr's death) wrote a letter encouraging believers to persevere in hardship and suffering and to continue to live their lives in a way that pleased God.

The Message: Peter begins by encouraging the believers to rejoice in their trials and the hardships that they face: "These have come so that your faith—of greater worth than gold, which perishes even though refined by fire—may be proved genuine and may result in praise, glory and honor when Jesus Christ is revealed. Though you have not seen him, you love him; and even though you do not see him now, you believe in him and are filled with an inexpressible and glorious joy, for you are receiving the goal of your faith, the salvation of your souls" (1:7–9).

Peter reminds these new Christians that they have been called to live different kinds of lives than the ones they lived as unbelievers. "Be holy in all you do" (1:15). They are God's chosen people now and should set a good example for others. "Live as free men, but do not use your freedom as a cover-up for evil; live as servants of God. Show proper respect to everyone: Love the brotherhood of believers, fear God, honor the king" (2:16–17). Peter goes on to give advice to husbands and wives on how they should relate to each other in Christ (3:1–7). And he tells believers not to be surprised when they suffer for doing good—after all, Jesus did (4:12–14). Of course, Peter points out, there is a difference between suffering for your faith (being persecuted) and suffering for your sin—living with the consequences of your own foolishness (2:19–20; 3:13–17).

Peter concludes, "Be self-controlled and alert. Your enemy the devil prowls around like a roaring lion looking for someone to devour. Resist him, standing firm in the faith, because you know that your brothers throughout the world are undergoing the same kind of sufferings. And the God of all grace, who called you to his eternal glory in Christ, after you have suffered a little while, will himself restore you and make you strong, firm and steadfast" (5:8–10).

Key Verse or Passage

"But you are a chosen people, a royal priesthood, a holy nation, a people belonging to God, that you may declare the praises of him who called you out of darkness into his wonderful light." (1 Peter 2:9)

More on This Story in the Bible: Learn more about Peter—how he first became a disciple of Jesus and how he participated in Jesus' earthly ministry—by reading accounts in any of the four Gospels (Matthew, Mark, Luke, and John) and in Acts chapters 2–5 and 10–12. You can read more of Peter's writings in 2 Peter.

Words to Know:

refined: purified.

holy: perfect, pure, set apart for (and by) God.

imperishable: something that cannot perish, but will live forever.

submissive: obedient.

Think about It: Peter points out that when Christians face hardship and persecution—and even tragedy—it can actually be a wonderful opportunity to set a good example and be a witness to the power of God to touch hearts and change lives: "But in your hearts set apart Christ as Lord. Always be prepared to give an answer to everyone who asks you to give the reason for the hope that you have. But do this with gentleness and respect, keeping a clear conscience, so that those who speak maliciously against your good behavior in Christ may be ashamed of their slander" (3:15–16).

The right word, spoken at the right time, in the right way can have an enormous impact on our world.

2 PETER

The Book: 2 Peter

The Author: The apostle Peter

The Audience: Christian believers everywhere

The Setting: Written from Rome, between AD 65 and AD 68

The Story: In his first letter, Peter wrote to encourage Christians who were facing persecution. In his second letter he wanted to warn believers about the dangers of false teachers and to encourage the church to hold on to its faith, while it waited eagerly for the second coming of Christ.

The Message: Peter begins by urging the believers to grow in faith, goodness, knowledge, self-control, perseverance, godliness, brotherly kindness, and love. "For if you possess these qualities in increasing measure, they will keep you from being ineffective and unproductive in your knowledge of our Lord Jesus Christ" (1:8). Peter says he knows that they are firmly established in their faith, but still, it doesn't hurt to repeat a few instructions—especially since God has shown him that he's going to die soon (he'll be executed for his faith). He wants to teach the church everything he can while he still has the opportunity (1:12–15).

"We did not follow cleverly invented stories when we told you about the power and coming of our Lord Jesus Christ, but we were eyewitnesses of his majesty" (1:16). Peter reminds believers that in addition to the testimony of the disciples, they also have the Scriptures to guide them—the "word of the prophets," men who spoke from God as He directed them (1:19–21).

Just as there are true disciples and true prophets, there are false disciples and false prophets. Peter says God will deal with them: "The Lord knows how to rescue godly men from trials and to hold the unrighteous for the day of judgment, while continuing their punishment. . . . They will be paid back with harm for the harm they have done . . ." (2:9, 13).

In the meantime, believers must be on guard and hold fast to the truth, looking forward to the "day of the Lord" when Jesus will return to make all things new (3:1–13).

Key Verse or Passage

"The Lord is not slow in keeping his promise, as some understand slowness. He is patient with you, not wanting anyone to perish, but everyone to come to repentance." (2 Peter 3:9)

More on This Story in the Bible: Learn more about Peter—how he first became a disciple of Jesus and how he participated in Jesus' earthly ministry—by reading the accounts in any of the four Gospels (Matthew, Mark, Luke, and John) and in Acts chapters 2–5 and 10–12. You can read more of Peter's writings in 1 Peter.

Words to Know:

godliness: goodness; being like God in one's character and integrity.

disrepute: having a bad reputation.

blaspheme: to say disrespectful, even wicked things about God.

scoffers: those who mock or make fun of others.

repentance: turning away from one's sin; feeling sorry for having done wrong.

■ **Did You Know?** Have you ever wondered why there are so many different denominations in the Christian church, not to mention cults—which are twisted versions of the faith? How can Christians disagree on so many different things? Aren't we all reading the same Bible?

Well, most of us are—but some of us don't read it very carefully, while others take things out of context and build doctrines on shaky foundations. There are some things that the Bible simply doesn't address. We're left to try to apply general biblical principles instead of following specific commands. Some passages seem to have several possible interpretations, and different people understand these verses to mean different things. Then there are Scriptures that are downright difficult—confusing or hard to comprehend.

The apostle Paul, in particular, addressed some pretty heady topics and some especially complicated concepts. Peter points this out in his last letter to the church when he says: "This is just as our beloved brother Paul wrote to you with the wisdom God gave him—speaking of these things in all of his letters."

Then Peter adds, "Some of his comments are hard to understand, and those who are ignorant and unstable have twisted his letters around to mean something quite different, just as they do with other parts of Scripture. And this will result in their destruction" (2 Peter 3:16, NLT).

It's important that we learn how to read and study the Bible properly—carefully—asking God to give us wisdom and insight through His Holy Spirit. After all, He's the One who inspired the Scriptures in the first place, and Jesus said He would guide us into all truth.

1 JOHN

■ **The Book:** 1 John

■ **The Author:** John, the Beloved Disciple

■ **The Audience:** Christian believers everywhere

■ **The Setting:** Written from Ephesus, between AD 85 and AD 95

■ **The Story:** The churches in Asia were being infiltrated by false teachers who claimed to have a more advanced faith—and that salvation came through special knowledge ("gnosis"), rather than simple trust in Jesus Christ. The false teachings of these Gnostics included the idea that the spiritual world was "good" and that the material world was "evil." Therefore, Jesus (being good) could not have had a physical body—He came to earth only in spirit form. Furthermore, these teachers insisted that since the physical body was evil, either it didn't matter what you did with it (so sin all you want), or it should be punished and treated harshly until you could escape from it. John wrote to expose the heresy and the hypocrisy of these false teachers and to assure worried Christians that they had all the "knowledge" they needed to be truly saved.

■ **The Message:** John begins by reminding believers that the truths they have been taught came straight from the source—Jesus Himself and the disciples, all of whom were eyewitnesses to His life and death and resurrection (1:1–4). "This is the message we have heard from him and declare to you: God is light; in him there is no darkness at all" (1:5). Human beings, on the other hand, continue to struggle with their sinful nature. The good news is that "if we confess our sins, he is faithful and just and will forgive us our sins and purify us from all unrighteousness" (1:9).

John says there is a way to tell if a person truly knows God and loves God and walks in His light: "The man who says, 'I know him,' but does not do what he commands is a liar, and the truth is not in him. But if anyone obeys his word, God's love is truly made complete in him. This is how we know we are in him: Whoever claims to live in him must walk as Jesus did" (2:4–6).

John warns Christians not to let their hearts get too attached to worldly things. "Do not love the world or anything in the world. . . . The world and its desires pass away, but the man who does the will of God lives forever" (2:15, 17). He tells believers not to be led astray by false teachers, but to continue in the faith they were taught: "See that what you have heard from the beginning remains in you" (2:24).

Suddenly John exclaims: "How great is the love the Father has lavished on us, that we should be called children of God! And that is what we are! . . ." (3:1). What an incredible privilege! Over and over throughout his letter, John urges God's children to try grasp the love God has for them and to learn to love Him in return. We show our love by obeying His commandments (3:24).

Again, John urges believers to "test the spirits"—he gives them criteria to help them determine whether a teacher has the Spirit of God or the spirit of the antichrist (4:1–3). And he urges them to love one another, for "God is love" (4:16).

John concludes with some final words of reassurance to the churches that they are not uninformed or somehow inferior in their knowledge, as the Gnostic teachers have said. God has given us all the knowledge and understanding we need, "so that we may know him who is true. And we are in him who is true—even in his Son Jesus Christ . . ." (5:20).

Key Verse or Passage

"Dear friends, let us love one another, for love comes from God. Everyone who loves has been born of God and knows God. Whoever does not love does not know God, because God is love." (1 John 4:7–8)

More on This Story in the Bible: Learn more about John—how he became a disciple of Jesus and how he participated in Jesus' earthly ministry—by reading the accounts of any of the four Gospels (Matthew, Mark, Luke, John) and Acts 3–4. For more of John's writings, see the Gospel of John, 2 John, 3 John, and Revelation.

Words to Know:

overcome: to defeat or deal with a difficult problem.

atoning: making up for something done wrong.

sacrifice: an offering given to God.

lavished: generously or extravagantly given a great deal of something.

anointing: the mark of being chosen by or set apart for God.

antichrist: a false Christ; an enemy of Christ.

Did You Know? John was very close to Jesus during His earthly ministry; some Bible scholars believe they may have been cousins (John being the son of one of Mary's sisters). John is known as "the Beloved Disciple" because in the Gospel of John, he is often referred to as "the disciple Jesus loved." And in all of his other writings, he repeatedly emphasizes the importance of love—God's love for us, our love for Him, and the love we are to have for one another.

Making the Connection: Many people are familiar with the term "antichrist." It's most often used as a title, referring to one particularly evil individual (in a way, the opposite of Jesus) whose appearance on the world stage signals the beginning of the end: the final and ultimate showdown between good and evil, God and the devil. But as John explains here and in 2 John, anyone who teaches that Jesus is not the Son of God or that He did not come in the flesh to die on the cross for our sins—that person is an "antichrist" or has the "spirit of the antichrist."

John warns, "Dear children, this is the last hour; and as you have heard that the antichrist is coming, even now many antichrists have come . . ." (1 John 2:18).

Whenever and wherever we come across that spirit, John says, stay away! Have nothing to do with it or them. "You, dear children, are from God and have overcome them, because the one who is in you is greater than the one who is in the world" (1 John 4:4).

2 JOHN

The Book: 2 John

The Author: John, the Beloved Disciple

The Audience: The "chosen lady and her children"

The Setting: Written from Ephesus, between AD 85 and AD 95

▓ **The Story:** In the early days of the church, traveling evangelists spread the good news of the gospel far and wide. But not every teacher who came to town talking about Jesus was speaking the truth. In fact, false teachers were springing up all over the place, spreading all kinds of lies and deceit. So John wrote a letter to warn the church about the dangers of embracing these treacherous teachers.

▓ **The Message:** John writes that what he has to say to "the chosen" (or "dear") lady and her "children" (the members of her church) isn't anything they haven't heard before. "I am not writing you a new command but one we have had from the beginning" (v. 5). Yet it's so important, it bears repeating: "I ask that we love one another." John goes on to explain that we show our love by walking in obedience to God's commands (v. 6).

John warns the Christian community about the dangers of offering hospitality to false teachers—welcoming them into their homes and giving them the opportunity to spread their lies. "Many deceivers, who do not acknowledge Jesus Christ as coming in the flesh, have gone out into the world. Any such person is the deceiver and the antichrist" (vv. 7–8).

Christians need to continue in the faith they were taught. The truth is that Jesus did come "in the flesh"—not just in spirit (as the teachers of Gnosticism claimed). He had an earthly, physical body just like ours, a body that was literally, physically crucified and then raised from the dead in power and glory. "If anyone comes to you and does not bring this teaching, do not take him into your house or welcome him" (v. 10). John quickly closes his brief letter, not because he doesn't have more to say (in fact, he has a lot more he'd like to share), but because he hopes soon to visit the church in person himself (v. 12).

Key Verse or Passage

"Watch out that you do not lose what you have worked for, but that you may be rewarded fully." (2 John 1:8)

▓ **More on This Story in the Bible:** Learn more about John—how he became a disciple of Jesus and how he participated in Jesus' earthly ministry—by reading the accounts of any of the four Gospels (Matthew, Mark,

Luke, John) and Acts 3–4. For more of John's writings, see the Gospel of John, 1 John, 3 John, and Revelation.

Words to Know:

truth: what is real, true, honest, and accurate.

deceiver: someone who tricks people into believing something that isn't true.

antichrist: a false Christ; the enemy of Christ.

Think about It:
In this day and age and in our culture, it's hard to imagine that a "false teacher" would suddenly show up on our doorstep—or that we would welcome them in, if he did. But the truth is that false teachers show up all the time. And all too often, we do let them come right in. These teachers disguise themselves with helpful news and information and even entertainment. They twist and distort the truth to make it serve their own agenda. We welcome them into our homes through the TV shows and movies we watch, the books and magazines we read, the Web sites we visit. Sometimes, we even welcome these false teachers into our churches.

If we take a good look, we'll see that the ideas and values and beliefs these teachers promote contradict the teachings of the Bible. The advice they offer is the kind of "worldly wisdom" that doesn't come from God. We may think we can listen without being taken in—that they won't have an impact on our hearts and minds. But John warns us that all too easily, they can lead us astray. Furthermore, when we support these false teachers (financially or otherwise), we become partners with them in the evil that they do (2 John 11).

We need to think long and hard about the voices we listen to, the "teachers" we allow our families to learn from, and whether or not their message lines up with the truth of God's Word. If it doesn't, John says, we've got to show these "deceivers" the door.

3 JOHN

The Book: 3 John

The Author: John, the Beloved Disciple

▓ **The Audience:** A man named Gaius

▓ **The Setting:** Written from Ephesus, between AD 85 and AD 95

▓ **The Story:** An arrogant and ambitious man named Diotrophes was trying to take control of the Christian community in Asia. Diotrophes had spread malicious gossip about the disciples to undermine their authority and rejected those they sent to teach and train the church. John wrote a letter to his friend, Gaius, to commend him for not following Diotrophes' lead and to encourage him to continue extending hospitality to his brothers and sisters in Christ.

▓ **The Message:** John writes that he prays for God's blessing on Gaius, a man he led to Christ and considers a "son" in the faith. "I have no greater joy than to hear that my children are walking in the truth" (v. 4). He thanks Gaius for the hospitality he has shown the traveling evangelists and teachers that John sent him. "Dear friend, you are faithful in what you are doing for the brothers, even though they are strangers to you. They have told the church about your love . . ." (vv. 5–6). He encourages Gaius to continue this important ministry, "that we may work together for the truth" (v. 8).

Next, John addresses the problems Diotrophes has caused—problems he hopes to expose and rebuke when he visits (vv. 9–11). In contrast, John says, Demetrius (perhaps the one carrying John's letter to Gaius) is a man of Christian character and integrity—someone who can be trusted (v. 12). John sends his greetings to the rest of his friends in the church and says he looks forward to talking with them face-to-face soon (v. 14).

Key Verse or Passage

"Dear friend, do not imitate what is evil but what is good. . . ." (3 John 1:11)

▓ **More on This Story in the Bible:** Learn more about John—how he became a disciple of Jesus and how he participated in Jesus' earthly ministry—by reading the accounts of any of the four Gospels (Matthew, Mark, Luke, John) and Acts 3–4. For more of John's writings, see the Gospel of John, 1 John, 2 John, and Revelation.

Words to Know:

faithfulness: loyalty, reliability, trustworthiness.

pagans: people who are not Jewish, Christian, or Muslim; they may worship many gods or none at all.

hospitality: a generous and friendly way of treating people, making them feel comfortable and at home.

maliciously: purposely cruel and hurtful.

testimony: an eyewitness or firsthand account offered as evidence or proof.

Think about It: John says that Diotrophes "loves to be first" (3 John 9). But pride and ambition and political power plays have no place in the church—especially not among its leaders. When the disciples argued among themselves about which one of them was the greatest, Jesus told them: "If anyone wants to be first, he must be the very last. . . . The greatest among you will be your servant. For whoever exalts himself will be humbled, and whoever humbles himself will be exalted" (Mark 9:35; Matthew 23:11–12). Jesus Himself is our example: "For even the Son of Man did not come to be served, but to serve, and to give his life as a ransom for many" (Mark 10:45).

JUDE

The Book: Jude

The Author: Jude, the brother of Jesus

The Audience: Christian believers everywhere

The Setting: Between AD 60 and AD 95

The Story: Jude wanted to write to the body of Christ about "the salvation we share" (v. 3), but he became alarmed when he heard how easily false teachers had slipped into the church—confusing and deceiving the believers there. So he decided to warn the church instead.

▓ **The Message:** Jude urges Christians to "contend for the faith"—fight for the truth and reject Satan's lies. He lists some of the sins that the false teachers are committing—immorality, rebellion, slander, greed and selfishness, grumbling and fault-finding, boasting, and flattery—which they seem to think they will get away with. But Jude reminds the church of what will happen to those who continue in such sin—of what already *has* happened to others who walked the same road. God will deal with them. Jude closes his letter with words of encouragement, calling the body of Christ to persevere in dark times. "But you, dear friends, build yourselves up in your most holy faith and pray in the Holy Spirit. Keep yourselves in God's love as you wait for the mercy of our Lord Jesus Christ to bring you to eternal life" (vv. 20–21).

Key Verse or Passage

"To him who is able to keep you from falling and to present you before his glorious presence without fault and with great joy—to the only God our Savior be glory, majesty, power and authority, through Jesus Christ our Lord, before all ages, now and forevermore! Amen." (Jude 24–25)

▓ **More on This Story in the Bible:** Jude compares the sins of the false teachers to the sins of the angels (Genesis 6:1–2), Sodom and Gomorrah (Genesis 19), Cain (Genesis 4), Balaam (Numbers 31:8, 16), and Korah (Numbers 16). He also quotes respected writings/traditions from two of the books of the Apocrypha—the Assumption of Moses (v. 9) and the book of Enoch (vv. 14–15).

▓ **Words to Know:**

contend: to argue or fight; to try to deal with a difficult situation.

license: permission to do something freely.

slander/slanderous: lies that damage a person's reputation.

"love feast": another name for the Lord's Supper or Holy Communion.

scoffers: people who mock and make fun of others.

■ **Did You Know?** During Jesus' earthly ministry, his younger brothers and sisters (the children of Mary and Joseph) didn't know quite what to make of Him. They were too close to Him to see who He really was—to understand what He was doing and why. At one point, they even tried to "take charge" of Him, because they thought He had lost His mind (Mark 3:21; see also Mark 6:3). But later on, at least some of Jesus' siblings came to understand that He truly was—and is—the Son of God, their Savior as well as their "older brother." Several of them became leaders in the early church—including James and Jude, the author of this book.

REVELATION

■ **The Book:** Revelation

■ **The Author:** John, the Beloved Disciple

■ **The Audience:** The seven churches in Asia

■ **The Setting:** Written from the Island of Patmos, AD 95

■ **The Story:** Living in exile on the Island of Patmos, the last (and oldest) living member of the twelve disciples has a stunning vision—a revelation—of Jesus Christ. The message Jesus gives John for the seven churches has tremendous significance to them; they are suffering great persecution and desperately need encouragement if they are to hold on through the dark days ahead. But the words of Jesus are also for generations to come, believers who are still looking for His second coming—eagerly anticipating His return to earth.

■ **The Message:** The book of Revelation helps us see Jesus in a whole new way—as the King of kings and Lord of lords in all His glory and majesty and as the Shepherd of the church. John begins by sharing how Jesus appeared to him and gave him messages for the seven churches (1:1–11). These are messages of encouragement and instruction, challenge and rebuke (2:1–3:22). Jesus says He is coming soon and He wants the church—His bride—to be ready for Him.

Next, John is given a vision of future events—things that will happen in the last days. A voice says to him, "Come up here, and I will show you

255

what must take place after this" (4:1). He sees God on His throne, being worshiped by supernatural, heavenly beings (5:1–14). He sees God's judgment being poured out on the earth—wars, plagues, famine, disease (6:1–9:21). This judgment is well-deserved and long overdue; it is just punishment for those who have rejected God, embracing every kind of evil and immorality. Even in the midst of it, God gives the people of the earth a chance to repent and turn from their sins, but they will not (9:20–21).

John sees with spiritual eyes what has taken place in the history of humankind up to this point—the supernatural battle between good and evil. All this time Satan has been warring against the people of God. He tried to keep their Deliverer (Jesus) from coming in the first place; his failure has enraged him and emboldened him to launch a final, desperate attack on the kingdom of God (12:1–14:12). God has allowed it, because it has served His purposes. But when He is ready—when the time is right—He will put an end to the battle and destroy the devil once and for all, along with all of those who have taken his side (14–20). Jesus Himself will lead the armies of heaven to victory: "I saw heaven standing open and there before me was a white horse, whose rider is called Faithful and True. With justice he judges and makes war. His eyes are like blazing fire, and on his head are many crowns . . ." (19:11–12).

John says that this is the end of world as we know it. But that it's okay: "I saw a new heaven and a new earth, for the first heaven and the first earth had passed away. . . . And I heard a loud voice from the throne saying, 'Now the dwelling of God is with men, and he will live with them. They will be his people, and God himself will be with them and be their God. He will wipe every tear from their eyes. There will be no more death or mourning or crying or pain, for the old order of things has passed away'" (21:1–4). What follows is an awesome description of the paradise that believers have to look forward to for all eternity (21–22).

Key Verse or Passage

"Behold, I am coming soon! My reward is with me, and I will give to everyone according to what he has done." (Revelation 22:12)

■ **More on This Story in the Bible:** For more of John's writings, see the Gospel of John, and 1, 2, 3 John. There are all kinds of prophecies about the day of the Lord, God's judgment and deliverance, and a new heaven and a new earth, throughout both the Old and the New Testaments. There are also many references to the second coming of Christ in the New Testament, starting with the words of Jesus Himself in the Gospels (ex. John 14:1–3).

Understanding and interpreting some of these prophecies can be fairly complicated—there's a lot of historical background information you need to know before you can properly compare them or apply them to what is happening in the world today! If this is a subject that really interests you, you might pick up an in-depth Bible study on the book of Revelation, ask your pastor to recommend some reliable books on Bible prophecy and the end times, or sign up for a class on "eschatology"—the study of the end times—at a Christian college or university.

■ **Words to Know:**

blessed: specially cared for (protected and provided for) by God.

overcome: to defeat or deal with a difficult problem.

worthy: deserving.

revelation: something secret or hidden that is suddenly made known.

■ **Think about It:** The words of Revelation have gripped the attention—and the imagination—of people everywhere, ever since they were first recorded. John's vision has inspired countless books, poems, songs, stories, movies, and plays. Some of these are written from a biblical perspective to inspire Christians to remain true to their faith and to reach out to unbelievers (such as the Thief in the Night series of the 1970s or the Left Behind series of the 1990s). Others are secular interpretations of the fantastic themes of Revelation only loosely based on Scripture and made purely for entertainment purposes (such as *Armageddon, The Seventh Sign, End of Days*).

Many people are fascinated with biblical prophecy and "eschatology"—the study of the end times. They love to try to solve the puzzles, follow the clues, figure out the mysteries, and determine just how and when all of these amazing events will unfold. But some find the graphic descriptions of torture and suffering and martyrdom—not to mention the total destruction of life as we know it—to be downright terrifying, or at least deeply disturbing.

When you study Revelation and the end times, you don't want to squelch the curiosity of the more eager members of the family—after all, it's a good thing to be enthusiastic about the return of the King! At the same time, you want to be careful not to traumatize the more sensitive or fearful members of the family. Remind everyone that the most important thing is that we know how the story ends—we know who wins! And we know that Jesus is coming back soon. We don't have to figure out when; we just need to be ready whenever. Whatever suffering or hardship we may experience in this life ("end times" or otherwise), Jesus has promised He will never leave us or forsake us (Matthew 28:20). He'll always be with us. One day there will be a glorious new heaven and a new earth, and we will be safe there—in the arms of our heavenly Father—forever!

6

HOW TO STUDY THE BIBLE

Choosing a Translation

All Scripture is God-breathed and is useful for teaching, rebuking, correcting and training in righteousness."

2 Timothy 3:16

alk into the "Bibles" section of any bookstore today, and you'll be amazed at the selection available. Bibles in all different colors and shapes and sizes. Bibles for moms, dads, teachers, and students. Study Bibles, devotional Bibles. . . . The special titles have to do with the "extras"—the added material that appears in the front or back of the Bible and sometimes interspersed with the original text. This material may include study aids, maps and charts, devotional readings, and commentary from noted Bible preachers and teachers. It can all be very helpful. But the most important thing to note is the little letters on the spine, the letters that indicate the version of the Bible—the text of the Scripture itself. Most Bibles fall into one of three categories: a word-for-word translation, a thought-for-thought translation, or a paraphrase.

A **word-for-word translation** is a version of the Bible in which a team of Bible scholars has carefully translated each and every word from the original Greek or Hebrew into contemporary English. Examples of word-for-word translations include the King James Version (KJV), the New King James Version (NKJV), the English Standard Version (ESV), the New American Standard Bible (NASB), and the Amplified Bible (AMPLIFIED, which includes extended definitions of key words in the text).

A **thought-for-thought translation** is a version of the Bible in which a team of Bible scholars has carefully translated each and every thought or phrase (group of words) into contemporary English. Examples of thought-for-thought translations include the New International Version (NIV), the New Living Translation (NLT), the Contemporary English Version (CEV), and the New Century Version (NCV).

A **paraphrase** is a version of the Bible in which an individual (usually a Bible scholar) has rewritten the Scriptures in his or her own words, usually for the purpose of making the biblical text easier to read and understand. Examples of paraphrases include The Living Bible (TLB) and The Message. A paraphrase doesn't necessarily have the accuracy or authority of a translation, because it is one person's interpretation or understanding of the Scripture. However, the simple language and story-like feel of a paraphrase make it great for reading aloud. A paraphrase can also help shed new light on a familiar passage of Scripture or illuminate the meaning of a more challenging passage.

As far as reading comprehension, most translations and paraphrases fall somewhere between sixth and eighth grade level. However the King James, the New American Standard, and the Amplified version are considered eleventh or twelfth grade level.

For the sake of simplicity, every family should have one primary translation from which they do most of their reading, Bible study, and memorization. You might choose to use the version you are most familiar with, perhaps the one you grew up with or the one preferred by your church or denomination. Or—after a little research and reflection—the version you find the most clear, readable, and understandable. Then as you study the Scriptures, whenever you run across a particularly powerful, profound, or difficult verse, consult other translations and paraphrases to getter a better feel for the true meaning of the text. A **parallel** Bible offers several different versions of the text side-by-side, to make it easier to compare them.

USING A BIBLE DICTIONARY, ENCYCLOPEDIA, AND CONCORDANCE

"Study to shew thyself approved unto God, a workman that needeth not to be ashamed, rightly dividing the word of truth." 2 Timothy 2:15 (KJV)

Sometimes the more you read the Bible, the more questions you have about what you've read! We live in a different time, a different culture. Things that everyone understood when the Scriptures were written are completely foreign to us. That's where a Bible *dictionary* or *encyclopedia* or *concordance* can be really helpful. Dictionaries and encyclopedias are arranged in alphabetical order. Handbooks are often organized by topic or book of the Bible. These resources offer all kinds of information about the cultural and historical context of the Scriptures, the manners and customs of Bible lands:

HOUSETOP—the flat roof of a house. In Bible times, the housetop was used as a sitting area. Open to cool breezes in the evening, the housetop overlooked the streets of the city. It was an ideal place for proclaiming public messages; thus Jesus told the disciples to "preach on the housetops" (Matt. 10:27). Also see HOUSE.[1]

A concordance is an alphabetical index of important Bible names and key words found in the Scriptures. It comes in handy when you want to look up as many verses as you can find on a particular topic—or when you remember a part of a verse of Scripture but don't know where to find it in the Bible. A concordance entry usually offers a line from the Scripture in which a word appears (the word itself is indicated with an abbreviation), followed by the reference—the book of the Bible, chapter, and verse. If there are additional numbers at the end (as in the example

1. From the *Illustrated Dictionary of the Bible*, Herbert Lockyer, ed. (Nashville: Thomas Nelson, 1996), 496.

in Fig. 6.1), they refer to a Hebrew or Greek dictionary at the back of the concordance, for those who want to identify specific words in the original language of the Bible.

Fig. 6.1 Concordance Example

PEACE[2]

thou shalt go to thy fathers in *p* ...... Gen 15:15	7965
man wondering at her held his *p* ...... Gen 24:21	7965
good, and have sent thee away in *p* ...... Gen 26:29	7965
and they departed from him in *p* ...... Gen 26:31	7965
again to my father's house in *p* ...... Gen 28:21	7965
Jacob held his *p* until they were ...... Gen 34:5	2790
shall give Pharoah an answer of *p* ...... Gen 41:16	7965
and he said, *P* be to you, fear not ...... Gen 43:23	7965
get you up in *p* unto your father ...... Gen 44:17	7965
and Jethro said to Moses, Go in *p* ...... Ex 4:18	7965

A mini-concordance can be found at the back of most Bibles; an exhaustive concordance is a huge book that lists every single verse of Scripture in which a particular word occurs—including "a," "and," and "the"!

STUDY TIPS FOR PERSONAL BIBLE STUDY

"I will study your commandments and reflect on your ways. I will delight in your decrees and not forget your word." Psalm 119:15–16 (NLT)

There's something very special about having "devotions" or "quiet time" alone with God, connecting with Him through prayer and reflection and the reading of His Word. Ideally, every one of us should make time for this kind of personal Bible study each and every day. Unfortunately, it's not always possible. However, the truth is that any time you commit to growing in your relationship with God will produce fruit in your life— whether it's daily or weekly, two minutes or two hours. Do the best you

---

2. *The New Strong's Exhaustive Concordance of the Bible*, James Strong (Nashville: Thomas Nelson, 1996), 1010.

can. And remember, there's no "right" or "wrong" way to have a quiet time. How and where and when you spend time with God can be as unique and individual as you are. Here are just a few basic tips to get you started:

- Choose a Bible reading plan, a Bible study workbook, a devotional book—or your Bible, a concordance, and a list of topics you want to explore.

- Whenever you finish a paragraph or chapter of the Bible, review what you've read. See if you can answer the five Ws and an H: Who, What, When, Where, Why, and How. Ask God to help you understand the passage and learn something from what you've read. You might want to write your thoughts down in a notebook or journal.

- Memorize Bible verses that are meaningful to you, verses that encourage you or challenge you. Copy them onto sticky notes or file cards and put them where you will see them often—around the house, in the car or office, on the bathroom mirror.

- Keep a prayer journal or notebook in which you record specific things you're praying about. Leave some space next to each request so that later you can write down how and when God answered your prayers.

STUDY TIPS FOR FAMILY DEVOTIONS

"These commandments that I give you today are to be upon your hearts. Impress them on your children. Talk about them when you sit at home and when you walk along the road, when you lie down and when you get up." Deuteronomy 6:6–7

Conversations about the Scriptures, about God and life and faith, should be a part of everyday life. But it can also be very rewarding to set aside a specific time on a regular basis to gather as a family and study the Bible together. If the idea of family devotions is new to you, begin by calling everyone together and sharing your heart—why you feel it's important to study the Bible as a family. Explain what you hope to accomplish and why you want each one to participate in this special time.

Start with something simple. Consider the ages of your children and their attention span and your family's lifestyle and schedule. For some families, the half hour before bedtime works best. Others incorporate family devotions into (or just after) a sit-down meal. If necessary, you can even use a long commute to school or soccer practice—though of course, ideally, you want to choose a time and place when everyone can give their full attention.

- Read a passage of Scripture or a paragraph from a devotional book (involve older children by asking them to take turns reading). Follow up afterward with a few questions—give everyone a chance to respond and share their thoughts.

- Ask each member of the family to share either something they're thankful for—a "praise report"—or a prayer request. Put an older child in charge of writing down the requests in the family prayer notebook. Take turns praying over the list together.

- Sing a few hymns or praise and worship choruses together. If someone in the family plays a musical instrument, have them accompany you. If you're not as musical, try singing along with a favorite worship CD.

- With younger children, introduce arts and crafts or games that help illustrate a biblical principle. Sing songs with motions. Let them act out the story you've just read. Pray for wisdom and creativity to come up with ideas on your own—or pick up a book of Bible-based crafts and activities at your local Christian bookstore.

- Use the projects and materials your children bring home from Sunday school or children's church as a springboard for further discussion and Bible study.

- If the kids are really engaged and involved, keep it going—what could be more important? Otherwise, keep it short and sweet.

It's true that it takes discipline and commitment to make Bible study a regular part of your family life. And like diet and exercise, it's something you do because it's good for you—whether you feel like it or not. But if your family devotional time is frequently boring or burdensome, stop and reconsider. Do you need to try a different time, a different place, a different method? Don't be afraid to mix things up. Be sure your children have the opportunity to actively participate. Invite their input on what and how and where and when you study the Bible together.

As your children grow, encourage them to have their own private Bible study time as well. Make sure they have their very own Bible, perhaps one of those special Bibles "just for kids" or teens. Give them their own prayer journal that they can decorate, a set of Bible-marking pens or highlighters, a Bible cover, or a bookmark. During your family devotions, don't push—but do encourage them to share what God has been saying to them personally—what they've been learning on their own.

BIBLE READING PLANS

There are a lot of ways to incorporate daily Bible reading into your family life. For instance, you can start with a "verse-of-the-day" flip calendar that you read and discuss during mealtimes. Or choose a dramatized audio version of the Scriptures that you listen to in the car. Your church bulletin or newsletter may provide a list of Scriptures that the pastor suggests everyone read during the week. Christian bookstores offer a number of different versions of the Bible already arranged in such a way as to take you through all of the Scriptures in a particular amount of time (see the *90 Day Bible*, the *One Year Bible*, the *Two Year Bible*). There may also be a variety of reading plans in the front or back of the Bible you use now—give one of them a try! Or do a little research online. Go to any search engine and enter "Bible Reading Plan" and you'll find dozens of Web sites that provide different Scripture reading schedules. Some sites will even e-mail each day's reading to you, in the translation of your choice.

Here are some other things to try:

- Use the topical lists of Scripture verses provided in chapter 7 to do a daily or weekly study on a particular theme, such as "Bible heroes," the "miracles of Jesus," and "what the Bible says about heaven." Or use a concordance and a Bible commentary to create your own topical study on a subject that interests you and your family.

- The book of Proverbs has thirty-one chapters, one for each day of the month. Try reading the corresponding chapter each day—the fifth chapter on the fifth day of the month and so on.

- There are 150 chapters in the book of Psalms—all of them beautiful songs or prayers to the heart of God. Make it a practice to read one psalm every day. If you read five psalms a day, you'll finish the entire book in a month.

- Read through all four Gospels—Matthew, Mark, Luke, and John—in a month by reading three chapters a day.

- Start at the beginning and read straight through, from Genesis to Revelation. Four chapters a day will take you through the Bible in about a year. Or alternate reading a chapter each of the Old Testament and the New Testament every day (start with Genesis and Matthew).

Figure 6.2 is a chart you can use to check off your progress:

Fig. 6.2 Bible Reading Checklist

GENESIS

1	2	3	4	5	6	7
8	9	10	11	12	13	14
15	16	17	18	19	20	21
22	23	24	25	26	27	28
29	30	31	32	33	34	35
36	37	38	39	40	41	42
43	44	45	46	47	48	49
50						

EXODUS

1	2	3	4	5	6	7
8	9	10	11	12	13	14
15	16	17	18	19	20	21
22	23	24	25	26	27	28
29	30	31	32	33	34	35
36	37	38	39	40		

LEVITICUS

1	2	3	4	5	6	7
8	9	10	11	12	13	14
15	16	17	18	19	20	21
22	23	24	25	26	27	

NUMBERS

1	2	3	4	5	6	7
8	9	10	11	12	13	14
15	16	17	18	19	20	21
22	23	24	25	26	27	28
29	30	31	32	33	34	35
36						

DEUTERONOMY

1	2	3	4	5	6	7
8	9	10	11	12	13	14
15	16	17	18	19	20	21
22	23	24	25	26	27	28
29	30	31	32	33	34	

JOSHUA

1	2	3	4	5	6	7
8	9	10	11	12	13	14
15	16	17	18	19	20	21
22	23	24				

JUDGES

1	2	3	4	5	6	7
8	9	10	11	12	13	14
15	16	17	18	19	20	21

RUTH

1	2	3	4			

1 SAMUEL

1	2	3	4	5	6	7
8	9	10	11	12	13	14
15	16	17	18	19	20	21
22	23	24	25	26	27	28
29	30	31				

2 SAMUEL

1	2	3	4	5	6	7
8	9	10	11	12	13	14
15	16	17	18	19	20	21
22	23	24				

1 KINGS

1	2	3	4	5	6	7
8	9	10	11	12	13	14
15	16	17	18	19	20	21
22						

2 KINGS

1	2	3	4	5	6	7
8	9	10	11	12	13	14
15	16	17	18	19	20	21
22	23	24	25			

1 CHRONICLES

1	2	3	4	5	6	7
8	9	10	11	12	13	14
15	16	17	18	19	20	21
22	23	24	25	26	27	28
29						

2 CHRONICLES

1	2	3	4	5	6	7
8	9	10	11	12	13	14
15	16	17	18	19	20	21
22	23	24	25	26	27	28
29	30	31	32	33	34	35
36						

EZRA

1	2	3	4	5	6	7
8	9	10				

NEHEMIAH

1	2	3	4	5	6	7
8	9	10	11	12	13	

ESTHER

1	2	3	4	5	6	7
8	9	10				

JOB

1	2	3	4	5	6	7
8	9	10	11	12	13	14
15	16	17	18	19	20	21
22	23	24	25	26	27	28
29	30	31	32	33	34	35
36	37	38	39	40	41	42

PSALMS

1	2	3	4	5	6	7
8	9	10	11	12	13	14
15	16	17	18	19	20	21
22	23	24	25	26	27	28
29	30	31	32	33	34	35
36	37	38	39	40	41	42
43	44	45	46	47	48	49
50	51	52	53	54	55	56
57	58	59	60	61	62	63
64	65	66	67	68	69	70
71	72	73	74	75	76	77
78	79	80	81	82	83	84
85	86	87	88	89	90	91
92	93	94	95	96	97	98
99	100	101	102	103	104	105
106	107	108	109	110	111	112
113	114	115	116	117	118	119
120	121	122	123	124	125	126
127	128	129	130	131	132	133
134	135	136	137	138	139	140
141	142	143	144	145	146	147
148	149	150				

PROVERBS

1	2	3	4	5	6	7
8	9	10	11	12	13	14
15	16	17	18	19	20	21
22	23	24	25	26	27	28
29	30	31				

ECCLESIASTES

1	2	3	4	5	6	7
8	9	10	11	12		

SONG OF SONGS

1	2	3	4	5	6	7
8						

ISAIAH

1	2	3	4	5	6	7
8	9	10	11	12	13	14
15	16	17	18	19	20	21
22	23	24	25	26	27	28
29	30	31	32	33	34	35
36	37	38	39	40	41	42
43	44	45	46	47	48	49
50	51	52	53	54	55	56
57	58	59	60	61	62	63
64	65	66				

JEREMIAH

1	2	3	4	5	6	7
8	9	10	11	12	13	14
15	16	17	18	19	20	21
22	23	24	25	26	27	28
29	30	31	32	33	34	35
36	37	38	39	40	41	42
43	44	45	46	47	48	49
50	51	52				

LAMENTATIONS

1	2	3	4	5		

EZEKIEL

1	2	3	4	5	6	7
8	9	10	11	12	13	14
15	16	17	18	19	20	21
22	23	24	25	26	27	28
29	30	31	32	33	34	35
36	37	38	39	40	41	42
43	44	45	46	47	48	

DANIEL

1	2	3	4	5	6	7
8	9	10	11	12		

HOSEA

1	2	3	4	5	6	7
8	9	10	11	12	13	14

JOEL

1	2	3				

AMOS

1	2	3	4	5	6	7
8	9					

OBADIAH

1					

JONAH

1	2	3	4		

MICAH

1	2	3	4	5	6

NAHUM

1	2	3			

HABAKKUK

1	2	3			

ZEPHANIAH

1	2	3			

HAGGAI

1	2				

ZECHARIAH

1	2	3	4	5	6	7
8	9	10	11	12	13	14

MALACHI

1	2	3	4			

MATTHEW

1	2	3	4	5	6	7
8	9	10	11	12	13	14
15	16	17	18	19	20	21
22	23	24	25	26	27	28

MARK

1	2	3	4	5	6	7
8	9	10	11	12	13	14
15	16					

LUKE

1	2	3	4	5	6	7
8	9	10	11	12	13	14
15	16	17	18	19	20	21
22	23	24				

JOHN

1	2	3	4	5	6	7
8	9	10	11	12	13	14
15	16	17	18	19	20	21

ACTS

1	2	3	4	5	6	7
8	9	10	11	12	13	14
15	16	17	18	19	20	21
22	23	24	25	26	27	28

ROMANS

1	2	3	4	5	6	7
8	9	10	11	12	13	14
15	16					

1 CORINTHIANS

1	2	3	4	5	6	7
8	9	10	11	12	13	14
15	16					

2 CORINTHIANS

1	2	3	4	5	6	7
8	9	10	11	12	13	

GALATIANS

1	2	3	4	5	6	

EPHESIANS

1	2	3	4	5	6	

PHILIPPIANS

1	2	3	4			

COLOSSIANS

1	2	3	4			

1 THESSALONIANS

1	2	3	4	5		

2 THESSALONIANS

1	2	3				

1 TIMOTHY

1	2	3	4	5	6	

2 TIMOTHY

1	2	3	4			

TITUS

1	2	3			

PHILEMON

1				

HEBREWS

1	2	3	4	5	6	7
8	9	10	11	12	13	

JAMES

1	2	3	4	5	

1 PETER

1	2	3	4	5	

2 PETER

1	2	3			

1 JOHN

1	2	3	4	5		

2 JOHN

1				

3 JOHN

1				

JUDE

1				

REVELATION

1	2	3	4	5	6	7
8	9	10	11	12	13	14
15	16	17	18	19	20	21
22						

7

WHERE IN THE SCRIPTURES YOU'LL FIND . . .

STORIES FROM THE OLD TESTAMENT THAT EVERYONE SHOULD KNOW

Adam and Eve in the Garden of Eden: Genesis 2–3

Cain and Abel: Genesis 4:1–16

Noah and the Great Flood: Genesis 6–8

The Tower of Babel: Genesis 11:1–9

God Calls Abraham: Genesis 12:1–5

Abraham and Sarah: Genesis 18:1–15; 21:1–7

Abraham Offers Isaac Back to God: Genesis 22:1–19

Jacob and Esau: Genesis 25:19–34, 27–28

Jacob's Ladder: Genesis 28:10–22

Jacob Marries Rachel and Leah: Genesis 29:1–30

Jacob Wrestles with an Angel: Genesis 32:22–32

Joseph and His Brothers: Genesis 37; 39–50

Moses in the Bullrushes: Exodus 2:1–10

Moses and the Burning Bush: Exodus 3:1–4:17

The Plagues: Exodus 7–12

Moses Parts the Red Sea: Exodus 14
The Ten Commandments: Exodus 20:1–21
The Golden Calf: Exodus 32
The Twelve Spies in the Promised Land: Numbers 13–14
Joshua and the Battle of Jericho: Joshua 6:1–26
Deborah Rides into Battle: Judges 4–5
Gideon and the Fleece: Judges 6:33–7:24
Samson and Delilah: Judges 16:4–31
Ruth Follows Naomi: Ruth 1:1–22
Samuel Hears God's Voice: 1 Samuel 3
God Chooses David to Be King: 1 Samuel 16:1–13
David and Goliath: 1 Samuel 17
The Wisdom of Solomon: 1 Kings 3:5–15; 4:29–34
Elijah Routs the Prophets of Baal: 1 Kings 18
Elijah and the Chariot of Fire: 2 Kings 2:1–11
Elisha and the Invisible Army: 2 Kings 6:8–23
Nehemiah Rebuilds the Wall: Nehemiah 2:1–20; 4:1–23; 6:15–16
Queen Esther Saves Her People: Esther 2–9
God Tests Job: Job 1:1–2:10; 42:7–17
Isaiah Sees the Lord: Isaiah 6:1–8
Jeremiah at the Potter's House: Jeremiah 18:1–10
Shadrach, Meshach, and Abednego: Daniel 3:1–30
Daniel in the Lion's Den: Daniel 6:1–28
Jonah and the Great Fish: Jonah 1–3

STORIES FROM THE NEW TESTAMENT THAT EVERYONE SHOULD KNOW

The Birth of John the Baptist: Luke 1
The Birth of Jesus: Matthew 1–2; Luke 1:26–2:40
John Baptizes Jesus: Matthew 3:1–17; Mark 1:9–11; Luke 3:1–22; John 1:29–34
Jesus Is Tempted in the Wilderness: Matthew 4:1–11; Mark 1:12–13; Luke 4:1–13
Jesus Turns Water into Wine: John 2:1–11

Jesus Calls the Twelve Disciples: Matthew 10:2–4; Mark 3:13–19; Luke 6:12–16

Jesus Feeds the Five Thousand: Matthew 14:13–21; Mark 6:35–44; Luke 9:12–17; John 6:5–15

Jesus Casts Demons into a Herd of Pigs: Matthew 8:28–34; Mark 5:1–20; Luke 8:26–39

Jesus Calms the Storm: Matthew 8:23–27; Mark 4:35–41; Luke 8:22–25

Jesus Walks on Water: Matthew 14:22–32; Mark 6:45–52; John 6:16–21

Jesus Goes to Zacchaeus's House: Luke 19:1–10

Jesus Talks with Nicodemus: John 3:1–21

Jesus and the Samaritan Woman: John 4:1–30

Jesus and the Adulterous Woman: John 8:1–11

Jesus Raises Lazarus from the Dead: John 11:1–44

The Transfiguration: Matthew 17:1–13; Mark 9:2–13; Luke 9:28–36

Jesus Enters Jerusalem: Matthew 21:1–11; Luke 19:28–38; John 12:12–19

Jesus Clears the Temple: Mark 11:15–18; John 2:13–17

The Last Supper: Matthew 26:17–30; Mark 14:12–42; Luke 22:7–22; John 13:1–30

Jesus Prays in the Garden of Gethsemane: Matthew 26:36–46; Mark 14:32–42

Judas Betrays Jesus: Matthew 26:47–50; Mark 14:10–11, 43–46; Luke 22:47–48; John 18:3–6

Peter Denies Jesus: Matthew 26:69–75; Mark 14:27–72; Luke 22:34–62; John 18:15–27

Jesus Is Crucified: Matthew 27:11–66; Mark 15; Luke 22:47–23:56; John 18–19

Jesus Is Raised from the Dead: Matthew 28; Mark 16; Luke 24; John 20

Jesus Ascends into Heaven: Acts 1:1–11

The Holy Spirit Comes at Pentecost: Acts 2

Peter and John Heal a Crippled Beggar: Acts 3:1–4:4

Ananias and Sapphira: Acts 5:1–11

The Stoning of Stephen: Acts 6:8–7:60

Philip and the Ethiopian: Acts 8:26–40
Saul Becomes Paul: Acts 9:1–31
Peter's Vision: Acts 10
Peter Escapes from Prison: Acts 12:1–19
Paul and Silas in Prison: Acts 16:16–40
Paul's Shipwreck: Acts 27:1–44
John Receives a Revelation: Revelation 1:9–19; 22:8–10

BIBLE HEROES: MEN

There are many men who played a very important role in the history of God's people—as husbands and fathers, prophets and priests, judges and kings. None of them were perfect; they all made mistakes. But their faith, courage, and wisdom are still an inspiration to us today (see Hebrews 11–12:1). Here are just a few:

Adam: Genesis 2–5:5; Romans 5:12–15
Abel: Genesis 4:1–16; Hebrews 11:4
Enoch: Genesis 5:21–24; Jude 14–15
Noah: Genesis 5:28–9:29
Abraham: Genesis 11:27–25:10
Isaac: Genesis 17:19; 21:1–22:19; 25:19–28:5; 35:29
Jacob: Genesis 25:19–49:33
Joseph: Genesis 37; 39–45; 50
Moses: Exodus 2–24; 31:18; 32–34; Numbers 5–14; 16–17; 20–21; Deuteronomy 31–34
Joshua: Deuteronomy 31:1–8; Joshua 1–24
Samson: Judges 13–16
Samuel: 1 Samuel 1–3; 7–10; 12–13:15; 15–16; 19:18–24; 25:1
David: 1 Samuel 16–30; 2 Samuel 1–12; 15–24; 1 Chronicles 11–22; 28–29
Solomon: 1 Kings 1:29–11:43; 2 Chronicles 1–9; Proverbs; Ecclesiastes; Song of Songs
Elijah: 1 Kings 17–21; 2 Kings 1–2:11
Elisha: 1 Kings 19:19–21; 2 Kings 2–13:20
Job: Job 1–42

Isaiah: Isaiah 1–66
Jeremiah: Jeremiah 1–52; Lamentations 1–5
Daniel: Daniel 1–2; 4–12
Shadrach, Meshach, Abednego: Daniel 1–3
Jonah: Jonah 1–4
Joseph, Husband of Mary: Matthew 1–2; Luke 2
John the Baptist: Matthew 3; 11:1–15; 14:1–12; Mark 1:1–11; 6:14–29;
    Luke 1; 3:1–19; 7:18–23; John 1:14–34; 3:22–36
Jesus: See Matthew; Mark; Luke; John; Acts 1:1–11; 9:1–19; Revelation
    1–3; 19; 21–22
The Twelve Disciples: Simon Peter and Andrew, James and John, Philip
    and Nathanael (Bartholomew), Thomas, Matthew, James, Thaddaeus,
    Simon the Zealot, and Judas Iscariot. See Matthew; Mark; Luke; John;
    Acts 1–8; 9:32–12:19; 1–2 Peter; 1–3 John; and Revelation 1.
Stephen: Acts 6:8–7:60
Paul: Acts 8:1–3; 9:1–31; 13–28; see also Paul's letters to the Romans;
    Corinthians; Galatians; Ephesians; Philippians; Colossians; Thessa-
    lonians; Timothy; Titus; and Philemon.

BIBLE HEROES: WOMEN

The Bible is full of women who played a very important role in the history of God's people—some as wives and mothers, others as prophets,
judges, and queens. None of them were perfect; they all made mistakes.
But their faith and courage and wisdom are still an inspiration to us today
(see Hebrews 11–12:1). Here are just a few:

Eve: Genesis 2–5
Sarah: Genesis 11:29–30; 12:10–20; 16:1–6; 17:15–18:15; 21:1–7;
    1 Peter 3:5–6
Hagar: Genesis 16:1–16; 21:8–21
Rebekah: Genesis 24–27
Leah and Rachel: Genesis 29:16–35:20; Ruth 4:11
Jochebed: Exodus 2:1–10; Hebrews 11:23
Miriam: Exodus 2:1–10; 15:1–21; Numbers 12:1–15
Rahab: Joshua 2:1–21; 6:1–25

Deborah: Judges 4–5
Ruth and Naomi: Ruth 1–4
Hannah: 1 Samuel 1–2:11, 21
Abigail: 1 Samuel 25:1–42
Huldah: 2 Kings 22:11–20; 2 Chronicles 34:21–28
Esther: Esther 1–10
Elizabeth: Luke 1:1–58
Mary: Matthew 1–2:11; Luke 1:26–56; 2:1–39; John 2:1–11; 19:25–26
Anna: Luke 2:36–38
Mary and Martha: Luke 10:38–42; John 11:1–44
Mary Magdalene: Matthew 27:56–61; Mark 16:1– 9; Luke 8:1–3; John 19:25; 20:1–18
Joanna and Susanna: Luke 8:1–3
Salome: Mark 15:40; 16:1
Priscilla: Acts 18:2, 18–19
Phoebe: Romans 16:1–2
Lydia: Acts 16:13–15, 40

BIBLE HEROES: KIDS AND TEENS

Many great Bible heroes began serving God at an early age. Some of them are most famous for things they accomplished during their childhood or teenage years. The Scriptures teach us that you're never too young (or too old) to give your heart to God and live your life for Him.

"Don't let anyone look down on you because you are young, but set an example for the believers in speech, in life, in love, in faith and in purity." (1 Timothy 4:12)

Kids and Teens on a Mission for God

Joseph the Dreamer: Genesis 37; 39–45; 50
Miriam Watches over Moses: Exodus 2:1–10
Samuel Hears God's Voice: 1 Samuel 3:1–21
David Kills a Giant: 1 Samuel 17
Good King Josiah: 2 Kings 22:2–23:3

A Servant Girl Shows the Way: 2 Kings 5:1–14
The Prophet Jeremiah: Jeremiah 1:1–19
Daniel, Shadrach, Meschach, and Abednego: Daniel 1–3; 6
Mary, the Mother of Jesus: Luke 1:26–56; 2:1–39
Jesus as a Boy: Luke 2:39–52
Timothy, Missionary/Pastor: Acts 16:1; 18:5; 19:22; 1 Corinthians 4:17;
1 and 2 Timothy

**Other Stories, Instructions, and Words of Encouragement
for Kingdom Kids**
Honor your father and mother: Exodus 20:12
Wisdom doesn't only come with old age: Job 32:6–9
How can a young man keep his way pure? Psalm 119:9
Before we were born, God knew each one of us by name: Psalm 139
Even a child is known by his actions: Proverbs 20:11
God pours out His Spirit on the young and the old: Joel 2:28
Jesus tells His disciples that they must become like little children: Matthew 18:1–5
Jesus blesses the little children: Matthew 19:13–15; Mark 10:13–16;
Luke 18:15–17
Jesus says when you welcome a child, you welcome Him: Mark 9:36–37;
Luke 9:47–48
Children praise Jesus as He enters Jerusalem: Matthew 21:15–16
Jesus raises Jairus's daughter from the dead: Mark 5:21–43
Jesus rejoices that God has revealed His truth to little children: Luke 10:21
Children, obey your parents in the Lord: Ephesians 6:1–4; Colossians
3:20
There comes a time to grow up, physically and spiritually: 1 Corinthians 13:11
Paul encourages Timothy to set a good example for older believers:
1 Timothy 4:12

THE MIRACLES OF JESUS

Here are some of the miracles Jesus performed during His earthly ministry—though as His disciple, John, pointed out, no list will ever be complete: "Jesus did many other things as well. If every one of them were written down, I suppose that even the whole world would not have room for the books that would be written" (John 21:25). And He's still working miracles in the hearts and lives of His people today!

Jesus Shows His Power over Nature

He turns water into wine: John 2:1–11

He provides a huge catch of fish: Luke 5:1–11

He calms the storm: Matthew 8:23–27; Mark 4:35–41; Luke 8:22–25

He feeds five thousand: Matthew 14:13–21; Mark 6:35–44; Luke 9:12–17; John 6:5–13

He walks on water: Matthew 14:22–33; Mark 6:45–52; John 6:16–21

He feeds four thousand: Matthew 15:29–39; Mark 8:1–10

He sends Peter to catch a fish that has a coin in its mouth: Matthew 17:24–27

He makes a fig tree wither and die: Matthew 21:18–22; Mark 11:12–14, 20–25

He provides another huge catch of fish: John 21:1–11

He appears and disappears, suddenly and mysteriously: Matthew 28:9, 16–17; Mark 16:9–19; Luke 24:13–32, 36–39, 51; John 20:10–17, 19, 26–27; 21:1–14; Acts 1:1–11; 9:1–7

Jesus Shows His Power over Sickness and Disease, Demons, and Death

He heals a man with leprosy: Matthew 8:1–4; Mark 1:40–44; Luke 5:12–14

He heals the Roman centurion's servant: Matthew 8:5–13; Luke 7:1–10

He heals Peter's mother-in-law: Matthew 8:14–17; Mark 1:29–31; Luke 4:38–39

He delivers two demon-possessed men: Matthew 8:28–34

He heals a paralyzed man brought on a mat: Matthew 9:1–8; Mark 2:1–12; Luke 5:17–26

He heals two blind men: Matthew 9:27–31

He delivers a man mute and possessed by a demon: Matthew 9:32–33

He heals a man with a withered hand: Matthew 12:9–13; Mark 3:1–5; Luke 6:6–11

He delivers a man blind and mute and possessed by a demon: Matthew 12:22

He heals the Canaanite woman's daughter: Matthew 15:21–28

He heals a boy with epilepsy: Matthew 17:14–18

He heals two blind men near Jericho: Matthew 20:29–34

He delivers a man from an evil spirit: Mark 1:23–26; Luke 4:33–36

He raises Jairus's daughter from the dead: Mark 5:22–42

He heals a deaf, mute man: Mark 7:31–37

He heals a blind man: Mark 8:22–26

He heals a blind man named Bartimaeus: Mark 10:46–52; Luke 18:35–43

He raises a widow's son from the dead: Luke 7:11–15

He heals a woman with bleeding: Luke 8:43–48

He heals a crippled woman: Luke 13:11–13

He heals a man with dropsy: Luke 14:1–4

He heals ten men with leprosy: Luke 17:11–19

He heals the ear of the high priest's servant: Luke 22:50–51

He heals the royal official's son: John 4:46–54

He heals the man at the pool of Bethesda: John 5:1–9

He raises Lazarus from the dead: John 11:1–44

He is raised from the dead himself: Matthew 28; Mark 16; Luke 24; John 20

THE TEACHINGS OF JESUS

Jesus taught His disciples many things about who God is, what His heart is toward us, and how we can live a life that pleases Him. Here is a list of many of these teachings and where you can find them in the Scriptures.

General Teachings

The Beatitudes ("Blessed are the . . ."): Matthew 5:1–12

You Must Be Born Again: John 3:1–21

The Golden Rule: Luke 6:31

The Lord's Prayer: Matthew 6:5–15
The Sermon on the Mount: Matthew 5–7
Let Your Light Shine: Matthew 5:14–16
Be My Witnesses: Matthew 28:18–20; Acts 1:8

"I Am" Sayings
The Bread of Life: John 6:25–59
The Gate: John 10:7
The Good Shepherd: John 10:1–21
The Living Water: John 4:1–26
The Light of the World: John 8:12
The Vine (and You Are the Branches): John 15:1–17
The Way, the Truth, and the Life: John 14:6

Parables
Canceled Debts: Luke 7:41–43
The Cost of Discipleship: Luke 14:28–33
The Faithful Servant: Luke 12:42–48
The Good Samaritan: Luke 10:30–37
A Great Banquet: Luke 14:16–24
The Growing Seed: Mark 4:26–29
Hidden Treasure/The Pearl of Great Price: Matthew 13:44–46
Honor at a Banquet: Luke 14:7–14
A Lost Coin: Luke 15:8–10
A Lost Sheep: Matthew 18:12–14; Luke 15:3–7
A Mustard Seed: Matthew 13:31–32
The Persistent Widow: Luke 18:2–8
The Prodigal Son: Luke 15:11–32
The Sheep and the Goats: Matthew 25:31–46
The Sower: Matthew 13:1–8, 18–23; Mark 4:3–8, 14–20; Luke 8:5–8,
    11–15
The Talents: Matthew 25:14–30
The Tenants: Matthew 21:33–44; Mark 12:1–12; Luke 20:9–18
The Ten Virgins: Matthew 25:1–13
Two Sons: Matthew 21:28–31

The Unmerciful Servant: Matthew 18:23–34
The Wedding Banquet: Matthew 22:2–14
Wise and Foolish Builders: Matthew 7:24–27; Luke 6:47–49
Workers in the Vineyard: Matthew 20:1–16

VERSES TO HELP YOU
CELEBRATE HOLIDAYS

The Bible is full of stories of and instructions for special holidays (holy days), feasts and festivals, and celebrations. Here are some verses you can use in family devotions or as themes for your holiday celebrations.

Valentines Day: Love and Friendship
John 3:16
John 13:34–35
John 15:13
1 Corinthians 13
Ephesians 5:1–2
Colossians 3:14
1 Peter 4:8
1 John 3:1
1 John 3:16, 18
1 John 4:7–9, 11

St. Patrick's Day: Missions
Isaiah 52:7
Matthew 28:19–20
John 15:13
Acts 1:8
Romans 10:14–15

Easter
Isaiah 53
Matthew 26–28
Mark 14–16
Luke 22–24

John 1:29, 18–21
1 Corinthians 15:3–4; 55–57
Philippians 2:5–11
Revelation 5:9–10, 12–13

Thanksgiving
1 Chronicles 16:8–9
Psalm 35:18
Psalm 100
Ephesians 5:19–20
Colossians 3:16–17
1 Thessalonians 5:16–18

Christmas
Genesis 3:15
Isaiah 7:14
Isaiah 9:6
Isaiah 52:7
Matthew 1:18–2:11
Luke 1:1–2:38
Luke 4:17–22
John 1:1–12
John 3:16

VERSES TO HELP YOU
SHARE YOUR FAITH

Being a "witness" can be as simple as sharing with your family and friends what Jesus has done for you. But sometimes it helps to have some Scriptures you can point your friends to, Bible verses that explain what it means to be a Christian and how to put your faith in Christ. Here are a few to get you started.

The Roman Road: A Step-by-Step Series of Verses from the Book of Romans
Romans 3:23: "For all have sinned, and fall short of the glory of God."

Romans 6:23: "For the wages of sin is death, but the gift of God is eternal life in Christ Jesus our Lord."

Romans 5:8: "But God demonstrates his own love toward us in this: While we were still sinners, Christ died for us."

Romans 10:9–10: "If you confess with your mouth, 'Jesus is Lord,' and believe in your heart that God raised him from the dead, you will be saved."

Romans 10:13: "Everyone who calls on the name of the LORD will be saved."

Other Important Scriptures

Hebrews 9:27: Everyone will die one day and face God's judgment.

Ephesians 2:8–9: Salvation is a free gift from God; it can't be earned or achieved.

John 3:16: God so loved the world that He sent His one and only Son.

Isaiah 53:5: He was punished in our place; He paid the penalty for our sin.

Acts 4:12: Salvation comes through faith in Jesus alone; there is no other way.

Acts 16:30–31: Believe in Him, and you will be saved.

John 11:25–26: Believe in Him, and you will live forever with Him in heaven.

1 Corinthians 2:9: Heaven is a place so wonderful, it's impossible to describe!

The Sinner's Prayer

Many people have put their faith in Jesus—inviting Him into their hearts and lives—by praying something like this:

Dear Jesus, I know I am a sinner and that it was my sin that sent you to the cross. You took the punishment in my place. Thank you for sacrificing your life to save mine. Please forgive me and help me to live my life in a way that pleases you. Amen.

VERSES TO HELP YOU
GUARD YOUR HEART

The Bible has a lot to say about "guarding our hearts"—keeping our hearts, our minds, and our spirits pure, being sure to fill them with things that please God and help us to honor Him. It's a great idea to study some of these verses and memorize them so that you can make wise decisions about the things you watch or listen to or read or even just think about!

Guard Your Heart
Deuteronomy 5:29
Psalm 19:14
Psalm 51:10
Proverbs 4:23
Romans 12:2
Mark 12:30
Ephesians 5:15–16

Things to Put In
Deuteronomy 6:6–9
Psalm 119:9, 11
Proverbs 3:3, 5–6
Proverbs 15:30
Proverbs 18:15
Isaiah 26:8
1 Corinthians 13
Galatians 5:22–23
Ephesians 4:2–3, 32
Philippians 4:6–8
Colossians 3:1–2

Things to Keep Out
Psalm 119:36–37
Proverbs 6:16–19
Proverbs 14:30

Proverbs 16:5
Matthew 6:25–34
Ephesians 4:29–31
Ephesians 5:3–4
Colossians 3:5–10

VERSES TO HELP YOU FACE YOUR FEARS

Fear is a big issue for many kids—and grown-ups, too. There are silly fears and not-so-silly fears, impossible fears and very real fears. But the Bible says, "Fear not"—at least sixty or seventy times! Here are some verses to read and study and memorize, verses that will help you face your fears and overcome them.

Verses about Fear Itself
Deuteronomy 31:8
Psalm 23:1–5
Psalm 27:1–5
Psalm 56:3
Isaiah 41:10
Romans 8:14–16
Philippians 4:6–7
1 Peter 3:14
1 John 4:18

Verses of Hope, Comfort, and Peace
Psalm 4:8
Psalm 23
Psalm 91
Psalm 119:65
Psalm 121
Isaiah 26:3
Isaiah 43:1–3
John 14:27
John 16:33
Romans 8:28, 31–32, 37–39

Romans 15:13
Romans 16:20
Philippians 4:6–8
1 John 3:18–20
1 John 4:4
Revelation 21:1–4; 22:3–5

WHAT THE BIBLE SAYS ABOUT HEAVEN

The Bible tells us that one day the world as we know it will come to an end. "The heavens will disappear with a roar; the elements will be destroyed by fire, and the earth and everything in it will be laid bare" (2 Peter 3:10b). But then, God promises that He will resurrect or recreate the earth to be everything He always meant for it to be (Revelation 21:1). This new earth will be our home for all eternity, a perfect world unblemished, untarnished, undamaged by the consequences of our sin. Often, we refer to this new earth as "paradise" or "heaven."[1]

C. S. Lewis beautifully described this recreation in *The Last Battle*, the final book of his children's series, The Chronicles of Narnia. In one of the last scenes, Peter and Lucy and the other characters are confused. They have just witnessed the complete destruction of the land of Narnia —and yet they now find themselves in a world very like it, only better! Lord Digory is the first one to grasp the situation:

"That was not the real Narnia. That had a beginning and an end. It was only a shadow or a copy of the real Narnia, which has always been here and always will be here. . . ."

It was the Unicorn who summed up what everyone was feeling. . . .

"I have come home at last! This is my real country! I belong here. This is the land I have been looking for all of my life, though I never knew it till now. The reason why we loved the old Narnia is that it sometimes looked a little like this. Bree-hee-hee! Come further up, come further in!"[2]

---

1. Some Bible scholars suggest that the words "paradise" or "heaven" should really be used to refer to an intermediate (still wonderful) place where Christians who die before Jesus returns go to wait until it's time for all of us to join them. What we think of as "heaven"—our eternal destination—is actually the new earth.

2. C. S. Lewis, *The Last Battle* (1994 ed., New York: Harper-Collins, 1956), 211–213.

Lewis writes, "All their life in this world and all their adventures in Narnia had only been the cover and the title page: now at last they were beginning Chapter One of the Great Story, which no one on earth has read: which goes on forever: in which every chapter is better than the last."[3]

We live now in what C. S. Lewis called the "Shadowlands." Our life here on earth is only a pale copy—a faulty, imperfect imitation—of what is to come. And what we think of as the end (death) is really just the beginning. Unlike life in the Shadowlands, our adventures in heaven will never end.

The Bible tells us, "'No eye has seen, no ear has heard, no mind has conceived what God has prepared for those who love him'—but God has revealed it to us by his Spirit . . ." (1 Corinthians 2:9–10).

There are a lot of things we don't know about heaven—a place so wonderful, so beautiful, so amazing—sometimes it's hard to even imagine. But we do know that believing in Jesus is what it takes to get there (John 15:6; Acts 4:12; Romans 10:9–10). Here are some other things we know, from what the Scripture teaches directly and what it reveals about the nature of God and His creation:

Jesus has gone to heaven to prepare a place for us, and one day He'll come back to take us there himself (John 14:1–3).

In heaven, there are angels—powerful supernatural beings created by God to be His servants and messengers (Hebrews 12:22; Revelation 5:11).

Also in heaven are all the men and women of God down through the ages, our friends and family members who have gone on before us (Hebrews 12:1, 22–24).

Heaven is an exciting place, full of happiness and joy. There will be all kinds of places to go, people to meet, things to explore—all the best

---

3. Ibid., 228.

things from this life and more (Hebrews 12:22; John 5:17; Matthew 25:23; Isaiah 65:21)!

There, we will see God face-to-face—and we will be like Him (1 Corinthians 13:12; 1 John 3:2). We will shine like the sun (Matthew 13:43).

God will give each of us a new and a secret name that is just between us and Him (Revelation 2:17). He will write His own name on our foreheads (Revelation 22:4). Our names are also written in the Lamb's book of life (Luke 10:20; Revelation 21:27).

We will have new and perfect bodies in heaven. Unlike our earthly bodies, these heavenly bodies will never get sick or grow old (1 Corinthians 15:40; 2 Corinthians 5:1). But we'll still be ourselves—we'll be recognizable to our family and friends (Job 19:26–27; Luke 16:25; 24:39; Matthew 8:1).

In heaven there will be meaningful "work" for us to do—things that bring us joy and fulfillment—but rest from all of the hard work and suffering that is a part of our earthly life (John 5:17; Matthew 25:23; Isaiah 65:21; Revelation 5:10; 20:6; Job 3:17; Revelation 14:13). There will be no hunger or thirst, no crying, no pain, no curse of sin, no darkness (Isaiah 25:8; 1 Corinthians 15:26, 54; Revelation 7:16–17; 21:3–5).

Although we won't *have* to eat or drink, we will—just for the enjoyment of it (Revelation 21:6; Isaiah 25:6; Revelation 22:2)! We will celebrate with Jesus when He is united with us, His church, at a feast called "the wedding supper of the Lamb" (Revelation 19:9).

Some things—like being born, getting married, having children, dying—are only for this life (Luke 20:35–36). (That doesn't mean that we won't still be especially close to people in heaven whom we were especially close to on earth!)

There will be animals in heaven (maybe even extinct ones!). We don't really know if our pets will join us there. They don't have the same kind of spirits (or souls) that we do. But many Bible scholars say it's possible that God will resurrect our pets or recreate them or give us new ones, just because He loves us and loves to give us things that fill our hearts with joy (Isaiah 11:6–9; 65:25; Romans 8:21–23; Revelation 5:13)!

Although being good doesn't get us into heaven—only faith in Jesus does—our good deeds in this life will earn us heavenly rewards (Matthew 6:20; Luke 6:35; Daniel 12:3; Matthew 10:42; Ephesians 6:8; Romans 2:10; 2 Timothy 4:8; James 1:12; 1 Peter 5:4).

Those who have suffered for Jesus in this life will receive special honor in heaven (Matthew 5:11–12; Romans 8:18; 2 Corinthians 4:17; 2 Timothy 2:12; Hebrews 10:34; Revelation 7:13–17).

Heaven is better than anything we know in this life (2 Corinthians 5:8; Philippians 1:23).

We will live in heaven forever and ever and ever (2 Timothy 1:10).

8

MAPS OF BIBLE LANDS

Traditional route of
the exodus

From Egypt to the Promised Land

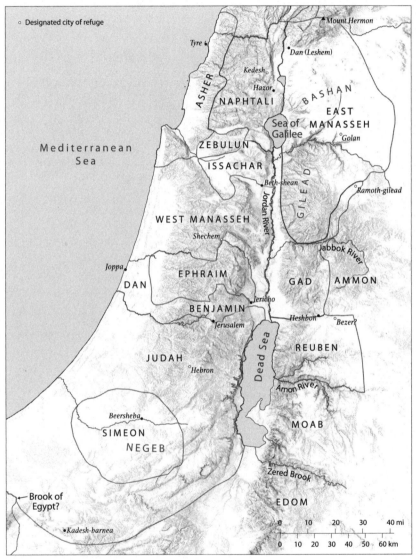

Twelve Tribes of Israel

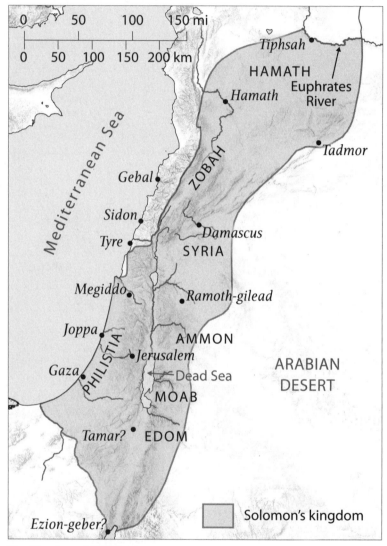

The Kingdom of Israel

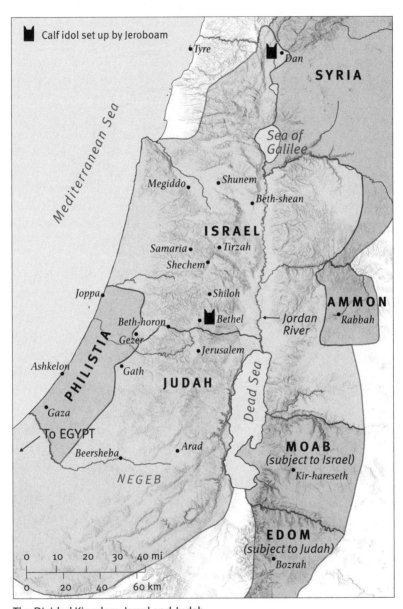

Calf idol set up by Jeroboam

Tyre

Dan

SYRIA

Mediterranean Sea

Sea of Galilee

Megiddo•
•Shunem

•Beth-shean

ISRAEL

Samaria•
•Tirzah

Shechem•

Joppa•
•Shiloh

Beth-horon•
•Bethel
← Jordan River

AMMON
•Rabbah

Gezer•

•Jerusalem

Ashkelon•

PHILISTIA
•Gath

JUDAH

Dead Sea

•Gaza

To EGYPT

Beersheba•
•Arad

MOAB
(subject to Israel)
•Kir-hareseth

NEGEB

EDOM
(subject to Judah)
•Bozrah

```
0    10    20    30    40 mi
0      20      40      60 km
```

The Divided Kingdom: Israel and Judah

Palestine in the Time of Jesus

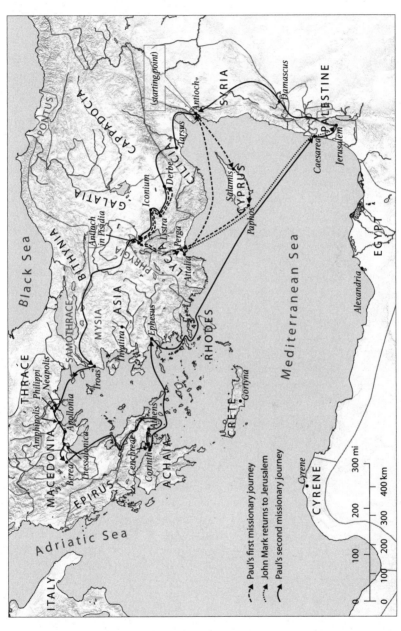

Paul's First and Second Missionary Journeys

Legend:
- - - - Paul's first missionary journey
········ John Mark returns to Jerusalem
——— Paul's second missionary journey

(starting point)

ITALY

Adriatic Sea

EPIRUS

MACEDONIA
Amphipolis
Philippi
Neapolis
Apollonia
Berea
Thessalonica

THRACE

SAMOTHRACE

Black Sea

BITHYNIA

PONTUS

CAPPADOCIA

GALATIA

Troas

MYSIA

ASIA

Thyatira

Ephesus

PHRYGIA

Antioch
in Pisidia

Iconium

Derbe

Lystra

CILICIA

Tarsus

Antioch

SYRIA

Damascus

ACHAIA
Athens
Corinth
Cenchrea

RHODES

LYCIA

Perga
Attalia

CYPRUS

Salamis

Paphos

PALESTINE

Caesarea

Jerusalem

CRETE

Gortyna

Mediterranean Sea

EGYPT

Alexandria

CYRENE

Cyrene

0   100   200   300 mi
0   100 200 300 400 km

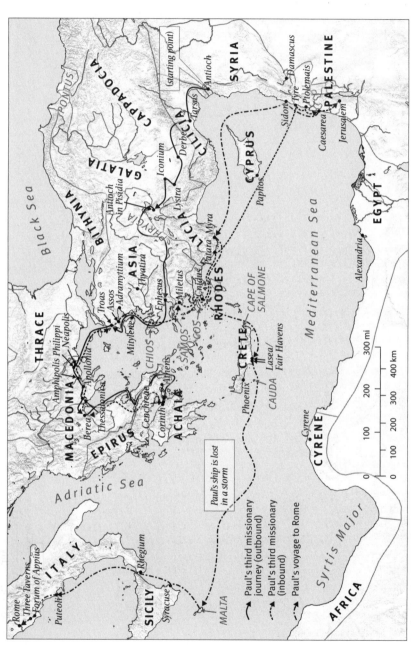

Paul's Third Missionary Journey

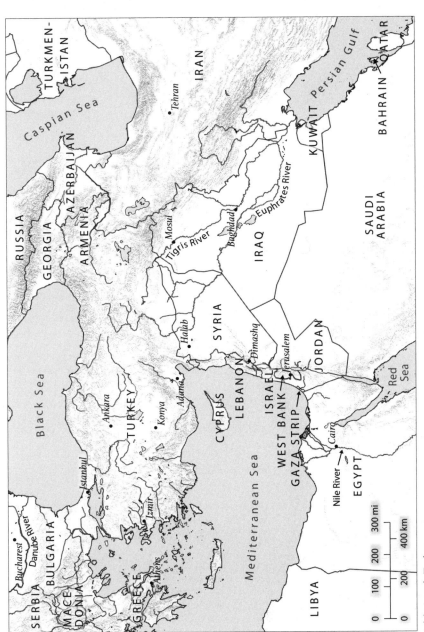

Bible Lands Today

9

FIND OUT MORE

BOOKS

Countless Bible commentaries, companions, encyclopedias, and handbooks are available to families today. These books can help you get more out of your own personal Bible study, answer questions that come up during family devotions or Bible story time, and shed new light on familiar passages of Scripture. Many include detailed maps and charts, and illustrations of Bible lands and archaeological artifacts. Here are just a few family-friendly resources to get you started:

- *The Crossway Illustrated Bible Handbook* by Tim Dowley, editor (Wheaton, IL: Crossway, 2005).

- *Daily Life at the Time of Jesus* by Miriam Feinberg Vamosh (Herzlia, Israel: Palphot, 2001), www.palphot.co.il.

- *Food at the Time of the Bible: From Adam's Apple to the Last Supper* by Miriam Feinberg Vamosh (Herzlia, Israel: Palphot, 2004), www.palphot.co.il.

- *The Illustrated Everyday Bible Companion* by George W. Knight with Rayburn W. Ray (Uhrichsville, OH: Barbour, 2005).

- *The International Children's Bible Dictionary* by Ronald F. Youngblood, F. F. Bruce, and R. K. Harrison (Nashville, Tommy Nelson, 2006).

- *What the Bible Is All About* by Henrietta Mears (Ventura, CA: Regal/Gospel Light, 1998).

- *What the Bible Is All About For Young Explorers* by Henrietta Mears with Frances Blankenbaker (Ventura, CA: Regal/Gospel Light, 1998).

- *Who's Who and Where's Where in the Bible* by Stephen M. Miller (Uhrichsville, OH: Barbour, 2004).

- *The Zondervan Handbook to the Bible* by Pat and David Alexander (Grand Rapids: Zondervan, 1999).

Maps, Charts, and Time Lines

These are great tools to use in an in-depth family Bible study or when you are teaching from the Bible in a Sunday school class, children's church, or a Christian school or home school setting. Some of the following are available as pocket-sized or wall-sized charts; others come as reproducible handouts.

- *Nelson's Complete Book of Bible Maps and Charts* (Nashville: Thomas Nelson, 1999).

- Rose Publishing (www.rose-publishing.com) handles visual aids on biblical topics:
  - How We Got the Bible
  - Christian History Time Line
  - Bible Overview: OT and NT
  - The Ten Commandments
  - Creation and Evolution
  - Christianity, Cults, and Religions
  - And many more!

Software

Publishers are always coming out with new Bible software. Most CD-ROMs include multiple translations of the Scripture along with a variety of Bible dictionaries, commentaries, concordances, maps, and charts. Stop by your local Christian bookstore or shop online to compare titles such as *QuickVerse*, *eBible*, *Bibleworks*, *The Amazing Bible Expedition*, and *Treasures of the Bible*. A number of Bible-themed trivia and video games are available for kids, such as the *Beginner's Bible Activity Pack*.

Movies

As filmmakers and audiences the world over have discovered, movies can be a powerful and uplifting way to communicate biblical truth. Literally hundreds of great Bible-based titles exist for Christian families today, from *Praise Baby* to *Veggie Tales*, *The Ten Commandments* and *Ben Hur* to *Jesus of Nazareth* and *The Passion of the Christ*. And don't forget movies that feature biographies of famous Christians or have strong Christian themes, like *The Hiding Place* and *Chariots of Fire*, even C. S. Lewis's *The Lion, the Witch and the Wardrobe*. These movies can be a great way to reinforce the things your family has been learning in your Bible study time together at home or at church. They can also encourage conversation (and lead to further study) on important issues as they relate to family life and faith.

Of course, it's important to preview films to make sure that they are in keeping with your standards and appropriate for the members of your family. Remember that many biblical epics—while wonderful and inspiring films—can be a little less than a hundred percent accurate. It's not uncommon for scriptwriters to invent characters and scenes to fill in the details or change things to make the story flow. Before or after you watch the movie, find the original story in the Bible and re-read it together. Be sure to clarify which elements of the movie version you know to be true from Scripture and which are the product of someone's creativity and imagination!

Organizations and Online Sites

The following Web sites offer all kinds of information for Christian families—articles and columns, devotionals and Bible reading plans, online Bible dictionaries and concordances, even a virtual reconstruction of the temple—as well as activity pages you can print out for the kids. Check them out!

- American Bible Society, www.americanbible.org.
- Bible Gateway, www.BibleGateway.com.
- Christianity Today, www.ChristianityToday.com.
- Crosswalk, www.crosswalk.com.
- Gospel.com, www.gospel.com.
- Israel Wonders: Go Israel, www.tourism.gov.il.
- Jerusalem Archaeological Park, www.archpark.org.il.

Places to Visit
Keep your eyes and ears open for information about family Bible conferences and retreats in your area. Many churches and Christian ministries sponsor mission trips, camps, cruises, and even tours of the Holy Land. If taking the whole family overseas isn't something you can do right now, you might still enjoy a visit to The Holy Land Experience in Orlando, Florida—a "living Biblical museum and park that brings the world of the Bible alive." The park features dramas, musical performances, activities, and exhibits—including the world's largest model of the city of Jerusalem as it was during the time of Christ and the largest private collection of biblical texts and artifacts in the United States.

For more information about The Holy Land Experience (4655 Vineland Road, Orlando, FL 32811), visit: www.theholylandexperience.com.